MEMOIRS OF A
BRITISH AGENT

R. H. BRUCE LOCKHART

MEMOIRS OF A
BRITISH AGENT

Being an account of the author's
early life in many lands and of his official
mission to Moscow in 1918

PAN BOOKS

First published in hardcover 1932 by Putnam

First published in paperback 1950 by Penguin

New edition published 1974 by Macmillan London Ltd

This edition published 2002 by Pan Books
an imprint of Pan Macmillan Ltd
Pan Macmillan, 20 New Wharf Road, London N1 9RR
Basingstoke and Oxford
Associated companies throughout the world
www.panmacmillan.com

ISBN 0 330 41493 3

Text copyright R. H. Bruce Lockhart 1932
Introduction copyright © R. H. Bruce Lockhart 1974, 1985

3 5 7 9 8 6 4 2

A CIP catalogue record for this book is available from
the British Library.

Printed and bound in Great Britain by
Mackays of Chatham plc, Chatham, Kent

CONTENTS

ILLUSTRATIONS

[1]Radio Times Hulton Picture Library.   [2]Keystone.   [3]*Daily Express.*

"I AM NOT SURE *that what I feel is remorse. I have seen the ocean when, lashed by something in itself or out of itself, it wrecked and ruined, and I have seen the ocean when it carried my barque in safety. It was the same ocean, and what is the use of words.*"

INTRODUCTION

WHEN WARNER BROTHERS turned *Memoirs of a British Agent* into a film in 1934 with Leslie Howard, Kay Francis and a cast of five thousand, they described the book as "The Greatest Human Document of the Century", "The Book that Startled the World". The film was hailed as "The Most Important Dramatic Event of the Year" and Warners claimed to have spent more money on *British Agent* than on any film they had previously produced. The film was, I understand, the first ever to be made based on the life and experiences of a person during his lifetime.

After making due allowance for the extravagant claims of the film moguls, the treatment Hollywood gave to the film was, nevertheless, a reflection of the rapturous acclaim given by the press to *Memoirs of a British Agent* when it was first published in 1932. The response from the reading public was tremendous. In a few weeks it had climbed to the top of the best-seller lists in both this country and in the United States. In America, where best-seller lists were published for five major cities (New York, Boston, Chicago, Philadelphia and Washington), it was the only book to figure simultaneously on all five lists – and this from a first-book author who was competing for a place in the lists against established writers such as H. G. Wells and Sinclair Lewis who had also brought out new books at the same time. It was the Book Society "Book of the Month" choice on both sides of the Atlantic, and it was serialised in many newspapers.

In London, Putnam, the original publishers, were busy producing reprint after reprint, as were Putnam in America. Within a matter of months of its original publication in London, translated editions had appeared in French, German, Italian, Swedish, Danish, Polish and Finnish. Throughout the 1930s, numerous editions were published in many languages and there have been several post-war editions – including paperbacks – in a number of languages. Unfortunately, no complete record exists of total sales, but these must be very considerable.

"A book in a thousand . . . exhilarating and unforgettable. It is a magnificent book. I must read it all again," wrote Harold Nicholson. "Holds our attention to the last page," said the *Sunday Times*. "He is a far more real personality, when met in print, than Lawrence of Arabia," was the view of the *New York Times*. "One of the sensations of the current publishing season," trumpeted the *Daily Express*. "A first class book sensational enough to satisfy the cravings of the most rabid spy-fans," *News Chronicle*. More sedately, G. K. Chesterton described *Memoirs of a British Agent* as "a most important book" while Hugh Walpole called it "a fine contribution to history – one of the most honest and vivid that we have had". Personally, I liked the comment of the *Sunday Express* writer to whom the book gave a sleepless night: "The book of the day. I could not put the damned tome down till the last page was lit by a gloomy day."

Most reviewers drew attention to the fascinating pictures my father drew of revolutionary Russia, of "historic events in the making" (*Chicago Tribune*), of "history from the inside" (*Spectator*), and of the principal architects of the revolution: "striking vignettes of the Russian revolutionary leaders" (*Daily Telegraph*), "Lenin, Trotsky and a score of others are etched unforgettably in these vivid pages" (*Daily Herald*).

Much was written by the critics about the unusual personality of the "Boy Ambassador" to Red Russia and his irrepressible sense of adventure – my father was only thirty years old when Lloyd George sent him to Moscow to treat with Lenin and Trotsky on behalf of Great Britain – but most reviewers and readers were principally interested in his graphic first-hand description of the Moscow of 1918. This was to be expected, as he was virtually the only person from the outside world who had been in daily touch with the Bolshevik leaders.

Nevertheless, *Memoirs of a British Agent*, although a fascinating account of a fascinating period in history – and my father shows the revolution as few have shown it – is essentially the gripping story of one man's lonely struggle with the Bolsheviks to keep Russia in the war and of his battles against those in Whitehall who believed that the Bolshevik regime was certain to collapse and a Tsarist regime would be restored.

Of all the many columns of comment written by so many people about *Memoirs of a British Agent*, I myself like best that of the *Christian Science Monitor* which said succinctly and so very truly: "It is a personal story extremely well told and enormously worth telling." If this book is the story of an individual set against a background of great happenings, it is still very much a personal story in which the author stands out clear and distinct.

The events leading up to the Russian Revolution moved with the inexorable march of a Greek tragedy which human effort seemed powerless to avert. Later, they moved so fast that to be in the middle of them must have been like watching one of those flickering films of the early cinema. A sense of impending doom overhangs the narrative and the characters stand out against an increasingly tragic background although many light-hearted and witty stories are distilled into all the excitement and tragedy. What is perhaps remarkable is that, at a time of extreme political tension, my father made and kept friends on both sides of the struggle and succeeded in writing about events and people objectively and of himself with candour. All the figures that move across the pages are real and human men at issue with destiny. It has been said that in his self-revelation he introduced a new technique into literature which had never been previously used – not even by Rousseau. Certainly he wrote exactly as if a friend in the next room was going to tell the whole truth about him anyway, and in *Memoirs of a British Agent* he first showed his facility, not of letting the reader look over the author's shoulder, but of looking over the reader's shoulder at himself.

It may well be true, as Arthur Ransome once wrote, "No better picture of the galloping weeks of the summer of 1918 in Moscow has been or is ever likely to be painted." But it is because the author is part of the picture himself and strays over the canvas arm-in-arm with the reader, introducing him to a living procession of men and moments of one of the greatest social and political upheavals in history, that *Memoirs of a British Agent* is so immensely readable and has become a minor classic.

He knew and talked freely with Kerensky, Lenin, Trotsky, Derjinsky – the formidable head of the Cheka – and many other Bolshevik leaders. His delightful portraits of these men fit admirably into a story which helps make intelligible the whole Bolshevik psychology. Flitting across the pages also is the shadowy figure of master spy Sidney Reilly – the real instigator of the "Lockhart Plot" for which my father was imprisoned in the Kremlin. Of Lenin, the author wrote: "He looks at first glance more like a provincial grocer than a leader of men. Yet in those steely eyes . . . He was impersonal and almost inhuman. His vanity was proof against all flattery."

British statesmen and their advisers in the First World War who had to deal with revolutionary Russia cannot have been pleased with the revelations made in *Memoirs of a British Agent*. The book is in many ways a record of misapprehensions and missed chances, as most of my father's recommendations and warnings fell on deaf ears.

My father considered that the assumption of the Supreme Command by the Tsar himself was "the first milestone on the way to Golgotha". He sympathised with the revolution but not with the Bolsheviks. Lenin was successful because he promised peace, and my father could not share the general belief of all the so-called Russian experts in London that the Bolshevik regime could not last more than a few weeks. "I deprecated as sheer folly," he wrote, "our militarist propaganda because it took no account of the war-weariness which had raised the Bolsheviks to power."

Memoirs of a British Agent, apart from being as thrilling and "unputdownable" as any masterpiece of fiction, is also an indictment by the man on the spot of the total failure of politicians and diplomats in Western Europe to grasp the significance of the Russian Revolution – the consequences of which we still have to live with today.

The casual reader might not realise from these memoirs that for some time my father's personality and fate were a matter of moment to a large part of the world – the man over whose disputed body two world systems battled. Like a Daniel in the lions' den, he was imprisoned in the Kremlin and nearly executed – indeed he was condemned to death *in absentia* after his return to England – and was labelled as pro-Bolshevik in Britain. At the time, he probably had a considerably more realistic and objective view of the causes and likely repercussions of the Russian Revolution than anyone. Had the British Government but heeded the still, small voice of their "Boy Ambassador" crying in the wilderness of Red Russia, the course of modern history might well have been changed.

Ditchling, Sussex   ROBIN BRUCE LOCKHART
February 1974

NOTE TO THE PAPERBACK EDITION

THE PUBLICATION of my father's diaries with their brief but fascinating entries covering his time in Russia during the First World War, the rise to power of Bolshevism, the "Lockhart Plot" and his imprisonment in the Kremlin revived public interest in *Memoirs of a British Agent*. Public demand for a new edition of the book has been aroused by last year's television serialisation of my own book *Reilly – Ace of Spies* – the ubiquitous spy who played a leading role in the "Lockhart Plot". (My father's eventual release from the Kremlin in exchange for Litvinoff, whom the British had arrested in London as a reprisal, was the precursor of the various exchanges of agents between Soviet Russia and Britain that have taken place subsequently.) In this, my father's first and most memorable book, the whole amazing story of his experiences in Russia is set out in complete detail.

It is my very sincere hope that readers who have already read *Memoirs of a British Agent* in an earlier edition will relive their original thrills when reading this new illustrated paperback edition. To readers who have not yet had the good fortune to read this stirring tale, I say your good fortune is now in your hands.

Hove, Sussex   ROBIN BRUCE LOCKHART
December, 1984

BOOK I

MALAYAN NOVITIATE

BULAN TRANG, bintang berchahaya;
Burŏng gaga' memakan padi.
Kelau Tuan ti'ada perchaya,
Belah dada' melihat hati.

(The moon is clear. The stars shine bright above.
The crow is feeding in the rice apart.
If Thou, my Lord, misdoubt my plighted love,
Come, cleave my breast, and see my wounded heart.)

Malayan Pantun.

CHAPTER ONE

IN MY STORMY and chequered life Chance has played more than her fair part. The fault has been my own. Never at any time have I tried to be the complete master of my own fate. The strongest impulse of the moment has governed all my actions. When chance has raised me to dazzling heights, I have received her gifts with outstretched hands. When she has cast me down from my high pinnacle, I have accepted her buffets without complaint. I have my hours of penance and regret. I am introspective enough to take an interest in the examination of my own conscience. But this self-analysis has always been detached. It has never been morbid. It has neither aided nor impeded the fluctuations of my varied career.

It has availed me nothing in the eternal struggle which man wages on behalf of himself against himself. Disappointments have not cured me of an ineradicable romanticism. If at times I am sorry for some things I have done, remorse assails me only for the things I have left undone.

. . . . .

I was born in Anstruther in the county of Fife on September 2nd, 1887. My father was a preparatory schoolmaster, who migrated to England in 1906. My mother was a Macgregor. My ancestors include Bruces, Hamiltons, Cummings, Wallaces and Douglases, and I can trace a connection back to Boswell of Auchinleck. There is no drop of English blood in my veins.

My childhood memories are of little interest to anyone except myself. My father was a keen Rugby football player and a member of the Scottish Rugby Union Selection Committee. My mother's brothers were well-known Scottish athletes. I therefore received my first "rugger" ball at the age of four and, under the tuition of various Scottish Internationals, could drop a goal almost as soon as I could walk. What is stranger is the fact that my father, who was no player, was also an ardent cricket enthusiast. When my third brother was born, I clapped my hands and exclaimed delightedly:

3

"Now we shall have one to bat, one to bowl, and one to keep wicket!" Then, repairing to the kitchen, I stole a raw beefsteak and placed it in his cradle in order that he might the quicker develop bone and muscle. I was seven at the time!

In other respects, my education was normal. I received my fair share of corporal punishment—chiefly for playing football or cricket on the Sabbath, which my father observed strictly. At the age of twelve I gained a foundation scholarship at Fettes, where I spent five years in the worship of athleticism. This exaggerated devotion to games interfered sadly with my studies. In my first term at Fettes I was first in the Latin sentence paper set for the whole school, with the exception of the VIth form, and corrected by the headmaster himself. During the rest of my school career I was never again within the first fifty, and, although I succeeded in reaching the VIth form, I was a grievous disappointment to my parents. In order to rid me of an unwholesome fetish, my father sent me to Berlin instead of allowing me to go to Cambridge, where a few years later my second brother was to distinguish himself by obtaining two Blues, forfeiting in the process the firstclass "honours" in modern languages which otherwise he almost certainly would have secured.

To Germany and to Professor Tilley I owe much. Tilley was an Australian who had become more Prussian than the Prussians, even to the extent of dropping the "e" from his name and signing himself after the manner of the great German soldier of fortune. His methods were Spartan and pitiless, but he showed me how to work—a virtue which, in spite of many backslidings, I have never entirely lost. He taught me two other valuable lessons—respect for institutions and customs other than English and the secret of mastering foreign languages. The first has helped me throughout my life in my relations with foreigners. The second was to stand me in good stead when seven years later I went to Russia. If Tilley is still alive, I hope he will see this tribute to his thoroughness. In my life his was the one influence which I can describe as wholly beneficial.

From Berlin I was sent to Paris, where I came under the influence of that good and godly man, Paul Passy. From him I acquired an excellent French accent and my first insight into Welsh revivalist methods. Passy, who was the son of Frédéric Passy, the eminent French jurist and pacifist, was the gentlest of Calvinists. As a young man he had wanted to be a missionary and, serious in all things, he had trained himself for his arduous career by eating rats. An affection of the lungs prevented this great scholar from burying himself in the wilds of China or the remoter South Sea Islands. The heathens' loss became science's gain, and to-day the name of Passy is linked eternally with the names of Sweet and Viëtor in the honours list of the pioneers of modern phonetics. In spite of his absorption in his linguistic studies, Passy never abandoned his good works or his reclamation of sinners. When first I knew him he was under the influence of Evan Roberts, the Welsh evangelist, and for the only time in a varied career I had the strange experience of appearing on the platform and singing Welsh revivalist hymns in French before a Paris slum audience. Passy said the prayers and played the harmonium with three fingers, while I sang the solos supported by a chorus of three trembling English students.

If life is a succession of accidents, the series in my own life has been rapid. After three years in France and Germany, I returned to England in order to undergo a final preparation for the Indian Civil Service. Fate and my own genius for drifting ruled otherwise. In 1908, my uncle, one of the pioneers of the rubber-growing industry in the Malay States, came home from the East and fired my imagination with wonderful tales of the fortunes that were to be made almost for the asking in that elusive and enchanting land. Already the travel-bug had entered my blood, and in my desire for new worlds and new adventures, I decided to throw in my lot with the rubber-planters and to go East.

My student days in Berlin and Paris had been serious and blameless. In Germany a passionate devotion to Heine—even to-day I can recite by heart most of the Intermezzo and the

Heimkehr—inspired me with an innocent attachment to the daughter of a German naval officer. I sailed my boat on Wannsee by moonlight. I sighed over my Pilsener on the terrace of a Schlachtensee café. I sang—in the presence of her mother—the latest and most romantic Viennese and Berlin Lieder. And I mastered the German language. But there were no adventures, no escapades, no excesses. In France I steeped myself in the exotic sentimentalism of Loti, whom I once met and whose eccentricities and mincing manners failed to cure me of an admiration which I feel to this day for the charm and beauty of his prose. But my tears were shed over "Les Désenchantées" in solitude. I learnt the farewell letter of Djénane by heart. Three years later it was to be of good service to me in my examination for the Consular Service. But I learnt it for the mortification of my own soul. I made no attempt to imitate the long series of "Mariages de Loti." Now the East was to lead me along the broad highway of her unrestricted temptations.

CHAPTER TWO

NO JOURNEY will ever give me the same enchantment as that first voyage to Singapore. It remains in the memory as a delicious day-dream in which I can recall every incident and which never fails to console me in moments of sadness. Far more clearly than the numerous travelling companions I have since met, I can see in my mind's eye the captain, the smoking-room steward, the deck hands, the obese and romantic purser, and the three German naval officers who were my only serious rivals for first place in the deck sports. But the real magic of that journey was in the kaleidoscope of wonderful colours and haunting landscapes which every twenty-four hours was unfolded before my eyes. This pageant I enjoyed for myself and by myself. I rose in the dark to catch that first flutter of the breeze which heralds the approach of the Eastern dawn and waited with a delicious tremor of anticipation until the great fire-ball of the sun burst through the pall of greyness and revealed where sky ended and the calmest of seas began. Alone in the bows I watched the saffron-tinted sunsets with their changing panoramas of ships and armies, of kings and castles, of knights and fair women, of adventures far more enthralling and vivid than the most thrilling film-story. I was only twenty-one, and my thirst for knowledge was unquenchable. I devoured every travel-book on which I could lay my hands. Some of the books I read then are still among my greatest treasures. Jules Boissière's "Fumeurs d'Opium" remains the best book of its kind that I know. Others, like Swettenham's "Unaddressed Letters," which bears its date on every page, seem almost comic to-day. Then, however, they were tremendously real. Loti was my hero, and like Loti I wrapped myself in a mantle of melancholy solitude. At ports I fled instinctively from my countrymen and, unaccompanied by any fawning guide, explored at random what I conceived to be the native quarters. With the exception of Victor Corkran, who, years older than myself, probably found a whimsical pleasure in drawing me out and in listening to the extravagant dreams and confident ambitions of an all-too-conceited, because self-conscious, youth, I made few friends. Nevertheless, he was kind, and concealed his amusement behind a mask of sympathy. He had travelled widely and knew strange scraps of history and folk-lore which were not to be found in guide-books. On board the *Buelow* he was a Roman in a horde of Goths, and to-day I am grateful to him for many a valuable lesson which, doubtless, he was unaware that he was imparting.

Above all, I learned to appreciate the beauty of warm colours and luxuriant vegetation. An orchid in the Malayan jungle meant more, means more to me to-day, than the most beautiful "cattleya" on the breast of the most beautiful woman. The glowing warmth of the tropical sun became a necessity to my physical existence and a stimulant to my mind. Even to-day I cannot think of those cloudless Eastern skies, those long stretches of golden sand with their background of cooling palms and lofty casuarinas without a feeling of longing which is almost akin to physical pain. Like Fauconnier's hero I have come to believe that every country where a man cannot live naked in all seasons, is condemned to work, to war, and to the hampering restraint of moral codes. To-day, the fogs of an English winter are to me as grim a nightmare as the walls of my Bolshevik prison.

And yet in this Malaya, which I love, which remains as the pleasantest regret in my life, and which I shall never see again, I was a failure. On my arrival in Singapore I was sent as a "creeper" to a rubber plantation outside Port Dickson. Earth knows no gem more beautiful than this tiny harbour which lies at the entrance to the Straits of Malacca. At that time it was unspoilt by the intrusion of the white man. The climate was almost perfect. Its coast-line was like an opal changing in colour with every angle of the sun. The stillness of its nights, broken only by the gentle lapping of the sea on the casuarina-crested shore, brought a peace which I shall never know again.

I enjoyed every minute of my year there. But I was an indifferent planter. The pungent odour of the Tamil coolies I could not abide. I learnt enough of their language to carry out my duties. To-day, beyond stock-phrases of command and a string of oaths, I have forgotten every word. The Chinese, with their automatic accuracy, made no appeal to me, and the actual estate work, the filling in of check rolls, the keeping of accounts, bored me. My head-manager, a brother-in-law of the late Lord Forteviot, was easy-going and benevolent to my short-comings. Very quickly I entered into the life of the British planter. I learnt to drink the inevitable "stengah."[1] Once a month I went with my chief to the neighbouring town of Seremban and imbibed vast quantities of gin "pahits" in the Sungei Ujong Club. At week-ends I travelled about the country playing football and hockey and making hosts of new acquaintances. The hospitality of the Malaya of those golden, prosperous days of 1908 was for a youngster almost over-whelming, and few there were who survived it unscathed.

During my stay at Port Dickson I had one minor triumph, the echo of which I hear faintly to this day.

Within a few months of my arrival in the country, I went up to Kuala Lumpur to play "rugger" for my State, Negri Sembilan, against Selangor. Kuala Lumpur is the capital of Selangor and of the Federated Malay States. Selangor itself has the largest white population of any State and, at that time, its "rugger" side contained several international players including that gargantuan and good-natured Scot "Bobby" Neill. In those days Negri Sembilan could hardly muster fifteen "rugger" players. Certainly, we had never beaten Selangor, and I doubt if we had ever beaten any other state. Notwith-standing the climate, "rugger" is the most popular of all spectacles in Malaya, and, in spite of the apparent disparity in strength between the two sides, a large gathering of Euro-peans and natives turned out to see the match, which was played on the Kuala Lumpur Padang. Those who witnessed this classic encounter were rewarded with one of the greatest surprises in the history of sport. The match was played about Christmas time, and Selangor were not in training. Perhaps

[1] Whisky and soda.

they rated their opponents a little too lightly. At any rate at half-time Selangor were leading by a try and a penalty goal dropped by the ponderous "Bobby" to a try scored by myself. Soon after the beginning of the second half, it was obvious that Selangor were tiring, and the crowd—a Selangor crowd—delighted at the prospect of a surprise victory, cheered us on. I was fortunate enough to score a second try, and with five minutes to go the scores were level. Then, from a line-out, a big New Zealander, who had played a sterling game for us, threw the ball back to me, and from just inside half-way I dropped a goal.

We had perpetrated the greatest joke for years, and the Selangor team and the spectators were sportsmen enough to appreciate it. I was carried off the field in triumph to the "Spotted Dog," the once famous club which stands on the edge of the Padang. There I was surrounded by a host of people whose names I did not know, but who were old Fettesians— Scotsmen, who knew my brother or my father, and who slapped me on the back and insisted on standing me a drink. Long before dinner time I must have had a drink, perhaps several drinks, with nearly everyone in the room. By the time I arrived at the F.M.S. Hotel, where an official dinner was being given to the two teams, both teams and guests were in their places. I was met at the door by "Bobby" Neill, who informed me that the chair was being taken by the acting Resident-General, and that I had been unanimously voted into the place of honour on his right-hand at the top table. This was my first experience of the limelight of publicity, and I did not like the ordeal. My crowning achievement, however, was my conversation with the R.G., to whom I talked like a father of my experiences in the East. They must have been too vividly described, for he informed me reprovingly that he was a married man.

"Tamil or Malay, sir?" I asked him politely.

"Hush!" he said. "I've three children."

"Black or white, sir?" I continued with irrepressible affability.

Fortunately, he had a sense of humour and a blind eye for the failings of twenty-one, and, when next year's match came round, he asked me to stay with him, came to see me play, and in his speech referred to me—alas! no longer the fleet-footed speed-merchant of the previous year—as "faint yet pursuing."

That fitful triumph had an unpleasant sequel. As the youngest and, therefore, most insignificant and innocent member of the visiting team, I had been quartered with the parson, a fine athlete but a trifle strait-laced—especially for a padre in the tropics. Kuala Lumpur, like Rome, being built on seven hills, I had some difficulty in finding the good man's bungalow in the early hours of the morning. Thanks, however, to the faithful "Bobby" and to other kind friends I was steered safely to my room, and by a great effort I succeeded in putting in an appearance at breakfast the next morning—Sunday morning with a three-course Sunday breakfast to celebrate it! Cold water had done wonders, and I looked not too bad, but my voice had gone. As I croaked out my answers to a fusillade of questions regarding my health and how I had slept, Mrs. Padre looked at me pityingly.

"Ah, Mr. Lockhart," she said. "I told you, if you did not put your sweater on after the game, you would get a chill."

With that she rushed from the table and brought me a glass of cough-mixture, which in that spirit of shyness, which even to this day I have never quite overcome, I was too weak to refuse. The result was instantaneous, and without a word I rushed from the room. Never before, or since, have I suffered as I suffered on that Sunday morning. I often wonder how much Mrs. Padre knew. If she intended to teach me a lesson, the rewards of the schoolmaster can never have been sweeter.

These wild excursions, however, were but episodes in a life which in spite of the monotony of my work provided me with countless new interests. The Malay gentleman at large, with his profound contempt for work, made an instant appeal to me. I liked his attitude to life, his philosophy. A man who could fish and hunt, who knew the mysteries of the rivers and forests, who could speak in metaphors and make love in "pantuns," was a man after my own heart. I learnt his language with avidity. I studied his customs and history. I found romance in the veiled mystery of his women-folk. I devoted to my Malays the energy and enthusiasm which should have been expended on the Tamil and Chinese coolies of my rubber estate. Despising the unintellectual existence of the planter, I sought my friends among the younger government officials. I showed them my poems. They invited me to admire their water-colours. There was one soulful young man—to-day he has reached the heights of Colonial eminence—with whom I played duets on the piano.

I made friends, too, with the Roman Catholic missionaries—splendid fellows, voluntarily cutting themselves off from Europe and even from the Europeans in the East and devoting their whole life to tending their native flock and to reclaiming and educating the half-caste population.

In the columns of the local newspaper I made my first essay in journalism, and, although my morbid efforts to expose the Japanese traffic in fallen women met with little favour, I achieved editorial recognition and a demand for more work of a similar nature as a result of a leader on the defects of Esperanto. Above all, I read, and read seriously. The average planter's library might contain a varied selection of the prose and poetry of Kipling, but its chief stand-by in those days was the works of Hubert Wales and James Blyth. I do not know what authors have taken their place to-day, but to me Hubert Wales was neither lurid nor instructive. I made a rule never to buy a novel, and to the weekly packet of serious literature, which I received from Singapore, I owe my sanity and my escape from the clutches of the Eastern Trinity of opium, drink and women. All three were to spread the net of their temptations over me, but reading saved me from the worst effects of a combined offensive.

CHAPTER THREE

IT WAS MY youthful craving for solitude which led me finally into serious trouble. I was always tormenting my uncle with requests for a job on my own. At last I was sent to open up a new estate at the foot of the hills. The place, which for over a year was to be my home, was ten miles away from any European habitation. No white man had ever lived there before. The village on which my estate bordered was the headquarters of a Sultan who had been deposed and who was, therefore, not too friendly towards the English. My house, too, was a ramshackle affair, verandahless and, although slightly better than the ordinary Malay house, in no sense of the word a European bungalow. A death-rate for malaria unequalled in the whole State did not enhance the attractions of the place. My only links with civilisation were a push-bike and the Malay police corporal who lived two miles away. Nevertheless, I was as happy as a mahout with a new elephant. During the day my time was fully occupied. I had to make something out of nothing, an estate out of jungle, to build a house for myself, to make roads and drains where none existed. There were, too, minor problems of administration which were a source of constant interest and amusement to me: Malay contractors who had an excuse for every backsliding; Tamil wives, who practised polyandry on a strictly practical basis—two days for each of their three husbands and a rest on Sundays; an outraged "Vulliamay," who complained that "Ramasamy" had stolen his day; Chinese shopkeepers, who drove hard bargains with my storekeeper, and Bombay "chetties" who stood round on pay day and held my coolies in their usurious clutch.

With this mixed collection I held sway as the sole representative of the British Raj. I dispensed justice without fear or favour, and, if there were complaints against my authority, they never reached my ears. During these first four months I was entirely care-free. I worked hard at my Malay. I wrote short stories which subsequently earned the unsolicited

13

encomiums of Clement Shorter and were published in the
"Sphere." I began a novel on Malay life—alas, never finished
and now never likely to be—and I continued my reading with
praiseworthy diligence. For amusement there was football and
shooting and fishing. I felled a piece of land, laid out a football
ground, and initiated the Malays of the village into the
mysteries of "Soccer." In that glorious hour before sunset I
shot "punai," the small Malay blue pigeon, as they were
flighting. I dabbed for "ikan harouan"—the coarse fish of the
Malayan rice-ponds—with a small live frog to take the place
of a daddy-long-legs. Marvellous to relate, I made friends with
the deposed Sultan and especially with his wife, the real ruler
of the royal household and a wizened up old lady with betel-
stained lips and an eye that would strike terror into the boldest
heart. Rumour had it that she had committed every crime
in the penal code and many offences against God and man
which were not included in that list of human shortcomings.
She was, however, the Queen Victoria of her district, and,
although we subsequently became enemies, I bear her no
grudge.

Among my own household I acquired an entirely unmerited
reputation as a revolver shot. My primitive bungalow was
infested with rats, which during meal-times would run down a
round beam from the palm-thatched roof to the floor. My
little fox terrier would then rout them out, while I stood with
a rattan cane in my hand to knock the rats down as they ran up
the beam again. I killed scores of them in this manner. Still
better fun was shooting them with a revolver as they crawled
out from the "ataps" on to the ledge of the wall and sat staring
at me impudently. This practice certainly improved my shooting. Then came the great day which was to invest me in native
eyes with the magic skill of a wizard.

The whole estate, including my own bungalow, was served
by a large well, round and deep, with great cracks in its earthy
sides between the water and the surface. One morning, as I
was breakfasting in solitary state, there was a fiendish gibbering
in the compound outside my office door. The chatter of many

tongues was accompanied by a chorus of women's wails. Infuriated, I rushed out to discover the reason for this matutinal interlude. A Tamil coolie was lying groaning on the ground. Two hundred of his compatriots surrounded him, shrieking, explaining, imploring. A batch of Malays and the whole of my Chinese household stood round to offer advice and see the end of the tragedy. The unfortunate wretch had been bitten by a snake. In jerks and pieces and with many contradictions, the wildly excited crowd told its story. There was a cobra— a giant cobra. It was in the well. It had built its nest in a crack in the side. It was a female. There would be eggs and then young. The well was unapproachable. Armagam had been bitten. The master must build a new well at once. With the aid of the estate dispenser I lanced the two tiny blue punctures in the wretch's leg, cauterised the wound, gave him a bottle of gin, and sent him off in a bullock cart to the hospital twelve miles away. (He recovered!) Then, accompanied by two Tamil "Kenganies" and the Malay overseer, I went out to examine the well. My rifle was still at Port Dickson. My gun I had lent to the District Officer at Jelebu. My only weapon was my rat-shooting revolver. At the well all was still. The Tamil "Kengany" pointed out the hole some eight feet down, in which the cobra had made her home, and with a long bamboo pole my Malay overseer hammered at the entrance. Then life moved with cinematic swiftness. There was a warning hiss. A black hood showed itself at the hole, raised an angry head, in indignation, and sent my companions running for their lives. I took careful aim, fired and likewise retreated. There was a commotion from the well. Then all was still. I had shot the cobra through the head. In its death struggle it had fallen from its hole into the water. The victim of my wizardry was exposed to the public gaze and to the public awe. My reputation was made. In future I could go anywhere.

It was a fortunate chance, because the nearest way to Seremban and civilisation lay through a Chinese mining village with a bad reputation for gang-robberies. Already my bank clerk had been held up by "Kheh" desperadoes, who, disappointed with the contents of his wallet, had cut off his finger as the most convenient means of removing his ring.

To this danger I was no longer exposed. Even in the mining village it was well known (1) that I could shoot rats and cobras with a single bullet, (2) that I never travelled without my revolver, and (3) that I never carried money. I travelled, therefore, in peace. I confess, however, that nothing in life has thrilled me quite so much as riding an ordinary push-bike through the jungle in the middle of the night. This ordeal, terrifying and yet enchantingly mysterious, was my experience every time I went into the chief town and stayed for dinner. As I had to be on my estate before six o'clock the next morning, I used to set out on the return journey about midnight From the fourth to the tenth milestone I did not pass a single house and for six miles I rode for dear life through a forest of giant trees which in the moonlight cast fantastic shapes and shadows across my path. In the distance, like King Solomon's mountains, loomed the hills of Jelebu, mysterious, intimate and yet unfriendly. In the face of this unknown world, which quickened my senses, until like the soldier in the fairy-tale I could put my ear to the ground and hear people whispering some miles away, I was afraid, but there was fascination in my fear. Always I was glad when I reached home. But never was I too afraid to accept a dinner invitation in Seremban or to face the journey home through the jungle. It was a good apprenticeship for Bolshevik Russia. Familiarity soon conquers fear. I grew used to the nightly concert of owls and night-jars. Occasionally, I heard a tiger roaring to its mate. Once I nearly ran into a black panther. But these were rare interludes, and in the end, although I never quite conquered the feeling of eeriness, my fears left me.

I was now to seek other adventures. I have said that I cultivated good relations with the deposed Sultan and his wife. My diplomacy bore fruit, and shortly before the fast of Ramazan I received an invitation to a "rong-geng"—a kind of dancing competition at which the professional dancing girls dance and sing Malay love quatrains. And as they sing, they throw challenges to the would-be poets and dancers among the local youth. To the European it is not a particularly enthralling performance. The dancers do not dance in couples, but shuffle side by side, the man endeavouring to follow the steps of the professional lady. To the Malay, however, it is a romantic adventure with an irresistible sex appeal. Occasionally, a young man, his blood heated to boiling point, will lose all restraint and try to hurl himself on one of the girls. Then the local bodyguard steps into action, and the delinquent is removed forcibly from the arena for the rest of the evening. He is disgraced but envied.

A model of decorum and European propriety, I sat between the Sultan and his virile spouse. The Sultan, old and shrivelled, maintained a dignified silence. His activities were confined to plying me with sweet lemonade and whisky. His virago was more voluble. She discoursed to me on the wickedness of the younger generation and, particularly, of the young women. I enjoyed her conversation. According to local report she had been the wickedest woman of her own generation. Her lovers had been as numerous as the seeds of a mangosteen, but none had ventured to criticise her conduct or to exert the customary Malay rights of a jealous husband or paramour. Even then, with her betel-stained lips and her wrinkled face, she was more than a match for any man. She reminded me of Gagool in "King Solomon's Mines" and inspired me with the same awe and respect.

On the whole, however, it was a tedious entertainment. I did not dare to turn my head to inspect the ladies of the "istana" who, with "sarong" drawn over their heads, revealing only their dark, mysterious eyes, stood behind me. I retired early, determined to requite the hospitality I had received by a far more gorgeous spectacle. The next morning I engaged from a neighbouring state two "rong-geng" girls, whose beauty was a byword even in this remote village. I cleared a space in my own compound, erected seats and a miniature grandstand, and sent out invitations broadcast for the following week.

The village, headed by the Court, turned up in full force.

In the moonlight the bright "sarongs" of the Malays acquired a new and strange splendour. The palm-trees, still as the night itself, cast a ghostly shadow over the earthen floor. Myriads of stars shone from the dark blue canopy of heaven. It was a ballet setting, of which Bakst himself might have been proud, and with the removal of the first restraint my guests gave themselves up to full enjoyment of the sensuous scene. To add lustre to my own brilliance, I had invited the Commissioner of Police, a genial Irishman, whom with some trepidation I placed between the Sultan and his wife. I was thus free to organise the proceedings and to superintend the arrangements for my guests. *And then I saw her.* She was standing among the ladies of the "istana"—a radiant vision of brown loveliness in a batek skirt and a red silk coat. A "sarong" of blue and red squares was drawn over her head, exposing only the tiniest oval of a face and eyes which were as unfathomable as the night.

CHAPTER FOUR

THERE ARE moments in life which photograph themselves indelibly on the brain. This was such a moment—what the French call the *coup de foudre*. I have been in one of the worst earthquakes in Japan. I have seen Tsarist ministers shot before my eyes as a premonitory example of what my own fate was to be if I did not speak the truth. I have had the roof lifted off my house by a "Sumatra." But none of these cataclysms was as tremendous or as shattering as the first explosion of love in my heart when I saw Amai. I was twenty-three. I had spent four years in France and Germany. I had been through my calf love, but I had had no affairs, no dangerous attachments. I had been living for six months in splendid isolation from my fellow countrymen. I had not spoken to a white woman for over a year. Steeped in an unhealthy romanticism, I was ripe for temptation. My life was abnormal enough for me to take my temptation with tragic seriousness. And serious it was in its consequences to both of us, changing the course of both our lives.

For the rest of that evening I was in a fever. A fierce longing to be rid of my guests consumed me. I left the Sultan and his malignant wife to the cares of the Commissioner and, crossing to the other side of the arena, I walked up and down, staring across at the frail beauty of this Malayan girl, who had so suddenly disturbed the monotony of my life. Just above her head there was a torchlight, which seemed to shine on her alone, making her stand out like a pearl on a black background. And, indeed, she was passing fair for a Malay, her skin being far lighter than the skin of the peasant women, who worked in the fields. I was soon to discover why.

Letting impatience get the better of discretion, I summoned Si Woh, my Malay headman, whom I had brought from Singapore and whose relations with the villagers were none too good.

"The girl standing behind the Sultan—who is she?" I whispered fiercely.

His face never changed. Slowly he swept the arena with his eyes as though following the movements of the dancers. He showed no astonishment. He roused no suspicion. Then, talking as though he was discussing some detail of estate work, he answered slowly:

"The crow does not mate with the bird of Paradise. That is Amai, the Sultan's ward. She is married and is about to divorce her husband. When the divorce is through, she will be married to the Sultan's cousin."

I waited impatiently until the last guest had gone. Then, with my new knowledge adding to my ardour, I unburdened myself to my Commissioner friend. His warning was more explicit than Si Woh's. In a few terse sentences he told me to put Amai out of my head now and for always. Otherwise there would be trouble—serious trouble. Native women were all the same anyway. There were others more easily attainable and less dangerous.

The advice was good. I should have taken it. Instead, I set in motion such machinery as I possessed in order to establish contact with my goddess. I took Si Woh into my confidence. Through him I enlisted the services of an old woman attached to the "istana"—a betel-stained old hag who pleaded my suit for me. My progress was slow, but I never relented. Every day at five o'clock Amai used to walk from her house to the "istana," and every day at five o'clock I stood at the corner of the road to watch her pass. We made no sign. I remained motionless. To have spoken would have ruined everything. She never unveiled. She never slackened her pace. And on these daily two minutes of transient passing I lived for six weeks. Then one evening, soon after the divorce proceedings had been completed, I went to my usual trysting-place. The sun was setting and had settled like a ball of fire on the highest mountain peak. A cooling breeze brought a rich fragrance from the jungle. I waited for a few minutes, drinking in the warm beauty of the Malayan sunset, a gnawing hunger in my heart. For once the road was empty. My eyes were fixed on the little footpath which led from her house to the road. At last she came, a crimson "sarong" over her head and small green slippers on her feet. Would she pass me by again as she had passed me on so many occasions before—without a sign, without even a glance? She seemed to be walking more slowly than usual. When she was nearly opposite me, she paused, drew her "sarong" back until it showed the lotus-blossom in her hair, and looked straight into my eyes. Then, like a startled hare, she turned and, quickening her steps, disappeared into the gathering darkness.

I went home on fire. I summoned Si Woh. I summoned the old "bidan."[1] A meeting—a real meeting must be arranged at once.

Two days later the "bidan" came back. She looked more sinister than ever. With many prayers for her own safety she told me that everything had been arranged. The meeting was for that night. I was to wait at the edge of the jungle opposite the ninth milestone at nine o'clock, and Amai would come to me. I was to be punctual and very careful. I was to avoid the road.

Very deliberately I made my preparations. I oiled my revolver, put on a pair of rubber-soled gym shoes, and slipped an electric torch into my pocket. Then, trembling with excitement, I set out on my wild adventure. I had about a mile to walk through a narrow jungle path which led to a disused tin mine. There was the river to cross by a rickety bamboo bridge which even by daylight was a balancing test for any white man. It was not a journey which I would have made for money. No woman will ever tempt me to make it again. Fear lent speed to my limbs, and, when I arrived at the footpath across the rice fields by which Amai had to come, I was a quarter of an hour before my time. The waiting was worse than the walking. In the stillness of the Malayan night my hearing was intensified a hundredfold. The harsh call of the night-jar filled me with forebodings. A giant moth, attracted by my silver buttons, embedded itself in the folds of my coat, striking terror into my heart. There was no moon—not a star in the sky. Crouching

[1] The Court medicine woman.

on my haunches like a native, I waited, gun in hand, while the minutes passed in an agony of slowness. Had the old "bidan" played a trick on me? If so, she would pay dearly for it on the morrow. Had Amai's courage failed her at the last moment? For her the ordeal was a thousand times more dangerous than for me. Then, when despair had almost driven me away, I heard a splash. Some living creature had slipped in the marshy water of the "Padi" field. Then silence, followed by a footstep and, before I could distinguish whether it was a man or beast, a figure loomed suddenly out of the darkness not two paces in front of me. I jumped to my feet. The figure stopped. A faint smell of perfume filled my nostrils. She had come. It was Amai. For one fierce moment I held her in my arms, her body trembling like the quivering of lalang grass at the first touch of the morning sun. Then, taking her by the hand, I led her swiftly from the night down that murky jungle path, across that rickety bridge, back to the friendly shelter of my bungalow. She was never to leave it again until I myself was to be led, half-corpse, half-man, on to the boat at Port Swettenham which was to bear me for ever from the shores of Malaya.

The rest of the story is all tragedy or all comedy according to the romanticism or cynicism of the reader. After that first night Amai remained in my bungalow. Her presence was not merely a visible proof of her love; it was also inspired by fear of her own people. In short, the affair of Amai provoked a great scandal. My bungalow underwent a kind of siege. My Malayan Gagool came to interview me on my doorstep. She came to cajole and entice and remained to threaten. She enlisted the services of her nephew, a ruling prince and a charming young man with whom I had frequently played football. His embarrassment was great. He liked Europeans and he liked me. Over our "stengahs" we discussed the situation from every angle. He offered me the fairest "houri" of his principality. But Amai I must surrender. She was of the blood royal. It was an insult to his aunt and, worse still, it was dangerous to me. The Malays of my village were not civilised like himself. There would be trouble—very serious trouble. He shook his head and smiled, just like my Police Commissioner, but he might as well have talked to the wind as tried to over-ride my Scottish obstinacy. I did not wish to quarrel with the man, still less did I wish to hurt his pride. The affair had made some stir even in European circles. It had reached the ears of the Resident, and I had found it necessary to take counsel's opinion.

I went to Mr. C., an important government official, who had married a Malay, and who was a member of a family with a distinguished record of service in the East. His unofficial advice—his official advice was like "Punch's" advice about marriage—was given from the dearly-bought store of his own Oriental wisdom.

"This is a question of face-saving," he said. "You must gain time. You must say you are preparing to become a Mohammedan."

In my interview with Gagool's nephew I bethought myself of this advice. When all else had failed, I turned to him and said: "I am ready to become a Mohammedan. I have written to the Archbishop of Canterbury to obtain the necessary permission."

When a man is infatuated with a woman, there are almost no limits to the baseness of his conduct. In the eyes of other men my conduct was base and sordid—but not in my own. To keep Amai I *was* prepared to embrace Mohammedanism. It is not an episode in my life of which I am proud or for which I seek to make my youth and my loneliness an excuse, but at the time it was—in the literal sense of the words—deadly serious. It was not merely infatuation. Something of the lust of battle was in my soul—the same spirit which in Rugby football has always made me prefer a struggle against odds to an easy victory. I was playing a lone hand against the world, and I was determined to play it to the last trick.

The Prince professed himself satisfied. Gagool and the village did not. Amai and I became outcasts. My football team deserted me. Akbar, my best half-back, who held the nominal post of bendahara or minister of war under Gagool, betook himself to the jungle. I was warned that he was preparing to run "amok." My Chinese cook left me. He was afraid of what might happen to my food.

And then I fell ill. Day after day a particularly virulent form of malaria wasted my flesh and blood. Every afternoon and every morning I ran a temperature with the regularity of an alarum clock. My doctor came. Like every one else the good man was immersed in the rubber boom. His charge was by the mile, and, as my estate was his most distant call, I could not afford him very often. He drenched me with quinine, but to little purpose. As the months passed, my illness became aggravated by a constant vomiting. I could not keep down any solid food. In three months my weight declined from twelve stone eight to under ten stone. I became depressed and miserable. All day I lay propped up in my long chair, trying to read, cursing my half-caste assistants and the "kenganies" who came to disturb me about the estate work, making myself a burden and a nuisance to everyone. But Amai I would not give up. This determination, this obstinacy, was the one thing that saved me from suicide.

For Amai herself I have nothing but praise. She was an incurable optimist. She was not afraid of any man and she ran my house with a rod of iron. Her cheerfulness, it is true, became a strain almost greater than I could bear. She liked noise which in Malaya means that she liked the gramophone. It was not safe for her to go ouside the compound. She, therefore, stayed at home and played "When the Trees are White with Blossom, I'll return." To-day, I should break the record, or throw it at her head, but at that time I was too weak. Instead, I made a martyr of myself. My only relief from the gramophone was the piano. When I could bear the blossom of the trees no longer, I would offer to play the tin-kettle upright which I had borrowed from my cousin. Amai would then help me to the piano-stool, put a shawl over my shoulders, and sit beside me, while with chattering teeth and palsied fingers I strove to recall the harmonies of my Viennese and Berlin days. Her taste in music was entirely primitive. Obviously, she would have liked negro spirituals and, more than negro rhythmics, the languorous melodies of the Tsiganes. But in those days the "Blue Danube" was the supreme thrill of her musical sensuousness, and, if Wolff and Buresh could have descended on my bungalow with that combined artistry which has made them supreme as exponents of the Viennese waltz, she would have transferred her affections on the spot.

Perhaps I do her an injustice. She had her full share of pride of race. She despised the women who worked in the fields. The irregularity of her own position worried her not at all. Marriage and my own Mohammedanism never entered her mind. As mistress of the only "Tuan" in the district, she held her head proudly. She had the only gramophone and the only piano in the village. Moreover, she saved my life. Suspecting that I was being poisoned, she allowed no food, which she had not prepared herself, to pass my lips. And when I failed to recover, she sent Si Woh for Dowden, the government doctor.

Dowden was a queer fellow—a cynical, morose Irishman, whom I had known in my Port Dickson days. He was unhappy in the East and vented his unhappiness in an aggressiveness which made him unpopular. His heart, however, was all gold, and, as the son of the Dublin Shakespeare and Shelley professor, he appealed to me intellectually more than any other white man in Malaya. He was not entitled to attend me professionally, but he was not the man to worry overmuch about questions of etiquette. He came at once. He saw and he grunted. And that night he went into the bar of the Sungei Ujong Club. The rubber boom was then at its height. Several planters, including my uncle, had made vast fortunes on paper, and in the club drink flowed as it always seems to flow in moments of sudden prosperity. My uncle was playing poker in the card-room—high poker with an "ante" of a hundred dollars. Dowden, who had something of the Bolshevik in his nature, tracked him down. My uncle had just raised the stakes. The doctor poured a douche of cold water on his exuberance.

"If you don't want to lay out your stake in a white man's coffin, you had better collect that nephew of yours at once."

My uncle was shocked. He acted immediately. The next

morning he came out with two Chinese "boys" in his car. In silence the "boys" packed my clothes. Wrapping me in blankets, my uncle carried me into the car. Amai had disappeared into the back room. She must have guessed what was happening, but she never came forward. There was no farewell. But, as the car turned in the compound drive, the sun cast a glint on her little silver slippers which were lying neatly on the bottom step of my bungalow entrance. They were the last I saw of her—the last I was ever to see of her.

CHAPTER FIVE

TO-DAY, ALTHOUGH I have travelled farther afield both by land and sea than even most Scotsmen, I never remember the name of a ship. I recall only vaguely the date and the route of my voyages. Perhaps it was my illness; perhaps first impressions and the memories of early youth are more easily retained; perhaps—and this is true—the first home-coming is the one a man remembers best. The fact remains that every moment of that long voyage from my uncle's bungalow in Seremban to my Highland home in Scotland is impressed on my mind as clearly as if it were yesterday. With great generosity my uncle sent me to Japan for two months. His doctor had said that, once I were removed from the source of infection and infatuation, I should be a new man in six weeks. But Dowden shook his head. He advised me to cut my traces and to go for good. I was given money and a ticket to Yokohama. Maurice Foster, the Worcestershire cricketer, brought me to Singapore. Ned Coke took charge of me on board the steamer. He had left the Rifle Brigade for big business in rubber in Malaya and in real estate in Canada, and his immense physique and vigorous personality overwhelmed me. I let myself be managed. The ship's captain, a German with a Captain Kettle beard, was kindness itself. Perhaps the other passengers objected to my constant retching. At any rate he gave me a cabin to myself on the upper deck. But the voyage itself was a nightmare. The sickness and the vomiting would not stop. My clothes hung in loose folds on my wasted frame. The other passengers had bets whether I should reach Japan alive. At Shanghai I was too ill to go ashore. My eyes were too weak to allow me to read. I wanted to die and was prepared to die. All day long I lay on my long chair and gazed with a fixed vacant stare at the pleasant panorama of hazy coast and island-studded sea. The ship's doctor had me watched in case I slipped overboard. But there was no thought of suicide in my mind—only an immense weariness of the body and of the soul. I was well enough to appreciate the beauty of the Inland Sea. I was well enough to write bad poetry—atrocious sonnets to Amai in which I still heard the surf beating upon Malaya's palm-crested shore with regret for the life and the love I had lost. I was well enough, when we landed in Yokohama, to hate the Japanese with all the prejudice of an Englishman who has worked with the Chinese. But I was not well enough to eat. I was too ill to withstand Ned Coke.

With military precision he had already decided my fate. He was sailing for England via Canada in ten days. If I wished to save my wretched carcase, I must sail with him. He had business in Canada which would detain him six weeks. I should spend these six weeks in the "Rockies." I should take the sulphur baths at Banff (of which more anon). The fever would leave my body, and I should land in Liverpool and be restored to my parents in the same state of healthy and seraphic innocence in which I had left them.

To me it seemed a complicated decision. Coke made it delightfully simple. He took me to a Tokio doctor who confirmed Coke's views about my salvation. He telegraphed both to my father and to my uncle for the necessary funds for this new journey, and both lots of money—more than double what was necessary for my needs—arrived three days later. He was the perfect organiser, and, if I qualify the perfection later, I cast no reflection either on his merits or on my own gratitude. If I were dictator of England at this moment, I should make him Earl of Leicester and leader of the House of Lords. He would soon find the necessary means of reinvigorating that palace of somnolence or, failing in his task, he would, like Samson, remove it on his broad shoulders and deposit it gracefully in the Thames.

Having paid this tribute to my rescuer, I must return to the narrative of my voyage. Everything worked out according to plan. Crossing the Pacific, I shivered and suffered tortures from ague. But at last I began to take nourishment without ill effects. I could even watch with zest a British admiral (long since dead) indulging in deck hockey with that ferocious youthfulness which makes us at once the envy and the laughing-stock of foreigners. When we arrived at Vancouver, I was introduced to Robert Service and for the first time for months the blood came back to my cheeks. I was a shy youth and could still blush, and Service, then at the height of his fame, was the first British author I had met. He gave me autographed copies of his "Songs of a Sourdough," and his "Ballads of a Cheechako." To-day, with the rest of my books, they are doubtless gracing the shelves of a Bolshevik library unless, which is highly probable, they have been burnt by the Moscow hangman as imperialistic effluvia and, therefore, noxious to the Moscow nostrils.

In the smoking-room of the C.P.R. Hotel I heard delirious conversation about speculators in real estate, who had made millions in a night, leaving in their trail a ruin which has lasted to this day. There, too, for the first time I heard the name of Max Aitken, who, having fought and beaten the millionaires of Montreal, had gone to seek new fields of conquest in England. It is a tribute to the honesty of my romanticism, if not to the soundness of my judgment, that at that moment Max Aitken meant nothing to me and Robert Service a good deal.

Be that as it may, I read Service's books, had a drink with him, and sniffed the Canadian air. The combined effort cured me of my infatuation for Amai and made me turn my eyes towards the West. And so to Banff.

Patriotism is the most abused of all sentiments. In its best sense it expresses an animal instinct of self-preservation. In its worst it is tainted with material interests and such sordid things as money and self-advancement. In the Englishman it manifests itself in a dumb contempt for everything that is not English. The Scot has a more practical patriotism. His contempt for foreigners includes the Englishman, but is carefully concealed. His jingoism is confined to cheering Scotland at Twickenham. It is racial rather than local. It concerns Scotland hardly at all. Its aim is the glorification and self-satisfaction of the Scot in whatever part of the globe the impulse of self-advancement drives him.

There is, however, another form of patriotism which may be truly expressed as love of country. This is the actual love which is in every man for the place in which he was born and brought up. It may be inspired by vanity, by the desire to see himself reflected again in the glory of his youth. It is especially strong in the man who has been brought up in beautiful surroundings, but it affects even the man from Wigan. It is strongest of all in the Highlander.

Banff with its glorious background of fir and pine was to me the first breath of returning life. Rarely have I felt so homesick, and this outpost of Scotland was already half-way home. The Rockies were grander than the Grampians, but they were like the Grampians. The Bow River made a sub-stitute for the Spey. The village itself was named after a Scottish town not twenty miles away from the scenes of my own early youth. I took Banff to my heart. I hired a launch and explored the Bow River (alas! I was still too weak to fish) and I visited the cold waters of Lake Louise and Lake Minnewanka. I talked with the Indians in the settlement. I discovered Parkman and read him voraciously. I devoured stories of Soapy Smith and the other brigands of the trail of '98. Klondyke was still on everyone's lips. In every township one found the scarred and frost-bitten victims of the gold rush. It was an age of romance—sordid enough when one looked beneath the surface, but in the luxurious comfort of a C.P.R. Hotel no one wanted to look. Motor-buses had not yet made the highways hideous. There was no army of American tourists to fill the mountain air with their dis-cordant rapture. Dangerous Dan McGrew was at any rate true to life and "Soapy" himself a nearer descendant of Dick Turpin than Al Capone. Above all, the mountain passes lit by the Arctic moon were a more fitting setting for romantic crime than the searchlights and machine-guns of the under-world fastnesses of Cicero.

If it is true that man creates his own atmosphere, Nature can make or mar the process, and in Banff Nature was a powerful ally. I bathed myself in the romance of the

Far West and felt better. I was now to bathe in a more literal sense.

Ned Coke was the agent of my undoing. My health was his constant preoccupation. My progress towards recovery delighted him, and, rightly, he took full credit for it. Unfortunately, he was unable to leave well alone. He had the mind of a prospector, and he was always seeking new fields of exploration. At Banff there were famous sulphur baths—open-air baths situated some 1,000 feet above sea-level. I had spent three years in an unhealthy climate almost on the equator. I was suffering from as bad an attack of malaria as mortal man could withstand and, if the desire to live had returned, death had not yet relaxed his grip on my enfeebled body. Commonsense might have pointed out to me the folly of bathing in the open air in a high and cooler altitude. I had, however, little commonsense and less will-power, and Coke was an experimentalist. He found an ally in the hotel doctor—a young enthusiast, who was impressed by Coke's persuasiveness and wished to share in the credit of the discovery of sulphur as a sovereign cure for malaria. Perhaps my faith was not as strong as Naaman's. At any rate I bathed in Banff's Jordan. I stayed in the bubbling sulphur the requisite number of minutes ordained by Coke and his McGill University admirer. Unaided, but with chattering teeth, I returned to the hotel; within ten minutes my temperature had risen to 103. I retired to bed. My friends piled blanket after blanket on top of me. An hour later my temperature had risen another point. Gasping and half-delirious, I raved for quinine. Prompted by Coke, the doctor gave me five grains of quinine and five grains of aspirin. Then they both withdrew to leave me to sleep. Fortunately, they left the bottles on my night-table. I made a sign to Harry Stephenson, who had remained with me, and Harry gave me fifteen grains more of both the quinine and the aspirin. For four hours I tossed in my delirium, half-way between life and death. And then the sweat broke. I dripped through my sheets. I dripped through my mattress. My bed was like a pool. But my temperature was down and, limp and weary, I changed beds and slept myself back to life.

The rest of my homeward voyage was accomplished without incident. I stayed a week in Quebec, read the "Chien d'Or," scaled the heights of Abraham and dreamed those first dreams of Empire, which were afterwards to make me a willing disciple of the policy of Lord Beaverbrook. The seeds of my Canadian visit bore fruit in 1916, when I was the first Englishman to celebrate Empire Day in Russia in a fitting and official manner.

The only fiasco was the actual home-coming itself. If the blue skies of the Canadian autumn had restored some of my former vigours, the fogs of Liverpool brought a return of my malaria and with it a fresh access of that moral cowardice which in moments of crisis has always been my bane in life.

I returned to the bosom of my family who were then rusticating in the Highlands. There was, however, no fatted calf for the returning prodigal. My mother welcomed me, as mothers will always welcome their first-born, that is to say, with gratitude to God for my escape from death and with sorrow for the disappointment of her fondest hopes. My father, himself the most austere of moralists, has always been tolerance itself in his attitude towards others. No word of reproach fell from his lips. I am, however, on my mother's side, a member of the Clan Gregarra, and until her death our family world moved on the axis of my grandmother—an Atlas of a woman who supported on her broad shoulders a vast army of children and grandchildren. She was a woman cast in the Napoleonic mould—an avatar of the old Highland Chieftains whose word was law and whose every whim a command which had to be fulfilled. She supported the clan with a generosity which is rare in these days, but the business of the clan was her business, and woe betide the scapegoat whose delinquencies were brought to her notice by any other members of the family than the offender himself.

She was a rigid and austere Presbyterian who ruled her ministers with the same iron rod with which she ruled her family. Nor was she tolerant of clerical opposition. On one occasion the elders of the Speyside congregation over which she presided dared to select as parish minister a candidate against whom she had turned her face. Her anger was as sharp as her decision. She deserted the church where her ancestors were buried, and half a mile away set up at her own expense a new church and a new manse for the candidate whom she herself had approved. Not until the offending minister had passed away did she relent. Then her repentance was as magnanimous as her anger had been petty. Her own church was joined to the old church and converted into a free library and concert hall. The manse was sold for the benefit of the parish, and she herself returned to the family pew in which she had sat in judgment on so many sermons. To-day her remains repose on the banks of the Spey beside those massive granite boulders of which she herself had been in life the living embodiment.

She was a great woman, but like most Presbyterians she worshipped material success. At the time of my return she had made a vast paper fortune out of her plantations in the Malay States. In Edinburgh she was re-christened the Rubber Queen, and the flattery had gone to her head like new wine. Already she saw herself controlling the Stock Exchange. Her financial success was the reward of her own foresight and business acumen. She refused to see anything exceptional in this most exceptional of booms and, heedless of the warnings of her brokers, she continued to buy rubber shares on a falling market. Within a few years her fortune had dwindled to proportions incommensurate with her scale of expenditure.

At that moment, however, her star was in the ascendant. Planters are not renowned for their intellectual attainments. Yet every planter had made money out of the rubber boom. I, who had been a scholar, had failed to profit by my golden opportunities. This was the measure of my business capacity in her eyes. I was a fool.

There was worse to come. The news of my moral delinquencies had preceded my arrival. There had been gossip.

My uncle had been accused of neglecting me, and, if he was too good a sportsman to bother to defend himself, other relatives in the Malay States had undertaken the task for him. The shadow on my grandmother's face, when she greeted me, was the shadow of Amai.

Every day I was made to feel myself a moral leper. I was dragged to church. If the sermon was not actually preached at me, it was interpreted in that sense afterwards by my grandmother. The scarlet woman was conjured up before my eyes on every conceivable occasion. I was too weak to fish or shoot. Instead, I went motoring with my grandmother. Every drive was the occasion for a lecture. Every scene of my boyhood was recalled and pointed to adorn a moral tale. I was told to lift up my eyes to the hills, until even my beloved Grampians became a plague-spot and a canker of self-torture. To this day I hate the right bank of the Spey, because that year my grandmother's shoot was on that bank.

That October in the Highlands undid all the good which Canada had done for my health, and, shattered in mind and body, I returned to the South of England to place myself once more in the hands of the doctors. I visited two malaria specialists in Harley Street. Their reports were grave. My heart was seriously affected. My liver and spleen were enlarged. My digestion was ruined. The process of recovery would be slow, very slow. I could never return to the Tropics. I must not walk up-hill. Exercise was out of the question. Even golf was forbidden. I must be careful, very careful.

I returned to my father's home in Berkshire and, freed from the moral domination of my grandmother's personality, began at once to recover. In spite of the English winter and frequent bouts of malaria, I put on weight. I cast my drugs and tonics into the outer darkness and confined my medicine to a brandy-flip a day. In three months I was playing Rugby football again. So much for the experts of Harley Street.

CHAPTER SIX

MY PARTIAL RECOVERY, however, did not solve the question of my existence. The malaria had left me with an impaired will-power and an unhealthy morbidness. If a certain amount of morbidity in the thoughts of a young man is normal, the lack of will-power, which is a characteristic reaction of tropical fevers, is serious and not easily remedied. I had no ambitions of any kind. In a delightfully vague manner I desired to be an author. I was given a special room in my father's home, and there I sat through the winter, writing sketches of Eastern life and short stories with morbid settings and unhappy endings. I engaged in desultory correspondence with various literary agents. At the end of six months I had succeeded in placing one short story and two articles. My receipts were smaller than my postages bill.

And then one May morning my father sent for me. There was nothing peremptory about the command, no reproach in what he said. He talked to me—as I hope I shall be able to talk to my own son when his turn comes—suggesting rather than ordering, studiously safeguarding my sensitiveness, solicitous only of my welfare even if that welfare entailed more sacrifices and more self-denial on his part. He pointed out to me what many others have pointed out before: that literature was a good crutch, but scarcely a pair of legs, that I did not seem to be making much headway, and that security of occupation was the master-key to happiness in life. At twenty-three I was too old for most government examinations. There was, however, the general Consular Service. It was a career in which my knowledge of foreign languages would reap their full benefit and which would give abundant scope to my literary ambitions. Had not Bret Harte and Oliver Wendell Holmes been members of the American Consular Service? In slow and measured sentences my father expounded the pleasures of a life of which he knew less than nothing. Then, like the Fairy Godmother, he produced his surprise packet—a letter from John Morley announcing that he had been able to procure for me a nomination for the next examination. Years before, my grandfather, a staunch Conservative and one of the earliest Imperialists, had opposed Morley at Arbroath, and such is the sporting spirit of English political life that twenty years afterwards the great man had seen fit to bestir himself on behalf of the grandson of the defeated candidate.

Before this new onslaught of my father's kindness, my defences broke down. Doubtless, his manner of dealing with a recalcitrant and self-indulgent offspring was too gentle. But I have studied at close hand the methods of the stern, relentless father, and the results have brought neither happiness to the parent nor discipline to the children. If, viewed from the angle of material success, my life has been a failure, my father has the consolation that in a flock of six I have been the only black sheep and that to all of us he has remained not only a wise counsellor but a friend and companion from whom not even the most shameful secret need be withheld.

As I read the Morley letter, I looked into the mirror of my past life. The reflection gave me no satisfaction. I had been an expensive investment for my parents. Hitherto I had paid no dividends. It was time that I began. To the unqualified relief of my father I graciously consented to burden the Civil Service Commissioners with the correction of my examination papers.

Before I could enter the precincts of Burlington House there were certain formalities to be fulfilled. Almost immediately I had to undergo a personal inspection by a committee of Foreign Office inquisitors. Dressed in my most sombre suit, I travelled to London, made my way to Downing Street, and was piloted into a long room on the first floor of the Foreign Office, where some forty or fifty candidates sat waiting their turn in various degrees of nervousness. The procedure was simple but tedious. At one end of the room there was a large door before which stood a Foreign Office messenger. At intervals of ten minutes the door would open, an immaculately dressed young man with a sheet of paper in his hand would whisper to the messenger, and the messenger, clearing his throat, would announce in stentorian tones to the assembled innocents the next victim's name.

By the time my turn came the room was nearly empty and my nerves had gone back on me. I was in agony lest there had been some mistake and my name had been forgotten. I saw myself forced into making some sheepish explanation. Only terror lest my boots should creak prevented me from tiptoeing to the messenger to set my doubts at rest. Then, just when I had given up hope, the frock-coated messenger raised his voice, and this time the rafters re-echoed with the name "Mr. Bruce Lockhart." With flushed face and clammy hands I crossed the threshold of my fate and passed into the inner temple. My mind was a blank. My carefully rehearsed answers were completely forgotten.

Fortunately, the inquisition was less formidable than the waiting. In a narrow oblong room six senior officials sat at a long table. For a moment I stood before them like a prize bull at a cattle show undergoing the scrutiny of six pairs of be-spectacled or bemonocled eyes. Then I was told to take a seat on the other side of the table. Again there was a pause while the inquisitors rustled with their papers. They were extracting my curriculum vitæ—that record of *suppressio veri* and *suggestio falsi* which like the questionnaire of an insurance company every candidate is obliged to produce before he can present himself for examination. Then, with the politeness of Stanley addressing Livingstone, the chairman smiled at me benevolently: "Mr. Lockhart, I presume," and, before I knew where I was, I was being questioned about my experiences as a rubber planter. I imagine most of the inquisitors were interested personally in the rubber market. At all events I underwent a rapid cross-fire of questions about the merits of different shares. As my knowledge was greater than that of my examiners, my confidence returned, and I expanded with volubility and authority on the dangers and possibilities of the Malayan Eldorado. I hope they took my advice. It was inspired with caution derived from the experiences of my own over-optimistic relations.

Then, just when I felt completely at my ease, I was brought back to earth with a sudden bump. Hitherto I had been playing the schoolmaster to a band of attentive and enthusiastic schoolboys. Now the rôles were to be suddenly reversed. Across the smooth plains of this pleasant and entirely satisfactory conversation came an icy blast from a stumpy little man with a wrinkled forehead and iron-grey moustache.

"And will you tell us, Mr. Lockhart, why you left this terrestrial Paradise?"

My knees rocked. Had the omniscience of the Foreign Office already discovered the escapade of Amai? It had been glossed over in my testimonials. It did not figure in my curriculum vitæ. The speaker was Lord Tyrrell—at that time plain Mr. Tyrrell—and there and then, with an instinct which has rarely played me false, I registered him as a potential enemy. With an effort I pulled myself together.

"I had a very bad attack of malaria," I said. And then I added feebly: "but I'm playing 'rugger' again now." This afterthought was a happy inspiration. A sportsman with a monocle and the lean spare figure of an athlete came to my rescue.

"Are you a relation of the Cambridge googly bowler?" he asked. (My brother—a double Blue and "Rugger" International—was then at the height of his athletic fame.)

"He is my little brother," I said simply. And with that password I received the official blessing and passed out again into the sunshine.

So far so good. There remained, however, the more serious obstacle of the written examination. The more I considered my chances, the less I liked them. In that year of grace there were only four vacancies. The number of registered candidates exceeded sixty. Practically all had been preparing for the examination for several years. Several had been in the first twenty the previous year. Half a dozen had taken first-class honours at Oxford and Cambridge. I had done no scholastic work of any kind for three years. Now I had only ten weeks in which to prepare myself for an examination, which not only was highly competitive, but which included, among its obligatory subjects, law and economics. Of law I had not read a single line. Political economy was to me an occult and mysterious science. Truly, indeed, the outlook seemed hardly worth the effort.

My father, however, was enthusiastically optimistic. I transferred myself to London and entered the most successful "crammer" of those days. The experience plunged me into even deeper gloom. For one long week I attended my classes with unfailing patience and punctuality. The other candidates were finishing off where I was beginning, and the lectures on law and political economy—doubtless, admirably given, but intended rightly for advanced students—were sheer waste of time. My despair roused me to action, and I took a rapid decision. I wrote to my father and told him that I must leave the "crammer" and that I proposed taking my chance on the other subjects and engaging the services of the law coach and the political economy coach for private tuition. My father agreed to the extra expense. As my fees for the term had been paid in advance, the "crammer" authorities made no objection.

My law coach was a born teacher. My political economy coach was a German genius who had gone to seed on snuff and whisky. Together we "gutted" Marshall and Nicholson, and, as we did our work in German, I was enabled to kill two subjects with one fee.

My plan of campaign involved three hours a day with my coaches and whatever work I chose to do by myself. There were, however, disturbing distractions. An uncle, who after ten years of incessant labour had made a fortune, had come to London to enjoy himself. He had fallen in love with a charming South American who required a chaperon. He required someone to engage the attentions of the chaperon, and the most tractable and easily managed someone was myself. He made me give up my modest rooms in Bayswater and took me to live with him in his hotel. Every evening we dined *en partie carrée*, went to a theatre and then to supper at the Ritz or the Carlton. It was scarcely the best preparation for a sadly unprepared candidate, but with the supreme egotism which characterises most successful business men my uncle had no idea of the harm he was doing. On the contrary, he hounded me off to my coaches' rooms every morning and informed me that if I failed to pass I should be cut out of his will. I laughed and continued to drink his champagne. He has since married twice, and the chances of my heritage have been wrecked, partly, on the quicksands of my own follies, but mainly through the arrival into this world of four flourishing cousins, who are young enough to be my own children. In the intervening years, however, he has rewarded my chaperonage a thousandfold, and to-day, but for my reckless extravagance, the sum total of his generosity would be yielding me an income of some five hundred pounds a year.

In this spirit of preparation I approached that fatal first week in August when with a strange lack of consideration the Civil Service Commissioners unfold the doors of Burlington House to the youthful hopes of the nation. I give a detailed account of the proceedings for the benefit of those pedagogues who believe in the futility of all examinations. In my own experience they will find an ample justification for their theories.

When on that Monday morning I took my place in the queue of perspiring candidates, my prospects were so poor as to relieve me personally of all anxiety. The disadvantages of my unpreparedness were obvious. Against them I could set two advantages: I was more of a man of the world than my fellow-competitors and, having, as I thought, no chance, I had no nerves. I had perhaps one other advantage and certainly one enormous piece of luck. That summer was the hottest summer England had experienced for many years, and I liked heat. That year, too, for the first time an essay was included in the French and German papers—an innovation which had escaped the vigilance of the "crammers" and which left the candidates to their own slender resources. In the choice of subjects for the French essay was included Kipling's tag of "East is East and West is West." I fastened on it eagerly, drawing on my Malayan experiences and paraphrasing whole pages of Loti which I knew by heart. I enjoyed that examination, feeling completely at my ease in the face of a new adventure. My one embarrassment was the paper on political economy. There were ten questions of which we had to answer not more than six. Unfortunately, my knowledge embraced only four. There was, however, one question on which I was a minor expert. I wrote pages on it, scribbled short and non-committal answers to the three other questions, and then added a polite footnote to the effect that two hours was too short a time in which to answer a paper of this nature.

On the Thursday evening, having completed my written papers, I said good-bye to my coaches, who had worked with me every night of the examination. As we shook hands, my German mentor handed me a sealed envelope.

"You will open it," he said, "on the day the result is declared. The envelope contains my prophecy of the successful candidates. I am rarely wrong."

As soon as he had gone, I opened the letter. He had placed me fourth, and in celebration of a joke which was truly "kolossal" I dined at the Carlton and went to the theatre.

There remained only the oral examination on the next day to complete my ordeal, and I considered I was entitled to some relaxation. Nevertheless, the oral examination was nearly my undoing. My German oral was at ten in the morning. I do not know if my late night was to blame, but with the German examiner I lost my head. He was altogether too suave and too enticing. Before I knew where I was, he had drawn me into a conversation about Malaya. From that starting point he proceeded to question me, for his own edification, on the different processes of tapping rubber. Even in English this is a technical and difficult basis for an ordinary conversation. In a foreign language it was frankly impossible, and, although my knowledge of German was considerable, I knew that I had made a failure of my German oral. I left the room cursing myself for my stupidity and determined not to be caught again in the same manner. When I came out into the sunlight, I was in a quandary. My French oral—the climax of my week's ordeal—was not until five o'clock in the afternoon. All my friends had left for Scotland or the Continent. How was I to fill in the long blank between eleven and five? I hesitated and then stepped boldly across the street. Opposite Burlington House was the "Bristol Bar," the favourite haunt of the foreign women who frequented the London of the pre-war days. Stimulating my courage with a sherry and bitters, I made the acquaintance of two elderly but extremely voluble Pompadours. I gave them a free luncheon and free drinks, in return for which they talked French with me. I went for an hour's walk in the Green Park and returned at three-thirty for more alcohol and more French. By a quarter to five my volubility was immense and my accent almost perfect. Then at five minutes to five I walked steadily across the road for my French oral.

Once again, like a convict with a warder, I was kept waiting in the long corridor until the examiner's cell was free. This time, however, all trace of nervousness was gone, and I entered the room with the courage of a seasoned veteran. A mild looking professor with pince-nez and a drooping moustache looked up from his desk and placed the tips of his fingers together.

"Can you tell me the name of the French Dreadnought recently launched at Brest?" he asked.

I shook my head and smiled.

"No, Sir," I said with a fine precision. "I do not know and I do not care. I have only half an hour in which to prove to you that I know French as well as you do. Let me talk of other matters."

Then I made a lucky shot. He had a slight English accent and, before he could interrupt me, I beat down his defences.

"You are Professor S——," I said, "and last week I reviewed a book of yours in the *Maître Phonétique*."

My conduct was a breach of the anonymity which is supposed to be enjoyed by all Civil Service examiners, and the Professor promptly reproved me without admitting or denying the accuracy of my identification. The damage, however, had been done. The conversation had been turned to phonetics in which science I was an expert and he only a beginner, and from that moment I was safe. For long past the regulation period the Professor continued to be absorbed in our conversation. I had wound up the mainspring of his interest, and, when finally I said goodbye to him, I knew that, however badly I had done in German, my French oral had been a brilliant success.

THAT NIGHT I left for the Highlands, and for the next four weeks I led a pleasant existence fishing in the Spey and shooting my grandmother's grouse. As September approached, I experienced vague pangs of uneasiness. I had prepared my parents for the disappointment which I had assured them was bound to come. My pessimism did nothing to relieve their anxiety about my future. My grandmother, in particular, continued to regard me as a scapegrace, who had no right to the good things of life. If I took a second glass of port at dinner, I was sure to find her reproving eye fixed upon me. I lived in an atmosphere of apprehensive disapproval and, resigning myself to an inevitable return to rubber-planting and the East, I endeavoured to extract as much enjoyment as I could from these last opportunities of luxury in much the same spirit as a condemned man eats a hearty breakfast before his execution.

Then on September 2nd, that blessed day which saw my birth, I went into the neighbouring town to play a round of golf. As I was putting on the third green, I was disturbed by a wild yell. I looked up from my ball and saw my two young brothers careering on bicycles across the mountainous slopes of our Highland course. Norman, who was later to die gloriously at Loos, had disappeared into a ditch. His front wheel was buckled, but his face was radiant with excitement. He waved a paper triumphantly in the air.

"You're in," he gasped breathlessly. "You're first!"

I took the paper from his hands. It was true. There it stood in black and white: first, R. H. Bruce Lockhart. I studied the cold marks sheet. I was first by seventeen marks. Fifty marks covered the first four candidates. I had done badly in German which was by far my best subject. I had qualified by one mark in the mathematical paper. I was second in law and first in political economy. I had collected thirty-five more marks in French than any other candidate. I had received ninety-nine marks out of a hundred for my French oral. The Pompadours had done it. I do not know if they are still alive.

44

I never discovered even their Christian names. But for such damage as I have inflicted on the might, majesty and dominion of the British Empire in my official capacity, they—and they alone—must bear the full responsibility.

I abandoned my game and returned home to announce the glad tidings to my parents. They had recently celebrated their silver wedding, and most of my numerous relations had assembled in the neighbourhood for the event. Great, indeed, was my welcome. Never before or since have I felt so completely virtuous. An unstamped envelope, bearing the inscription "On His Majesty's Service," had wrought a lightning metamorphosis in my existence, and overnight I had passed from the ranks of the ne'er-do-weels into the Valhalla of heroes. My grandmother took me to her ample bosom and with the infallibility of the truly great announced firmly that she had always believed in my success. She sent for her bag. She sent for her spectacles. And, there and then, she wrote me out a cheque for one hundred pounds. Her example was contagious, and that afternoon I collected nearly two hundred pounds in tips. A few days later, with my winnings still intact, I left for London in order to enter upon my official duties at the Foreign Office.

In that year of grace the Foreign Office was a very different place from what it is to-day. Then it combined space with elegance and ease. Now it is a rabbit-warren overrun by bespectacled typists and serious-looking and rather badly dressed young men. In 1911 there were still elderly gentlemen who wrote fastidiously with quill-pens. A certain standard of penmanship and a minute attention to margins were still demanded from youthful draft-writers. Otherwise, it was a leisurely and not unpleasant existence, fortified by regular hours and an adequate luncheon interval. If the hours were longer than Palmerston's comparison with the fountains of Trafalgar Square, "which played from ten to four," they were not a weariness of the flesh. Nor were they devoted entirely to work. In the department to which I was attached desk-cricket flourished under the skilful guidance of Guy Locock, to-day the presiding genius of the Federation of British Industries.

The war and the industry of Lord Curzon have destroyed this calm backwater in the rushing river of life. The corridors, where one used to play football with the Resident-Clerks, are now lined with heavy cases of archives. Staffs have been doubled. Papers have accumulated to such an extent that the conscientious official has to work late into the night in order to complete his daily task. The Foreign Office now works longer hours than most business houses. It has become efficient and more democratic.

In my day it had a highly developed sense of its own superiority. It was a home of mandarins, holding itself superbly aloof from the more plebeian departments of Whitehall. The Treasury was admitted to some degree of equality. After all, the allowances of even ambassadors were subjected to Treasury control. We are justly famed for our sense of the practical. I have yet to meet the Englishman who is not prepared to put his social pride in his pocket if by this action his pocket will benefit. The Board of Trade, on the other hand, was regarded in much the same light as the Shooting Eight at a public school—as a home for bug-shooters. Junior vice-consuls, whose main function is the fostering of British trade abroad, were, therefore, looked upon as unnecessary intruders. Their social position in the office was a kind of purgatory suspended between the Heaven of the First Division and the Hell of the Second.

In those days the procedure with regard to a junior vice-consul was as follows: before proceeding to a foreign post he was required to spend three months in the Consular and Commercial departments of the Foreign Office. Except for the fact that it gave me an opportunity to know some of the clerks in the office, it was sheer waste of time. In view of the official attitude towards trade, these two departments were the most inefficient in the Foreign Office. The senior clerks, who ran them, were men who had lost all ambition and who had abandoned hope of further promotion. They were the last stepping-stones to honourable retirement and a pension.

As head of the new list of vice-consuls, I was sent for my period of probation to the Consular Department. My "chief" was Lord Dufferin—a kind and generous man, who smoked countless cigarettes and who looked—and, indeed, was—a sick man. His only exaction from his subordinates was neatness, his only passion—red ink. My first fortnight in the office was sheer misery comparable only with one's first fortnight at a public school. Nobody spoke to me. Every day at eleven I made my appearance, dressed in the stiffest of white collars and the regulation short black coat and striped trousers. I minuted a few letters from distressed British subjects abroad. Occasionally, I wrote a draft demanding the repayment of sums advanced by British consuls to stranded seamen. Once I had a minor thrill. A letter arrived addressed to His Majesty, and beginning with the words "My dear King." It was from a young English girl of seventeen who had taken a post with a Russian landowner in the Volga district. She was miles from any railway station, and her employer was making love to her in a particularly violent and disgusting manner. This pathetic cry from the wilderness was given to me to answer, and my gorge rose with indignant emotion. I wrote a strong minute which was approved with commendable despatch. The telegraph wires were set in motion. The intervention of His Majesty's Ambassador was requested, and within thirty-six hours the little lady was set free and despatched at government expense to her home in Ireland. For the first time I had put my finger on the Empire's pulse. I had tasted power and felt duly elated.

On the whole, however, there was little to do, and I was left severely alone. Every day I lunched alone at the "Ship." I could not share my meals with Kaye, my consular colleague in the department, as we had alternate luncheon hours. Occasionally, in the corridors I passed the silently great and greatly silent figures of the Foreign Office hierarchy. Furtively, I studied their gait and their mannerisms: the long, raking stride of Sir Edward Grey, the automatic energy of Sir Eyre Crowe, the graceful elegance of Sir Ian Malcolm, and the ponderous roll of Sir Victor Wellesley. They were, however, vague and awe-inspiring shadows in my existence, and they gave me a proper sense of my own insignificance.

Gradually, as I came to know Guy Locock better, my lot improved. We lunched together. With Sir George Buchanan and Harold Nicolson he was one of the few Wellingtonians in the Foreign Office. As my brothers were playing for Marlborough, I took him to see the Wellington v. Marlborough "rugger" match. We played golf together. I was admitted to desk cricket and became an expert. From him I learnt the historical gossip of the office—wondrous tales of the practical jokes of Lord Bertie and of other stalwarts of bygone days. In return, with my weakness for self-revelation, I told him the story of my life. Our friendship progressed so rapidly that within a few weeks I was able to induce him to listen to the Eastern sketches which I had written and which English editors had been foolish enough to refuse. Doubtless, he found the performance more amusing than the writing of consular minutes.

This literary entertainment, provided of course during office hours, led to a strange turn in my fortunes. In the ordinary course of events, after completing my six weeks in the Consular Department, I should have been transferred to the Commercial Department, where I should have come under the tutelage of Sir Algernon Law, a fierce disciplinarian, of whom every youngster stood in awe. There had been, however, a change in my own department. Lord Dufferin had fallen ill and had been replaced temporarily by Don Gregory, who was then a junior assistant. In the meantime the Agadir crisis had broken out, and, as the political departments were working at high pressure, our staff had been reduced in order to provide extra help. One afternoon, as I was reading a particularly touching tale of a Catholic missionary in the East to Guy Locock, Don Gregory came into the room. The word "Catholic" must have caught his ear.

"What's this?" he said in his pleasant, rather fussy manner. Guy explained.

"We have a literary genius in the office," he said. "He's reading us a story about a Catholic missionary."

Gregory took my manuscript. The next day he asked me to dinner. I met Mrs. Gregory and liked her. I talked about my life in the East and gave her more manuscripts to read. I presented her with a couple of Japanese portraits which I had bought in Japan and about which I had written a sentimental sketch. Within a few days I was asked to dine again. My position in the office changed. Gregory gave me more work to do. I became, in short, his private secretary. Then one day he sent for me.

"We are very short-handed," he said. "You will gain nothing by going to the Commercial Department or by going abroad too soon. I can arrange for you to stay here for a bit to help us out. When the time comes for you to go abroad, I shall see that you will lose nothing by this arrangement in the selection of your post."

Of course I accepted. I was then still an Episcopalian, although my sympathies with Roman Catholicism were already strong. This, however, was enough. The generous, warm-hearted Don liked Catholics. What was more important he seemed to like me, and I owe him the full measure of my gratitude. As a departmental official he had few equals, and from him I learnt much that was to benefit me in future years. He put me wise about official life abroad. He told me much about Rumania, where he had been en poste, and about Poland, in whose fate he was deeply interested. He greatly stimulated my interest in Russia, which even then he realised was to be the storm-centre of Europe. Then, one evening about Christmas time, he summoned me to his room and showed me a despatch. It was an intimation from our Ambassador in St. Petersburg announcing that the Russian Government had approved my appointment as British Vice-Consul in Moscow.

"You will have to leave in a fortnight," he said with a smile.

Moscow! Like a flash the Russia of Seton Merriman—the only Russia I knew—passed before my eyes. Adventure, danger, romance photographed themselves in my mind. But one thought dominated everything. Moscow was Europe. It was only three days away from home. Six weeks ago, but for my luckless Eastern manuscripts, it was a thousand to one that like all new vice-consuls I should have been sent to Colon or Panama, or, at the best, to Chicago or Pittsburg. Gratefully I faltered out my thanks, and that night I left the office for good to rush home to tell the good news to my parents and to prepare for my departure.

There was to be one more adventure before I left. My father and mother gave a farewell dance for me. It was attended by all my—or rather their—friends in the neighbourhood. One house-party, which turned up in full force, brought with it a beautiful Australian girl, whom I had never seen before. I succumbed at once. I had only a fortnight in which to press my suit. In ten days we were engaged. Early in the New Year I left for Russia and she returned to Australia. We were married during my first leave the following year.

BOOK II

THE MOSCOW PAGEANT

"PEOPLE PASS. One has eyes. One sees them."

From the French.

CHAPTER ONE

MY ARRIVAL IN Moscow coincided with the visit of the British Parliamentary Delegation, which, on the invitation of the Russian Government, had descended upon St. Petersburg and Moscow in that January of 1912. It was an imposing body, headed by the Speaker of the House of Commons. Lord Ampthill, Lord Derby, and Lord Weardale represented the Peers, General Sir James Wolfe Murray the Army, Lord Charles Beresford the Navy, and four Bishops the Church. There were many others, and altogether the delegation was about eighty strong. Attached to it in the capacity of interpreter was the inimitable and indispensable Maurice Baring. By the time it had reached Moscow, several of its members had fallen by the way and had returned home. The hospitality of St. Petersburg had been too much for them. Now the remaining Parliamentarians had to face the far greater ordeal of Muscovite hospitality—an ordeal which I was to share to the full.

On my arrival at the Brest Station I was met by Montgomery Grove, my new chief. He was in full uniform and was just dashing off to the ballet for the gala performance in honour of the British visitors. Instructing the porter how to deal with my luggage, he whisked me into a sleigh, drove me to the Metropole Hotel, pushed a bundle of invitation cards into my hand, and, depositing me with the hall porter, rushed away to keep his engagement.

A little bewildered but full of curiosity I proceeded to examine my new surroundings. The hotel was full to overflowing, and the room reserved for me was on the top floor. Most of my neighbours were women, gaudily painted and gaudily dressed, who, after discovering by exhaustive telephone inquiries both my innocence and my modest purse, lost all interest in this new arrival. In any case, even had they so wished, Vice-Consuls could not compete with the Russian merchants of those days.

As I walked through the hall to the restaurant, my first impressions were of steaming furs, fat women and big sleek men;

of attractive servility in the underlings and of good-natured ostentation on the part of the clients; of great wealth and crude coarseness, and yet a coarseness sufficiently exotic to dispel repulsion. I had entered into a kingdom where money was the only God. Yet the God of roubles was more lavish, more spendthrift, less harsh, than the God of dollars .

The restaurant itself was a blaze of light and colour. The long high room was surrounded by a balcony on all sides. Along the balcony were gaily lit windows and doors opening into the private rooms—known in Russia as "kabinets"—where, hidden from prying eyes, dissolute youth and debauched old age trafficked roubles and champagne for gipsy songs and gipsy love. I do my beloved gipsies a wrong. Their morals were better than most people's. They kept themselves for themselves. The mercenary love, to which I refer, was Austrian, or Polish, or Jewish.

The restaurant itself was a maze of small tables. It was crowded by officers in badly cut uniforms, Russian merchants with scented beards, German commercial travellers with sallow complexions and close-cropped heads. And at every table a woman, at every table champagne—bad champagne at twenty-five shillings a bottle. At the hotel end of the room was a high balustraded dais, where an orchestra, resplendent in red coats, crashed out a Viennese waltz with a frenzy which drowned the popping of corks and the clatter of dishes and finally by its increasing furore subdued the conversation. And in a little pulpit all for himself, the Mephistophelian figure of Konchik—Konchik, the leader of the orchestra, Konchik the prince of cabaret violinists, Konchik—by that strange law of Nature which decrees that every leader in Russia shall be foreign—the Czech.

As I drank my first glass of vodka and for the first time ate caviare as it should be eaten—on a warm "kalatch"[1]—I realised I was in a new world, in which primitiveness and decadence lived side by side. Had an eldritch soothsayer appeared before me and foretold that seven years later I should again be sitting

[1] Kalatch: a warm roll with a handle like a basket.

in that hall, that I should be alone, divorced from all my friends and surrounded by Bolsheviks, that in the place where Konchik was now playing Trotsky would be denouncing the Allies in my presence, I should have laughed her to scorn. Yet it was here that in 1918, as the guest of Trotsky, I was to attend my first meeting of the Bolshevist Central Executive Committee and that I was to shake hands for the first and only time with Stalin.

At that moment, however, all my thoughts were fixed on Konchik. The tumultuous wave of the "Blue Danube" had died down. From a "kabinet" had come a command for "I do not speak to you"—that song once sung by Panina, the greatest of all gipsies. At its plaintive minor chords the room hushed, while Konchik, his eyes almost lost in his fat face, made his violin croon and sob and finally fade away in a whisper of despair and unrequited love.

Poor Konchik. The last time I saw him was four years ago in Prague. He was playing in a small restaurant frequented by soulless diplomatists and stolid Czech bourgeois. His savings had been engulfed in the revolution. His last possession was his violin. The mention of Russia brought tears to his eyes.

That first night in Moscow, however, he was a king in a palace of his own, and it was with praiseworthy resolution (alas! I make vain resolutions every time I make a change of surroundings) but with natural reluctance that I dragged myself to bed at eleven o'clock. I was well pleased with Moscow. The clear star-lit snow, the crisp, dry cold, the jingle of the sleigh bells, and the strange silence of the snow-banked streets, had stirred my pulses. Now Konchik's music had provided me with a new sensation, blinding me to the defects of a life, which was to put both my health and my character to an impossible test. To be strictly truthful, my early departure from the restaurant was not entirely due to a newly acquired sense of duty. Knowing nothing of Russia, I had assumed that thick clothes would be necessary to protect me from the cold. I had, therefore, invested in the thickest of woollen underwear. As in winter the tempera-ture of the average Russian room approaches that of a Turkish

bath, I suffered acute discomfort. After that first night I put
these offences away from me and have never worn them since.

For the next three days I lived in a turmoil of entertainment.
I did not even see the Consulate. Instead, I followed modestly
at the heels of the delegation, lunching now with this corpora-
tion, now with that, visiting monasteries and race-courses,
attending gala performances at the theatre, shaking hands with
long-bearded generals and exchanging stilted compliments in
French with the wives of the Moscow merchants.

On the third day this fierce round of festivities was wound
up with an immense dinner given by the Haritonenkos, the
sugar kings of Moscow. I describe it in some detail because it
gives an amazing picture of the Moscow which existed before
the war and which will never come again.

The Haritonenko's house was an immense palace on the far
side of the river just opposite the Kremlin.

To meet the British delegates every official, every notable,
every millionaire, in Moscow had been invited, and when I
arrived I found a throng like a theatre queue struggling on the
staircases. The whole house was a fairyland of flowers brought
all the way from Nice. Orchestras seemed to be playing in
every ante-chamber.

When finally I made my way upstairs, I was lost in a crowd
in which I knew no one. I doubt even if I shook hands with
my host and hostess. But at long narrow tables vodka and the
most delicious "zakuski," both hot and cold, were being
served by scores of waiters to the standing guests. I took a glass
of vodka and tried several of the unknown dishes. They were
excellent. Then an English-speaking Russian took pity on my
loneliness, and I had more vodka and more "zakuski." It was
long past the appointed hour for dinner, but no one seemed to
be moving, and presently it struck me that perhaps in this
strange country the people dined standing up. I had another
vodka and a second portion of reindeer tongue. Then, when my
appetite was sated, a footman came along and handed me a
card with a plan of the table and my own particular place, and
a few minutes later a huge procession made its way to the

dining-room. I do not wish to exaggerate. I say truthfully that I cannot remember the number of courses or the different varieties of wine which accompanied them. But the meal lasted till eleven o'clock and would have taxed the intestines of a giant. My immediate neighbours were a Miss von Meck, the daughter of a railway magnate, and Commander Kahovsky, the Russian flag-lieutenant, who had been attached to Lord Charles Beresford.

Miss von Meck spoke excellent English, and under the warm glow of her unaffected volubility my shyness soon melted. Before the meal was half-way through she had given me a lightning survey of Anglo-Russian relations, a summary of the English and Russian characters, a thumb-nail sketch of everyone in the room, and a detailed account of all her own realised and unrealised desires and ambitions.

Kahovsky, however, seemed nervous and ill-at-ease. I was soon to discover why. During dinner he was called away from the room and never returned. The next day I learnt that he had gone to the telephone to speak to his mistress, the wife of a Russian Governor, who lived in St. Petersburg. They had been on bad terms for some time, and with dramatic instinct she had chosen this moment to tell him that all was over. Kahovsky had then pulled out his revolver and, still holding the receiver, had put a bullet through his brain. It was very sad, very Russian, very hard on Lord Charles Beresford, and by way of example a little dangerous for a young and highly impressionable Vice-Consul.

Dinner having dragged itself to an end, we again went upstairs to another vast room, where a stage had been erected. Here for over an hour Geltzer, Mordkin and Balashova provided us with a delightful ballet divertissement, and Sibor, the leading violinist of the "Big Theatre" orchestra, played Chopin nocturnes to us.

What the evening must have cost I do not know. For me it was not to finish until the early morning. After the musical entertainment we danced. As far as I was concerned, it was not a successful experiment, and, strangely enough, in those days the Russians were poor ball-room dancers. Clinging firmly to the friendly von Meck girl, I repaired once more to the dining-room, where a continuous supper was in progress. Here I met my host's son, a young chubby-faced boy, who was still in his 'teens and who even at that age showed signs of the corpulence of good living. With flushed cheeks he informed us that, after the guests had gone, we were going on to hear the gipsies. We formed a minor conspiracy, collected half a dozen kindred spirits, and at four in the morning set out in "troikas"— private "troikas" drawn by magnificent Arabs—on the long drive to "Streilna," the kingdom of Maria Nikolaievna.

I can still visualise those "troikas" standing before the house: the fur rugs; the drivers, with tiny fur-capped heads protruding from the immense folds of their "shubas," for all the world like Gargantuan golliwogs; the beautiful horses straining at their bits; below us, the ice-bound river lit up like a silver thread by the moon, and immediately before us the ghostly towers of the Kremlin standing out like white sentinels before the starry camp of night.

We took our place—two of us to each troika. The drivers purred to their horses, and in a second we were off. For four glorious miles we tore at breakneck speed through the deserted streets, up the Tverskaia, past the Brest Station, past the famous night establishment of Yar, out into the Petrovsky Park, until with stinging cheeks and icicles on the drivers' beards we drew up before the miniature crystal palace which is "Streilna."

As in a dream I followed the others through the Palm Court, which is the main part of the building, into a large pine-walled "kabinet," with a roaring wood fire burning in an open fire-place. The proprietor rubbed his hands and bowed. The head-waiter bowed without rubbing his hands. A host of waiters in white uniforms bowed still lower and moved silently to their various tasks. In a few seconds the room was prepared for the great ritual. We guests sat at a large table near the fire. Before us was an open space and behind it a semi-circle of chairs for the gipsies. The wine waiter brought the champagne, and then

Maria Nikolaievna came in followed by eight gipsies, four men with guitars, and four girls, with eyes like sloes and sinuous graceful bodies. Both men and women were dressed in the traditional gipsy costume, the men with white-brocaded Russian shirts and coloured trousers, the girls in coloured silks with a red silk kerchief round their heads.

When I met her that night for the first time, Maria Nikolaievna was a plump, heavy woman of forty. Her face was lined, and there was a wistful sadness in her large, grey eyes. In repose she looked an old and lonely woman, but when she spoke the lines in her face vanished into smiles, and one realised the immense reserves of strength which she could call upon at will. The cynic will say that her task in life was to collect foolish and preferably rich young men, to sing to them, and to make them drink oceans of champagne until their wealth or their father's wealth was transferred from their pockets to her own. Commonsense may seem to be on the cynic's side, but there was nothing cynical in Maria Nikolaievna's attitude towards life. She was an artist—in her own way, a great artist—who gave full value for her money, and her kindness and generosity to those who were her friends came straight from the heart.

That night I heard her sing for the first time, and the memory of those great deep notes, which are the secret of the best women gipsy singers, will remain with me until I die. That night, too, I drank my first "charochka" to her singing. For a novice it is rather a trying ordeal. A large champagne glass is filled to the brim. The gipsy singer places it on a plate and, facing the guest who is to drink the "charochka," sings the following verse:

> "Like a scented flower
> Breathing out perfume,
> Bring the brimming glass;
> Let us drink a toast.
> Drink a toast to Román,
> Román our beloved,
> And until he drinks it down
> Pour him out no more."

The last four lines are a chorus, which is taken up with increasing frenzy by the whole troupe. The singer then advances towards the guest whom she is honouring, and holds out the plate to him. He takes the glass, bows low, stands erect, and then drinks the bumper in one draught, replacing the glass upside down on the plate to show that he has not left a drop.

It is an intimate ritual. Only the guest's Christian name is used, and, as there is no Robert in Russian, there and then Maria Nikolaievna christened me "Román," which is the Russian equivalent, and Román or Rómochka I have remained to my Russian friends ever since.

Maria Nikolaievna's art, however, was, as I discovered even then, on a far higher plane than the singing of mere drinking songs. When she sang alone, her voice now passionate, now appealing, then sinking to an infinite sadness, my heart melted. This gipsy music, in fact, is more intoxicating, more dangerous, than opium, or women, or drink, and, although champagne is a necessary adjunct to the enjoyment, there is a plaintiveness in its appeal which to the Slav and Celtic races is almost irresistible. Far better than words it expresses the pent-up and stifled desires of mankind. It induces a delicious melancholy which is half-lyrical, half-sensuous. Something there is in it of the boundless width of the Russian steppe. It is the uttermost antithesis of anything that is Anglo-Saxon. It breaks down all reserves of restraint. It will drive a man to the moneylenders and even to crime. Doubtless, it is the most primitive of all forms of music, somewhat similar in its appeal (may the spirit of Maria Nikolaievna forgive me for this sacrilegious comparison) to the negro spirituals. And it is very costly. It has been responsible for the bulk of my debts. Yet to-morrow, if I had thousands and the desire to squander them, there is no entertainment in New York, Paris, Berlin or London or, indeed, anywhere in the world, which I should choose in preference to a gipsy evening at "Streilna" in Moscow or at the Villa Rhode in St. Petersburg. It is the only form of entertainment which has never bored me and which, if I yielded to the temptation, I know would never fail to charm.

It would be foolish of me to pretend that my appreciation of gipsy music began on that first evening, or, rather early morning at "Streilna." Knowing not a word of Russian, I was, in truth, a little bewildered. I did not know my companions well enough to allow a loose rein to my Celtic temperament, and the heat of the room and the sweet champagne made my head ache. I was, therefore, not sorry when at six in the morning the party broke up, and we made our way home. Then it was that I discovered the innate subtlety of the Russian. Both in St. Petersburg and in Moscow he has his places of amusement far outside the town—not for any sinister or licentious purpose but merely in order that the drive back may cure him of the after-effects of his carouse. There is no such thing as a pick-me-up in Russia. The crisp, dry winter air is all the tonic that is necessary. By the time I had reached my hotel, I was fit enough to begin the evening all over again.

The Russia of those first three days of my Moscow life is gone for ever. I do not know what has happend to Miss von Meck. In 1930 her father—an old man of nearly seventy—was shot by the Bolsheviks as a dangerous counter-revolutionary. The Haritonenkos are dead. Their son is dead. Their elder daughter now lives in a two-roomed servantless flat in Munich. In 1930 she came over to England to protest to Lord Thomson, whom she had entertained in Russia, against the purchase of her father's house by the British Government. The house to-day is the headquarters of the British Embassy in Moscow. It was first confiscated by the Bolsheviks and then sold by them to His Majesty's Government.

The next afternoon, much to its own and everybody else's relief, the delegation left for England. It was to have one more adventure before it quitted Russian soil. As the train, which bore them back to sanity, drew into Smolensk late in the evening, a delegation of Russian clergy, headed by the local Bishop, stood on the platform to welcome them. They had come with bread and salt to greet the English Bishops. They found drawn blinds and darkened carriages. The unfortunate English were sleeping off the effects of ten days' incessant feasting. The

Russians, however, were insistent. They had faced the cold to see an English Bishop, and an English Bishop they would see even in his nightshirt. At last the train conductor, more terrified by his own clergy than by the prospective wrath of the foreign strangers, woke up Maurice Baring. That great man was equal to the occasion, and the dénouement was swift. Poking his head out of the window, he addressed the clergy in his best Russian:

"Go in peace," he shouted. "The bishops are asleep." And then, to clinch the matter, he added confidentially but firmly: "They're all drunk."

CHAPTER TWO

IF THE EXOTIC gaiety of these first three days was enough to turn the head of any young man, the departure of the British delegation soon brought me to my senses. The first sight of the British Consulate was a shattering blow. It was in the Consul's flat in a shabby side-street and consisted of a single room. There was no messenger, no door-keeper. The Consul's maid opened the door and, if she were out, I took her place. Montgomery Grove was a kind and tolerant chief, but he was married, had three children, was without private means, and in an extremely expensive post was shamefully underpaid. He was far poorer than the majority of the local British colony, which was composed mainly of Lancashiremen engaged in the cotton industry. Fortunately, the work was not very arduous. Every morning from ten to one I sat in the little ante-room, which was the Consular office. Its sole furniture consisted of two desks, a bookcase, a safe, a map of Russia and three chairs. If there was more than one visitor, Montgomery Grove fetched another chair from his drawing-room. I sat with my back to my chief, licked stamps, and whacked a typewriter. For the first few weeks I spent most of my time in translating commercial reports from the local German newspaper and in typing out copies of a stereotyped application in Russian for the renewal of the " *permis de séjour*," which was required by every foreigner in Russia and which was furnished by the local Russian Passport Department. We had, of course, no clerk. Such Russian correspondence as was necessary was done by Montgomery Grove. Before I had been six weeks in the Consulate I was tipped by a fat Russian merchant for opening the outside door for him. Fear of hurting his feelings made me pocket the twenty copecks.

I had seen much of official life in the Malay States. Even the young cadets had their punkah-wallahs, their clerks, their uniformed messengers. They sat, too, in luxurious offices and maintained a dignity which was respected by the whole business community. In Moscow the representative of the British

Empire was housed in surroundings of which a Malayan Sanitary Board inspector would have been ashamed. Montgomery Grove, who had been a dashing and good-looking officer in an Indian cavalry regiment, must have felt his position keenly. He was not in a position to entertain the rich Muscovite merchants and made no attempt to do so. He carried out his duties without complaint, was a pillar of the local English church, and steered a careful and on the whole skilful course through the rough waters of local British sectional interests and jealousies.

To myself the complete insignificance of my own position was a salutary lesson in humility, and, once I had recovered from the first shock, I accepted the situation with resignation and even managed to derive amusement from it. I had, of course, to leave my hotel. In those days a Vice-Consul with a salary of £300 a year could not afford to live at the Metropole, and the week I spent there cost me more than my first month's salary. Moreover, it was essential for me to learn Russian. Indeed, in the absence of an interpreter, Montgomery Grove could not go on leave until I did. I therefore transferred myself, body and baggage, to the bosom of a Russian family. Here, I must confess, I had an extraordinary stroke of luck. Every year half a dozen English officers came to Moscow to study Russian for their interpreter's examination. To meet their needs a certain number of Russian families specialised in teaching Russian. Most of them were squalid middle-class homes with nothing to recommend them in the way either of comfort or of intellectual uplift. By good fortune, the one family which had a vacancy at the time of my arrival, was the Ertels, and to the Ertels by the grace of God I went.

Madame Ertel, the head of the house, was the widow of Alexander Ertel, the well-known Russian novelist and a friend of Tolstoy. She was a plump and rather delicate little woman of about fifty, very intellectual, with a keen interest both in literature and in politics, fussy in a crisis, but a born teacher. She had a large flat with an excellent library on the Vozdvizenka. The other inmates of my new home were her daughter, a dark-eyed temperamental young girl more like an Italian than a Russian, her niece, tall, good-looking and English in appearance, an Armenian student called Reuben Ivanovitch (his surname, like Michael Arlen's, I can never remember), and a wondrously old lady, who was known as "babushka,"[1] who rarely spoke, and who appeared only at meal times. Into this new and modest existence I plunged myself with my usual enthusiasm and my genius for adaptability. My afternoons were my own, except on rare occasions, and I devoted them exclusively to the study of Russian. Every day I had a lesson from Madame Ertel and her daughter, and under their skilful tuition I made rapid progress. They did their best, too, to make me one of the family, and, although I feel that at times I must have been a sore trial to them, we never exchanged an unpleasant word.

This was a wholly delightful and instructive period of my Russian existence. Long before I had mastered enough Russian to take part in the general conversation, I suspected that the Ertels were bitterly opposed to the Tsarist form of Government, and that their sympathies were with the Cadets and Social-revolutionaries. As my Russian improved (in four months I could speak with considerable fluency), my suspicions were confirmed, and the knowledge that I was living in an anti-Tsarist stronghold gave a new thrill to my life and an added zest to my Russian studies. The thrill became almost a fear when one day over evening tea I was introduced to a woman whose husband had been shot during the 1905 revolution. I mentioned this episode to Montgomery Grove, who shook his head gravely and warned me to be careful. Nothing untoward, however, happened to me through this association. Later I was to realise that all the Moscow "intelligenzia" shared the Ertelian view.

The Ertels, in fact, were typical representatives of the intelligentzia. When at ten o'clock every evening they assembled round the samovar, they would sometimes sit far into the night discussing how to make the world safe by revolution.

[1] Grandmother.

But when the morning of action came they were fast asleep in bed. It was very harmless, very hopeless, and very Russian. But for the War and the antiquated inefficiency of the Russian military organisation, the Tsar would still be on his throne.

Let me create no false impression. My Russian friends were not obsessed by revolution. Politics, in fact, were reserved for special occasions such as unhappy political anniversaries or some outrageous political sentence in the Russian courts. At other times the conversation was stimulating and instructive.

Many writers came to the house: old friends of the late M. Ertel; young men with plays to read and novels to place; painters, musicians, actors and actresses; and, much impressed, I worshipped at the feet of all of them. It was at Madame Ertel's that I first met Olga Knipper, the widow of Chehoff and the leading Moscow tragédienne. It was Madame Ertel who first took me to see a Chehoff play performed by the Moscow Art Theatre players in that sober, solemn theatre where applause was forbidden and where a late arrival was shut out for the whole act.

During this period my life was divided into two watertight compartments: one, Russian and unofficial, and the other official and mainly English. My own preference was for the Russian and unofficial. Occasionally, I dined out at the houses of local British residents. More rarely I attended an official banquet at the German Consulate-General. I paid a few formal calls on my Consular colleagues, and once or twice a week I went to the local British Club at the Hotel National. Of the rich Russians, whom I had met during the visit of the British delegation, I saw nothing. Very soon I discovered that of Society with a big S in Moscow there was none. There was a small handful of nobles, who kept entirely to themselves. The rich merchants formed a group of their own. The intelligentzia were accessible, but only to those who were brought into their circle. Outside their business relations the English and the Russians remained severely apart.

Many of the local English, in fact, regarded the Russians as good-natured but immoral savages, whom it was not safe or proper to introduce into their home circle. It amused me to see Madame Zimin, a Moscow millionairess, lunching every Sunday and playing bridge with her three husbands—two ex, and one real. It showed a tolerance and an understanding which at that time were beyond the range of Western civilisation. The English wives, however, held up their hands in pious horror.

My introduction to the English colony was not very happy. Almost the first Englishmen I met were two brothers called Charnock. Both were Lancashiremen and both were connected with the cotton industry. At the time, Harry, the younger brother, was managing director of a large cotton mill at Oriechovo-Zuevo in the Province of Vladimir.

Now Oriechovo-Zuevo was one of the storm-centres of Russian industrial unrest, and as an antidote to vodka drinking and political agitation among his factory hands Charnock had instituted "soccer" football. His factory team was then champion of the Moscow League.

Through some confusion with my Cambridge brother the rumour had already gone round the British colony that I was a brilliant footballer. Without waiting to inquire whether "rugger" or "soccer" was my game, the Charnocks invited me to join the "Morozovtsi," which was the name of their factory team. Always ripe for adventure, I accepted. A few hours later I discovered that there was a British team in Moscow for which I was expected to play. The President of the Club did his best to persuade me to change my mind, but, having given my word, I was not prepared to go back on it.

At first there was some feeling against me, but I never regretted my decision. Later, when I came to know these North-countrymen better, I realised what splendid fellows they were. As for the Charnocks, they have remained my firm friends ever since, and I have always counted my football experiences with the Russian proletariat as a most valuable part of my Russian education. I fear the experience was more profitable to me than to my club. I was, in fact, hardly worth my place. Nevertheless, these league matches were great fun and excited immense enthusiasm. At Oriechovo we played before a crowd of ten to fifteen thousand. Except by foreign teams we were rarely defeated. Certainly, Charnock's experiment was a complete success. If it had been adopted in other mills, the effect on the character of the Russian working-men might have been far-reaching.

In my Russian football career I had only one exciting episode. This was in Moscow, when my factory team were playing the German champions. In an encouraging spirit of fairplay the Russian Football Association had invited a German to referee. The Germans were considerably bigger than our men and used their weight with unnecessary vigour. In particular, the German right half was unduly rough towards a young English schoolboy of seventeen—a nephew of Charnock and a brilliant footballer —who was playing outside-left to me. When the German had bowled him over most unfairly for the fifth or sixth time, I lost my temper and addressed him in language which I admit I should never have used in England. In a trice the referee was on my tracks.

"Be careful," he said in excellent English. "I heard what you said. If you use language like that again, I'll send you off the field."

The words I had used were not so very bad. They were an invocation to the Deity to blast the German and to consign him to the nethermost depths of Hell. But for a moment I shuddered. Like a flash I saw headlines in the English Press: "British Vice-Consul sent off the Field for Foul Language," and I apologised abjectly and profusely. I told the referee my fears after the game.

"If I'd known who you were," he said with a laugh, "I should have had you off without a warning."

During those first months of preparation there was one other influence which affected my life. This was my friendship with George Bowen, a young "gunner," who was studying Russian at the expense of the War Office. On the whole, I saw little of the military interpreters. Bowen, however, was an exception. He was a sandy-haired, little man, very serious and intelligent, but possessed of a quiet humour which rarely misfired. We became great friends and dined together at least once a week, when we found relief from our labours in comparing the idiosyncrasies of our Russian teachers. He was a hard worker and, as we made a kind of gastronomic competition out of our Russian knowledge (whoever was first "stumped" by a word in the menu paid for the dinner), our association did little harm to our Russian studies.

By June we had both been six months in Moscow and were able to talk together with considerable fluency—and inaccuracy —in "pidgin" Russian. With characteristic self-consciousness we did not practise these exercises in the streets, but reserved them for the seclusion of the parks and forests. We lived frugally and modestly, and only rarely did we permit ourselves to depart from the rigid economy which under Bowen's influence even I had learnt to practise.

There were, however, lapses. One digression in particular, nearly brought disaster in its train. In July my chief and his family had departed to the "dacha"—a kind of summer bungalow outside the town, whither all Russians, except the poorest, repair in order to escape the torrid heat of the Moscow summer. My family had gone to the country leaving me alone in the flat. Bowen was *"en villégiature"* with his family in a "dacha." I was lonely and miserable but still firm in my newly-found asceticism. Then one afternoon George Bowen walked into my flat. The sky was like ink. A storm was rolling up from the south and the heat, which had melted the pavement to a soft pulp, was stupefying. With flushed face George threw his hat on my bed and sank into a chair.

"I'm fed up," he said. "This dacha existence has defeated me. We have five grown-ups and three children in four rickety rooms. The walls are as thin as paper. The bugs stop me sleeping. The dog is sick daily in my room. Vasili Vasilievitch snores, and to-day I caught Maria Petrovna picking sprouts out of the dish with a hairpin. I'm through with Puritanism. To-night, I'm going Berserk!"

At that moment the storm broke, and for three-quarters of

an hour the lightning played fireworks round the blue and golden cupolas of the Kremlin. In the flooded streets the trams stood motionless like ships riding at anchor. The thunder shook the house to its foundations.

We closed the windows and, coatless, lay back in our chairs. The sweat poured down George's face in streams. My head ached. It was an hour of bitter agony not unmingled with fear.

Then suddenly the skies cleared and the sun came out. Quickly we opened the windows. A delicious freshness came from the monastery garden opposite. The trees, which an hour before had been parched and white with dust, were now radiantly green. The streets resumed their normal bustle. The trams moved, and we moved with them.

Very deliberately we laid our plans. George should stay the night with me. We should dine at the Hermitage. Later we should go to the Aquarium. No expense should be spared.

Cheque-book in hand, we walked down to Muir and Mirrielees—the Harrod's of Moscow—and handed in our cheques. Each was for twenty-five pounds—a month's salary for me and more for the rarely reckless George. With trepidation we watched the cashier's face. Hitherto, we had never cashed more than ten pounds. He paid without a moment's hesitation. In those days the credit of British officials abroad was still unassailable.

Happy and irresponsible, we drove into the beautiful summer gardens of the Hermitage. We chose our sterlet from the fish-tank fountain. We dined as young men generally do dine, recklessly, incongruously, sampling all the unknown Russian dishes and drinking more vodka and champagne than were good for us. Our extravagance commanded a new attention from the white-robed waiters, while in our honour Krysh, the sleek Jewish violinist, played all his English repertory to us. The dinner was a prolonged one, and we finished up with cigars and Napoleon brandy at ten roubles a glass. The brandy was not good; certainly, Napoleon never tasted it. But fools must learn their lesson by experience. In my case the lesson was well mastered. Since that day Napoleon brandy has never tempted me.

It was at the Aquarium a few hours later that the great adventure befell us. This vast open-air amusement park was presided over by a negro called Thomas—a British subject with whom the Consulate was frequently at variance over the engagement of young English girls as cabaret performers. The entertainment he provided consisted of a perfectly respectable operetta theatre, an equally respectable open-air music hall, a definitely less respectable verandah café-chantant, and the inevitable chain of private "kabinets" for gipsy-singing and private carouses. We had strolled into the café-chantant rather late and, taking the best box, had settled down to watch what even in our exalted state seemed a dreary performance. The rapid succession of talentless singers and dancers, who showed themselves on the stage for two minutes, smirked, and then rushed off to the dressing-room to change and join the tables below, soon wearied us, and even the "Macaroni Man," who drank incredible quantities of champagne in an incredibly short space of time, failed to relieve the gloom which was rapidly descending on us. Then suddenly the lights in the hall were dimmed. The band struck up an English tune. The curtain went up, and from the wings a young English girl— amazingly fresh and beautiful—tripped lightly to the centre of the stage and did a song and dance act. Her voice was shrill and harsh. Her accent was Wigan at its crudest. But she could dance, as Moscow had never seen an English girl dance. The audience rose to her. So did two young and suddenly refreshed Englishmen. The head-waiter was summoned. Pencil and paper were demanded, and then after bashful meditation—it was a new experience for both of us—we sent a combined note inviting her to join us in our box. She came. Off the stage she was not so beautiful as she had seemed ten minutes before. She was neither witty nor wicked. She had been on the stage since she was fourteen and took life philosophically. But she was English, and the story of her career thrilled us. I expect our shyness and our awkwardness amused her.

We were not allowed to enjoy our conversation without interruption. A waiter brought in a note and handed it to our guest. She read it, begged to be excused for a minute, and left the room. Presently, we heard high words outside the door— a male Cockney voice predominating. Then there was a scuffle and a final "blast you." The door opened and was hurriedly shut, and with flushed face our Lancashire lady returned to us. What was the matter? It was nothing. There was an English jockey—a mad fellow, always drunk, who was making her life a burden and a misery. We expressed our sympathy, ordered more champagne, and in five minutes had forgotten all about the incident.

We were not allowed to forget for long. An hour later the door was again thrown open. This time Thomas himself appeared, followed by a policeman. Outside the door was a mob of waiters and girls with scared faces. The negro scratched his head. There had been an accident. Would Missie go at once. The English jockey had shot himself.

Suddenly sobered, we paid our bill and followed the girl to the shabby furnished rooms across the road where the tragedy had taken place. We were prepared for the worst— scandal, possibly disgrace, and our almost certain appearance as witnesses at the inquest. For both of us the matter seemed terribly serious. In the circumstances the best course seemed to be to take Thomas into our confidence. He laughed at our fears.

"I will make that ol' right, Mistah Lockhart," he said. "Bless yo' heart, the police won't worry you—or the English Missie either. They'm shore used to tragedies like this, and this one has been coming for a long time."

He was right. Indeed, to anyone who was not a political suspect, above all, to anyone who had some official rank, the Russian police showed a deference, which, if generally reinforced by the concrete of hard cash, was not without its advantages. Still, some days were to elapse before our fears were finally allayed, and it was with grim forebodings that I awoke the next morning—or rather the same morning—to hear George Bowen splashing in his bath and crying to the Heavens to tell him who was the fool who said: "Joy cometh with the morning."

In that summer of 1912 I had the good fortune to see the Emperor twice—a rare opportunity in Moscow, for the Tsar of all the Russias seldom visited the ancient capital. The city had too many tragic memories for him, and the horror of the shambles of the Khodynka Field, where at his coronation celebrations hundreds of peasants were crushed to death, was ever present in his mind. Moscow, too, was the centre of Radicalism and, as such, was anathema to the Empress. On the first occasion, the Tsar came to unveil the statue to his father, the Emperor Alexander III. It was a strictly official ceremony, attended only by the nobles, the military and civil heads of departments, and a selected number of the leading merchants. I remember the visit for two reasons: first, because for weeks before the Moscow police had pestered us and, indeed, all the Consular Corps with idiotic questions regarding the political reliability of our various nationals who lived any-where near the route along which the Emperor was to pass, and, secondly, because on his way to the Kremlin the Tsar stopped at the spot where the Grand Duke Serge had been murdered, and knelt down alone on the cobbled stones and prayed. I could not help wondering what thoughts must have flashed through the mind of this least-to-be-envied of monarchs, as he knelt on the spot where the human débris of his uncle had once stained the ground. Boris Savinkoff, who had planned the Grand Duke's murder, was then in exile. He was to come back again in 1917, to become Minister of War in the Kerensky Government, to seek refuge once more in exile on the advent of the Bolsheviks, and to return finally on that sinister and still unexplained mission, when he cast his lot with the present rulers of Russia only to throw himself or to be thrown to his death from a Kremlin window close to the spot where the Grand Duke met his fate.

The occasion of the Emperor's second visit was the centenary of Borodino and the liberation of Russia from the yoke of Napoleon. This time the celebration was a national one and strikingly impressive in the demonstration of loyalty it aroused. Never have I seen a finer body of men than the Cossack troops who formed the Emperor's bodyguard. Well may the pre-war foreign military attachés be forgiven for over-estimating the military power of Russia. Yet the real symbol of Russia's strength was the frail bearded figure with the strange, wistful eyes, who rode at the head of his troops and whose feeble shoulders seemed incapable of supporting the mantle of autocracy which, like a shroud, hung over them. Even on that day, when revolution was far from most men's minds, the Tsar inspired pity and sympathy more than admiration. An Imperial visit was an ordeal which at any moment one felt might end in tragedy, and, as far as Moscow was concerned, everyone breathed a sigh of relief when the suspense was over and the Imperial train had left the city.

When the autumn came, I made another friend, who was to render me great services during my apprenticeship in Moscow. This was Michael Lykiardopoulos, the talented secretary of the Moscow Art Theatre. "Lyki" was a strange, lovable creature; one-third Greek, one-third Russian, and one-third English. His secretarial duties gave him a fixed salary. His real work in life was as a translator. He had real literary flair, an excellent Russian prose style, and a quite remarkable knowledge of eight or nine European languages. He knew most of the great writers of Europe and had translated their best works into Russian. It was through him that I first met H. G. Wells, Robert Ross, Lytton Strachey, Granville Barker, Gordon Craig, Aleister Crowley, not to mention numerous hangers-on of literature, who came to Moscow to worship at the shrine of Russian art. In his spare time he acted as ballet critic for one of the leading Moscow newspapers. He knew everyone in the literary, artistic, and dramatic world of Moscow, and, through him, many doors, which otherwise would have remained closed, were opened to me.

Poor "Lyki." During the war he ran our propaganda department in Moscow under my supervision—and ran it very well. His temperament was far too volatile to give any value to his political judgment. A Russian defeat depressed him almost to the point of suicide. The smallest victory drove him to the other extreme. Towards the end of 1915, when he had made up his mind that Russia was irretrievably ruined, he made a hazardous journey on our behalf into Germany, travelling as a Greek tobacco merchant and bringing back with him a mass of valuable information and a new optimism. The revolution finally destroyed all his hopes, and before the Bolsheviks had made their coup d'état he withdrew to Stockholm and eventually to England. Like many Russian Liberals he became a violent reactionary and spent most of his energy in writing anti-Semitic articles for the English Press. He was a born journalist, living only for the day, but his loyalty and his kindness to his friends were wonderful, and of all my Russian friends (in spite of his mixed nationality I can never regard him as anything but Russian) he is the one whom I miss most. He died in London in 1924.

CHAPTER THREE

AT THE END of my first year in Russia I returned to England to be married. Looking back on this experiment from a disappointing and disillusioned middle age, I find my conduct in the highest degree reprehensible. I had neither money nor position, and my prospects held out nothing more than a dreary and penurious career in the worst-paid service in the world. My wife was an Australian called Turner. Her grandfather had been the richest man in Queensland. On her father's death misfortune had overtaken the estate, and her mother was unable to allow her more than a hundred or two a year. My wife herself, who was delicate, had been brought up in England and Switzerland. All her friends were rich or well to do. She herself had been used to a life of luxury. To ask a girl, who had been brought up in this way and who was then only twenty-one, to share with me a life of poverty in a semi-barbarous town like Moscow was an effrontery for which there is no excuse. It is a tribute to her courage that she was able to adapt herself so quickly to a situation which imposed so many hardships upon her. My marriage was a contract from which I alone reaped any benefit.

Had I taken stock of myself at that time, I should have seen a young man of twenty-five, broad-shouldered and broken-nosed, with a squat, stumpy figure and a ridiculous gait. The young man's character was a curious mixture of Lockhart caution and asceticism and Macgregor recklessness and self-indulgence. Hitherto, the Macgregor had held the whip-hand over the Lockhart, and perhaps his chief failing had been an all-too-Celtic tendency to confound licentiousness with romanticism. Such accomplishments as he had—a good memory, a facility for languages, and a capacity for sudden bursts of hard work, were largely nullified by a lazy tolerance, which always sought the easiest way out of any difficulty, and by a fatal disposition to sacrifice the future for the cheap applause of the moment. In short, a still unformed and unattractive young man, whose self-consciousness at moments amounted almost to a disease. Had anyone told him that five years later he would be head of an important British Mission at a crucial moment in his country's history, he would have smirked, put his head on one side, and blushed with modesty.

This, I submit, is an accurate picture of myself as I was at the end of 1912. With marriage, however, my life changed, and I made a serious effort to conform to the conventionalities of my new state. The result was wholly beneficial. My night life was cast off, and a round of irksome social duties took its place. Intercourse with the British colony now became an obligation, and, as we were entertained, so we entertained in return. I found, however, a new zest for work. I continued my Russian studies and, until my wife learnt the language, I had to run the small flat we had taken, give orders to the servants, and superintend the household accounts. I read twice as much as when I was a bachelor. My knowledge of Russian was now tolerably good, and there was the whole field of Russian literature to explore. I began, too, to write for the English newspapers not so much from any internal urge as from necessity. The money was needed in order to supplement our scanty income, and afte· a little practice I found it not difficult to earn. I re-wrote and sold the short stories I had written in Malaya. I became a fairly regular contributor to the *Morning Post* and the *Manchester Guardian*, both of which newspapers were then interested in sketches of Russian life, and I found a ready home for more serious articles and even for short stories in the numerous British reviews which then flourished. These literary efforts were written under a pseudonym (in those days diplomatists and consuls were not allowed to write), but in my first year as a free-lance journalist I earned nearly £200, and by the time the war came and put a stop to these activities, I was making a steady twenty-five to thirty pounds a month.

Nor did marriage interfere with my Russian friendships. On the contrary, it extended them. "Lyki" was a constant visitor to our flat and requited our hospitality by bringing us into contact with the wide orbit of his own literary, journalistic,

and artistic world. At the end of my first eighteen months in
Russia I knew most of the leaders of the Moscow intelligentzia.

This contact, necessitating as it did the constant discussion
of politics, gave me my first interest in foreign affairs. Through
the Charnocks and other Englishmen connected with the
cotton mills, I kept my finger on the pulse of industrial unrest.
To complete my equipment as an intelligence officer there
remained only the nobility, the merchants—and the British
Embassy—to conquer. With the Embassy in St. Petersburg
we had practically no contact. The German Consul-General
might see his Ambassador once a month. French Consuls-
General might reasonably hope to finish their careers as
Ministers. But between the two British services there was an
impassable gulf which has not been satisfactorily bridged to
this day. Political reports from Moscow were not encouraged.
Commercial queries were positively discouraged. In the archives
of the Moscow Consulate there is—or was—a letter from a
certain British Ambassador, which we used to pull out in
moments of disgruntledness and which ran as follows:
"Dear Mr. ——, Please remember that I am not here to be
bothered with questions about trade."

The inadequate equipment of the Moscow Consulate was
not only a subject of grievance to the unfortunate Consular
officers. It attracted the attention of British visitors, who were
not slow to notice that, of all the Great Powers, Great Britain
was the only one which was not represented by a Consulate-
General. Invariably they expressed disgust, returned to
England, and did nothing. There was one exception. One
wintry afternoon in 1913, when I was alone in the Consulate,
there was a ring at the door. I sprang to my feet and admitted
an elderly, well-dressed man with a beard who handed me
his card. His name was Tennant, and, although I did not
realise it at the time, he was a relation of Mr. Asquith, who
was then Prime Minister. I took him into our dingy little
room.

"Can I see the Consul or the Vice-Consul?" he asked.

"The Consul is out," I replied. "I am the Vice-Consul."

He breathed heavily. The trudge up the three flights of stone stairs had shaken his wind.

"Is this all the British Consulate?" he asked at last. I told him it was. His chest heaved. His eyes flashed. Then with a great growl came his comment:

"More like a water-closet than a Consulate."

He invited me to lunch with him the next day. At luncheon he asked some pertinent questions. He made no promises, but, when he went away, I had a feeling that this time something was going to happen.

The weeks, however, passed into months, and gradually I abandoned hope. When the summer came, we shared a "dacha" with the Groves—a large, roomy wooden house at Kosino beside a lake where there were boats to row and pike and perch to catch. This risky experiment opened with a tragedy. My wife had bought a new toy—a pedigree French bulldog, called Pipo, who afterwards achieved immortality by being painted by Korovin. Naturally, she took him to the "dacha." Although in the Moscow flat he was as good as gold, his first night in the country was a disaster. The train journey must have upset his delicate constitution, for in the middle of dinner he forgot himself in the most offensive sense, and the carpet, a new investment of the Grove family, was irreparably ruined. Men are singularly ineffective on these occasions, and for the rest of that meal Grove and I kept our eyes firmly glued to the table. In spite of this inauspicious overture, the "dacha" concert turned out better than might have been expected. By the morning Mrs. Grove's very just anger had evaporated. With tearful eyes my wife begged for her dog. Pipo himself was profuse in his apologies. And Pipo remained.

With Pipo we had one more adventure, which might have ended disastrously for him and which for us had unpleasant consequences. Close to the lake there was a holy pool, where pilgrims from far and wide used to bathe in the hope of being cured of various diseases. One evening, when my wife was out walking, she passed the pool and with a natural modesty hurried away from the mass of naked bodies which sought relief from its stagnant waters. Pipo, however, was a gregarious animal and in a minute he was splashing wildly among the pilgrims. There was a shriek from the pool. At first my wife thought the bathers were playing with the dog, and she continued placidly on her way. Then the shriek grew into an angry roar, and the dog came tearing down the path with twenty naked figures in hot pursuit. My wife picked up her skirts and ran. Fortunately, the "dacha" was close at hand. Fortunately, too, I was at home. For five minutes I harangued the nudities from the "dacha" steps, and in the end my argument, backed by silver roubles, prevailed. More roubles had to be expended on the priest for the re-purification of the waters, and altogether the adventure was more costly than amusing. At first, too, I was afraid lest the outraged bathers might wreak their vengeance on the dog, and for some days Pipo had to be kept on a chain. In this, however, I did the Russians an injustice. Having made their peace, they bore no malice, and, as in future nothing would induce the dog to approach within a hundred yards of Siloam, no harm resulted.

Three years later economic duress forced us to sell him. He was a valuable dog, and he went to a millionaire's house. What his ultimate fate was I do not know. He was an aristocrat and must, therefore, have hated revolutions. I fear that, like Gorky's Great Dane, he may have been eaten by a starving population.

That summer, too, Sir Henry Wilson visited Moscow, and I dined with him and Colonel Knox, our military attaché, at the Hermitage. Even in those days Sir Henry was fully alive to the dangers of the European situation and had summed up all the possibilities in his far-seeing mind. In considering the relative strength of the European Powers, he had worked out all his facts to the smallest detail. In his opinion the French army was fully equal to the German. If ever it came to war, the Russian army would be the extra weight which would load the scales overwhelmingly in France's favour. Sir Henry was not the only expert whose judgments were to be rudely shattered by the tornado of 1914.

At the beginning of July came the repercussion to the Tennant visit. It came, too, in the form of what Fleet Street calls a bombshell. Moscow was elevated to a Consulate-General with a largely increased office allowance. The Groves were transferred to Warsaw, and Charles Clive Bayley, formerly H.M. Consul at New York and a scion of a family famous in Indian history, was appointed to reign in their stead. I shed a sympathetic tear over the departure of the Groves (they had been very kind to us) and with new hopes and new ambitions made ready to welcome my new chief.

CHAPTER FOUR

CHARLES CLIVE BAYLEY was then in his fifty-second year. He was a big, florid man with pouches under his eyes. The eyes could both twinkle and flash. Such hair as he had left was fair. His body was rather too heavy for his legs and, when he coughed or laughed, the veins stood out on his forehead. As he always laughed at his own stories, of which he had an inexhaustible fund (in two years I never heard him repeat himself once), I was in constant apprehension lest he should die of apoplexy. He wore an eyeglass and had a presence and a proper sense of his own importance.

He could speak neither French nor German. But he had served for ten years under Sir Thomas Sanderson in New York and knew all there was to know about running a Consular office. He combined what the Americans call "drive" with dignity, and no man could take liberties with him.

What was more important he had private means and was prepared to spend his own money on maintaining his position as Consul-General. He took a large flat for himself in the most fashionable street in Moscow and leased an adequate office for the Consulate-General on the first floor of a new house close at hand. He engaged an experienced clerk, two typists and a general factotum and commissionaire called Alexander Nechaeff, who, as a former Russian civil servant, knew every short-cut, legal and illegal, through the red-tape maze of Russian bureaucracy. In the eyes both of the Russians and of our Consular colleagues we acquired a new prestige. Alexander saw to that. He at once invested Bayley with the title of an Excellency, and within a month of his arrival every department, both civil and military, in Moscow knew through the agency of the devoted Alexander that the new British Consul-General was a man whose favour was worth courting and whose wrath was vastly to be feared. On occasions Alexander overplayed his hand and, when we caught him using the Consular seal in order to further his own personal ends, Bayley exploded. It required all my tact and all my pleading to prevent the old scoundrel's immediate dismissal. A man, who at a minute's notice could wangle a visa after office hours or a sleeping berth to St. Petersburg, when the Wagon-Lits office had been sold out for days, was not to be lightly discarded, and in the end Bayley relented.

Both in the office and outside it Bayley did his best to live up to the rôle for which the wily Alexander had cast him. All his life he had done himself well, and he knew how to entertain others. His wife, who was born a Ricardo, backed him up to the best of her ability. She was a kind, little woman, very shy and very English, but very hospitable and always willing to put herself out to promote her husband's interests. The Russians sat up and took notice. They ate the Bayley dinners. They liked the Bayley cocktails which I imagine he was the first man to introduce into Moscow. Almost they were prepared to take him at Alexander's estimate.

A few rays of this new glory were reflected on me. In the office Bayley drove me hard. Speaking no languages, he was dependent on my services for much of his information. On the other hand, he taught me how to run an office, how to handle all kinds and conditions of men, and how to coax or bully the various departments of the Foreign Office at home. "If you can't get things by asking politely, you must make yourself a nuisance," he used to say. He lived up to his own precepts, "kow-towing" to no man, and, if necessity arose, making himself a nuisance both to the Foreign Office and to the Embassy. To my astonishment I discovered that, by taking a high hand, he enhanced his own reputation. His stock rose. He went to St. Petersburg to see the Ambassador and came back with a mandate to inspect the other Consulates in Russia. In spite of a "peppery" temper (as a young man he had been on the Gold Coast and had acquired a liver) he was a splendid chief, and such merits as I ever possessed as a Consular Officer I owe entirely to his training. Outside the office he was like a father to me, and I was never separated from him. At his house I met scores of people, whom otherwise I should never have known, and whose friendship was afterwards to be of the greatest service to me during the war. Under Bayley's tutelage I developed from a shy and ignorant youngster into a self-reliant and tolerably efficient administrator.

In the spring of 1914 I had an amusing experience, while I was in charge of the Consulate-General during one of Bayley's tours of inspection. One Saturday afternoon I was summoned to the telephone by the Pristaff[1] of the Tverskoi district. Two Englishmen—a naval doctor and a Chief Petty Officer—had been arrested for shop-lifting. I put on my coat and hurried round to the Pristaff's house. The Pristaff—a bullet-headed, pimply-faced man with a military moustache, was polite but obdurate. The two men were under lock and key. They had been caught red-handed. He was having tea in his private apartment, when I called, and did not seem to relish my intrusion. At my request, however, he sent for the protocol and read it to me. On their own showing the two men had been sent out from the Tyne on a warship, which was being delivered to China, and, having completed their mission, were returning to England via the Trans-Siberian. During the four hours' stop in Moscow they had gone into a shop, had picked out some handkerchiefs, some socks, and a birch-wood cigarette case, and had put the goods in their pocket. Then, just as they were about to produce the money to pay for them, they had been seized by a shop detective. It was not a very plausible story. The evidence of the shop detective and of the policeman who had been called in to make the arrest was damning. The detective swore that he had watched the petty officer slip the cigarette case into his pocket with all the skill of a professional thief.

The only point in the men's favour was that between them they had about eighty pounds in English notes, and the total value of the goods found on them was less than three pounds. I made great play of this anomaly and also of the fact that a misunderstanding might have arisen over the language difficulty. I requested an interview with the two men.

My eloquence, however, was vain. The Pristaff smiled condescendingly.

[1] A police inspector of a district; generally an ex-army officer.

"You have your duty to do, Mr. Consul," he said. "I have mine. It is a bad case."

There seemed nothing for me to do except to retreat. At this moment a good-looking young man burst into the room.

"Papa," he said excitedly, "we've won."

Then he saw me, stared confusedly for a moment, rushed forward and shook me warmly by the hand.

"Mr. Lockhart," he said, "you don't remember me. I played against you last year. I'm the centre-half of the Union Club." His face glowed. He dashed back to his father. "Papa, this is Mr. Lockhart, who used to play for the Morozovtsi—the best team in Russia. He must have tea with us."

The Pristaff frowned and then smiled.

"Forgive me," he said. "In discussing our business, I forgot all about tea."

He rang the bell, ordered more cups and some vodka, and, as we sat and pledged each other, the boy told us the story of the afternoon's match. The Pristaff listened in silent admiration. Obviously, he doted on his boy. I, too, sat on, hoping for an unexpected dénouement to my own problem. When the boy had finished his recital, he turned again to me:

"And what are you doing here, Mr. Lockhart?"

The father blushed.

"Mr. Lockhart has some official business to discuss with me. I think you had better go."

When the boy had gone, there was an awkward silence. Then the Pristaff cleared his throat.

"Mr. Consul," he said, "I have been thinking over this case. I am convinced that you are right and that a British naval doctor with fifty pounds in his pocket would not steal a few worthless handkerchiefs. The devil of it is that the goods were found in both the men's pockets. If only all the goods had been in the gunner's pockets and we could call the doctor as witness, the case would not be so difficult."

He scratched his shaven head. Then he pushed the bell.

"Send me the policeman who made the protocol on this English case," he ordered.

The policeman appeared—a stout, honest fellow conscious of having done a good day's work and expecting to be praised.

"Did you make this protocol?" asked the Pristaff.

"Yes, sir,"

"Did you find the goods in the pockets of both men?"

"Yes, sir."

"Are you quite sure?"

"Yes, sir," said the policeman.

"Think again," roared the Pristaff in a voice of thunder.

The policeman blenched but made the same answer. Even for a Russian he was slow in the uptake.

The Pristaff returned to the charge.

"Do you think that a naval doctor, an officer of the English fleet, would steal a pair of socks and a handkerchief?"

The policeman shuffled.

"Yes, sir—I mean, no, sir," he stammered.

"Fool," growled the Pristaff. "What do you mean? Do you mean that you found all the goods in the petty officer's pocket and nothing in the pockets of the doctor."

This was said very slowly and deliberately, every word being punctuated with a tap of a large ruler on the table.

This time even the policeman understood.

"Yes, sir," he whispered hoarsely.

The Pristaff tore up the protocol.

"Go," he said. "Draw up a new protocol at once and don't let me catch you out in inaccuracies again."

He turned to me with a sheepish grin.

"That's all I can do," he said. "The case will have to go before the magistrate. I warn you there will be trouble over the detective who is a pig-headed fellow and who in any case is paid by results. But at any rate you have now a witness for the defence. The rest depends on you. I can release the doctor at once."

Football has its uses. I thanked him profoundly, begged him to send the doctor round to my flat, and rushed off to enlist the services of Alexander Wilenkin, the Consular lawyer.

That same evening we laid our plans. The naval doctor stuck

to his story that they had intended to pay for the goods, and Wilenkin, who knew England almost as well as he knew Russia, saw his way clear. The petty officer would have to stand his trial. The doctor's evidence would be valuable, but the chief witness for the defence was to be myself. This was Wilenkin's plan of campaign.

At once I raised objections. I was doubtful about the propriety of a British Consular officer appearing in a case of this kind. In any case I did not see how I could be of assistance.

"Leave it to me, my dear-r Lockhart," said Wilenkin in his guttural Jewish accent. And I did.

Wilenkin, who belonged to a rich Jewish family, had the reputation of being the best-dressed man in Moscow, and in his defence of the two Englishmen clothes played an important part.

On the Tuesday we all appeared before the examining magistrate, Wilenkin and I, complete in morning coats, striped trousers, monocles and top hats. Our entry into the squalid, crowded court made a sensation.

The case opened badly. The shop detective gave his evidence with overwhelming effect. The petty officer, dirty and unshaven after three days in prison, made an unfortunate impression on the bench. Wilenkin's speech, however, was a masterpiece. Basing his defence on the fact that the two men were well supplied with money, he pointed out the improbability of two such distinguished members of His Majesty's Navy risking their careers for the sake of a handkerchief and a pair of socks. Englishmen were, admittedly, queer people. They washed. They had a preference for clean linen. What more natural than that they should profit by their stay in Moscow to permit themselves the luxury of a wash and a clean handkerchief. The detective had erred on the side of eagerness. Finally, the matter had a profound political aspect. England and Russia were now friends—almost Allies. One day—how soon no one knew—they might be fighting side by side. Had the magistrate weighed in his mind the deplorable effect a miscarriage of justice might have on the present happy state of

Anglo-Russian relations? Autres pays, autres mœurs, and in order to demonstrate that English customs were different from Russian he had brought into this court a very busy man—the acting British Consul-General.

I stepped forward with all the dignity I could muster and took the oath.

"Is it quite a common occurrence in England for respectable people to enter a shop, pick up an article off the counter and put it in their pocket before they have actually paid for it?" asked Wilenkin.

"Yes."

"Have you done it on occasions yourself?"

"Yes," I answered without a blush.

The petty officer left the court without a stain on his character. But that night every newspaper in Moscow came out with large headlines: "British Consul in Moscow swears that in England shoppers may put goods in their pocket before paying for them!"

My reputation, however, survived this sarcasm. I was beginning to know my Moscow.

This was merely a minor achievement for Wilenkin. In peace time regarded by most people as a fop, he proved himself a lion of Judah in the war. He was, in fact, the bravest Jew I have ever met. He was one of the first Russians to enlist as a volunteer. By his physical courage as much as by his intelligence he rose from the ranks to be a junior officer. He won the St. George's Cross for bravery in action. Bemonocled and clean-shaven in his civil life, in war he grew a magnificent beard and mustachios. When the first revolution came, he threw himself heart and soul into the task of persuading his men to continue fighting. His skill as an orator raised him to the dignity of Vice-President of his Army Soviet, and it was he who brought back to St. Petersburg the troops which suppressed the first Bolshevik attempt at a coup d'état in July, 1917. After the Bolshevik revolution of November, 1917, he threw in his lot with Savinkoff and had a hand in almost every counter-revolutionary plot against the new régime. His indifference to danger amounted almost to foolhardiness, and on several occasions I warned him of the risks he was running. In July, 1918, he was arrested in Moscow as a counter-revolutionary. He was one of the first victims of the official terror, when, as a reprisal for the attempt on Lenin's life on September 1st, 1918, the Bolsheviks shot seven hundred of their political opponents.

Throughout the spring and early summer of 1914 my life ran on active and pleasant lines. I had sufficient work to keep me out of mischief. My interest in Russia and things Russian was amounting almost to a mania, and my ambition to make myself the best-informed Consular officer in Moscow was well on the way to fulfilment. My pride was pleasantly titillated, when the Austrian Consul-General borrowed our annual report (written mainly by me) in order to paraphrase it as his own. In the past he had always conferred this honour on his German colleagues. If I showed any disposition to "let up," a judicious mixture of praise and exhortation from Bayley kept my nose to the grindstone. It has been my fate in life to be the willing horse of various masters. My pleasures were few—a little tennis, an occasional game of billiards, and an odd week-end in the country. Yet I was not unhappy. My home life was peaceful and undisturbed. Obviously, if I was the last person any woman should have married, marriage was good for me.

In June, 1914, I had another surfeit of official entertainment. Admiral Beatty and a picked selection of the officers of the First Battle Cruiser Squadron paid an official visit to Moscow. The youthful appearance of the youngest Admiral since Nelson nearly led to my official undoing. Dressed in uniform and cocked hat, I had been sent by Bayley to meet the train and to welcome Beatty on the platform. It was my first encounter with the Navy, and I knew less than nothing of the distinguishing marks of the different ranks. On the platform I found the Prefect, the Governor, the General commanding the Moscow district, and other Russian officials to whom I should have to introduce the British admiral. The train drew up, and out of the special carriage stepped a brisk young man who

looked no older than myself and whom I naturally supposed
was Beatty's flag-lieutenant. I stood waiting for the emergence
of the great man himself, and there was an awkward pause.
It was ended very quickly by my supposed flag-lieutenant.

"How do you do?" he said. "I'm Beatty. Introduce me and
tell me whom I shake hands with first."

I went hot and then cold. When I told him afterwards of my
embarrassment, he laughed and took it as a compliment.

In my own defence I must admit that the Russians were
equally astonished by Beatty's youthfulness.

The visit was a tremendous success. Beatty's officers, who
included Admiral Halsey, Admiral Brock, and several other
captains, whose names were to become household words during
the war, went down with the Russians like a dinner. Their
clean-shaven, red-cheeked faces brought a breeze of health and
vigour into the parched atmosphere of the Moscow summer,
and Beatty's square jaw and the jaunty angle at which he wore
his cap gave a lasting joy to the Moscow caricaturists, who
were only too glad to have this opportunity of contrasting the
efficiency of the British Navy with the shortcomings of their
own. The climax to a whirlwind triumph came with Beatty's
speech at a dinner given by the town in a large marquee in the
Sokolniki park. After a succession of dreary orators the English
admiral arose, and in a voice which would have carried through
a gale, delivered a speech which stirred the sluggish Muscovites
to an extraordinary display of emotion. Never before had they
seen an admiral who had not a beard down to his knees. The
military strength of Britain might be insignificant, but the
British Navy was the real thing. To-day, I often wonder why
Lord Beatty has never gone into politics. That voice of his
would wake even the sleepers in the House of Lords. It was a
first-rate performance, and his visit did much to enhance
British prestige.

Then came tragedy—swift as an eagle in its descent and
pitiless in its consequences. On June 28th the Archduke Franz
Ferdinand was murdered, and, however secure London may have
felt, Moscow realised from the first moment that the red sun of

war had already risen. It was at this time that a tragedy occurred in my own family. In June my wife had been expecting a child. I had wished to send her home and had written to my grandmother in the hope that she would provide the necessary financial assistance. The reply had been stern and uncompromising. She herself had given birth to her first child under a bullock cart in New Zealand. A woman's place on those occasions was by her husband.

The doctor recommended to my wife was a German called Schmidt—a kind and gentle old man who was long past his best. I had misgivings and wished to employ a Russian. The English women in Moscow, however, were strongly prejudiced against Russian doctors. Schmidt spoke English, and my wife liked him.

The crisis came on June 20th and lasted all through the night. Inexperienced as I was, I soon realised that the birth was complicated. It was one of the hottest nights I have ever known in Moscow or anywhere else, and for hours on end I stood at the open window in the drawing-room, smoking cigarette after cigarette and trying to keep my mind a blank. At three o'clock Schmidt came into the room. The sweat, streaming from his face, had dripped on to his white overalls.

"It is difficult," he gasped, "very difficult. I must have another doctor."

He gave me the number, and I rushed to the telephone. Hours seemed to pass. Again I resumed my stand at the window, listening for the sound of the "droschke" wheels on the cobbled streets. After several false alarms the doctor arrived— a young man, whose efficient manner inspired me with a new confidence. Then he disappeared into the bedroom, and again there was an immense silence. At five o'clock all was over. Katja, the cook, tiptoed across the room, her apron up to her eyes. Then the young doctor came in.

"The mother is alive," he said gravely. "The girl will not live."

Very quickly he told me the details. The birth had been difficult. There had been great exhaustion, and they had had to use instruments. The first instruments had been defective. If he had been summoned sooner . . .

"The child is dead?" I whispered. He nodded.

In a dream I ordered coffee and biscuits for the doctors. In a dream I saw them off at the door. Then I sat down to wait for the morning. At seven o'clock my mother-in-law came in and took me into the room which would have been our nursery. The child was lying in a cot. They had dressed her in the clothes which for months past my wife had been making for her. Her eyes were open. There was not a mark on the little waxen face. She looked so fresh and sweet that it was impossible to believe that she was dead. The little cap which covered her head concealed the fatal bruise.

Mechanically I went about the tasks of the day. I telephoned to Bayley to tell him what had happened. I called on the chaplain to see what could be done about the burial, and in the afternoon I walked down to the Sadovaya to order the tiny coffin. As I passed the Hermitage, a street-woman accosted me. I walked past, and she came back to me. Silently I handed her five roubles; for a moment our eyes met; then she turned and ran. I think she thought I was mad.

Two days later I made the long "trek" out to the German cemetery, carrying the coffin on my knees. The sun beat down pitilessly from a cloudless sky, but I never felt the heat. An Englishman of seventy was being buried, and it was among strangers that I stood, while the chaplain read the burial service and the two coffins of the man who had lived his full life and of the nameless child were lowered into their common grave . . .

All through that burning July, while my wife lay in danger, first, of her life and then of her reason, I toiled at the Consulate-General, striving to kill my thoughts with a surfeit of work. And, as the days passed, the tension of the Russian people grew, until gradually it swelled into an angry murmur. Why was England hanging back? As July broke into August, scores of people telephoned daily to know the reason and, not receiving satisfaction, grumbled and threatened. Through the long white days troops in full marching kit tramped through the streets, singing their plaintive songs and leaving a cloud of dust in their trail. The heart of Russia was on fire with war.

On the morning of Wednesday, August 5th, I set out as usual on my short walk to the Consulate-General. At the street corner opposite the office a crowd of demonstrators impeded my progress. A band was playing, and raucous voices were calling for the Consul-General. Suddenly a man in the crowd recognised me. "Way for the British Vice-Consul," he roared. Strong hands passed me over the heads of the crowd to the entrance, while a thousand voices thundered: "Long live England." A bearded student kissed me on both cheeks. England had declared war on Germany. Another day's delay, and the demonstrators would have smashed our windows.

BOOK III

WAR AND PEACE

"EINE GROSSE Epoche hat das Jahrhundert geboren, aber der grosse Moment findet ein Kleines Geschlecht."

(The century has given birth to a great epoch, but the great moment finds a petty generation.)

Goethe

CHAPTER ONE

MY RECOLLECTIONS of those first war months in Moscow are remarkably vivid, although to-day in the light of after events they seem more like a strange dream than an actual experience. The contrast between 1914 and 1932 is too great. I have to shut my eyes to recall the enthusiasm of those early days. There in the patchwork of my memory I see again those moving scenes at the station: the troops, grey with dust and closely packed in cattle trucks; the vast crowd on the platform to wish them God-speed; grave, bearded fathers, wives and mothers, smiling bravely through their tears and bringing gifts of flowers and cigarettes; fat priests to bless the happy warriors. The crowd sways forward for a last handshake and a last embrace. There is a shrill whistle from the engine. Then, with many false starts, the overloaded train, as though reluctant to depart, crawls slowly out of the station and disappears in the grey twilight of the Moscow night. Silent and bare-headed, the crowd remains motionless until the last faint echo of the song of the men, who are never to return, has faded into nothing. Then, shepherded by the gendarmes, it files quietly out into the streets.

I come away with a hopefulness which overrides my better judgment. Here was a Russia which I had never known—a Russia inspired by a patriotism, which seemed to have its roots deep down in the soil. It was, too, a sober Russia. The sale of vodka had been stopped, and an emotional religious fervour took the place of the squalid intoxication which in previous wars had characterised the departure of Russian soldiers.

Among the bourgeoisie there was the same enthusiasm. The wives of the rich merchants vied with each other in spending money on hospitals. There were gala performances at the State theatres in aid of the Red Cross. There was an orgy of national anthems. Every night at the opera and the ballet the Imperial orchestra played the national hymns of Russia, England, France and Belgium, while the audience stood at attention in a fervour of exalted patriotism. Later, especially when the

97

number of Allied hymns assumed the dimensions of a cricket score, the fervour evaporated, and the heavy-paunched Muscovites groaned audibly at an ordeal which lasted over half an hour. But in those early weeks of 1914 Russian patriotism had much on which to feed itself. The beginning of the war, indeed, was all Russia, and, as the news of each Russian advance was made public, Moscow gave itself up to a full-throated rejoicing. If there were pessimists at that moment, their voice was not raised in the market-place. Revolution was not even a distant probability, although from the first day of the war every liberal-minded Russian hoped that victory would bring constitutional reforms in its train.

In St. Petersburg, it is true, these early Russian triumphs invoked covert sneers at the failure of the Franco-British effort. In drawing-rooms one heard whispers about English faint-heartedness, and pro-Germans spread slimy rumours about England's determination to fight until the last drop of Russian blood. In Moscow, however, the tongues of the slanderers were silent, and enthusiasm for the Russian victories was tempered by a generous sympathy for the difficulties of France and England.

Indeed, as far as Russia was concerned, the heart of the alliance was in Moscow. If ever Bayley or I appeared in public, we received an ovation. At the "Bat" Nikita Baleieff would come before the curtain, point us out, and say: "To-night we have with us the representatives of our ally, England." The band would then play "God Save the King," and the whole audience stood up and cheered. We pretended to be bored by these unaccustomed attentions, vowed to each other that we would avoid them in future, and returned as frequently as discretion permitted. There is no limit to the vanity of the very Great, and Bayley and I were only two very ordinary mortals.

On September 10th we attended in full uniform a gala performance at the theatre in honour of the capture of Lemberg by the Russians. I went with sadness in my heart. The German armies were on the Marne, and the fate of Paris hung in the balance. My brothers were in France, and here was I taking part in the celebrations of a Russian victory. Inside the theatre the uniforms of the officers made a brilliant setting to the jewels and costly dresses of the women. The play was a Russian adaptation of Rostand's "L'Aiglon," and Bayley and I shared a box near the stage and directly opposite the box occupied by the French Consul-General. During the first act the Frenchman was called away. He remained absent for some time. When he came back, his manner was agitated. Then the curtain fell, but the lights did not go up. In an instant the atmosphere became electrical. "The Russians had won another victory. They had captured 100,000 prisoners. They had taken Przemysl." In the darkness rumour ran riot. Then the footlights went up again; the orchestra filed into their places, and a young girl of eighteen, the daughter of the President of the French Chamber of Commerce, came on to the stage. With her white dress, her face free of all make-up, and her glorious golden hair, she looked like the Angel Gabriel. In her trembling hands she held a slip of paper.

The audience hushed itself in an expectant silence. Then, quivering with emotion and nervousness, the girl began to read: "The following official telegram has just been received from French headquarters." She stopped as if her tongue were chained. The tears streamed down her face.

Then, in a shrill crescendo, she read the message: "Je suis heureux de vous annoncer victoire sur tout le front.—Joffre."

The lights blazed up. The girl ran wildly off the stage. and in a storm of cheering the orchestra struck up the Marseillaise. Bearded men kissed each other. Women smiled and wept at the same time. Then, as the orchestra broke into the chorus, a miracle happened. From the gallery above came the tramp of marching feet, and four hundred French reservists, singing in a glorious unison, took up the refrain. They were leaving for France the next day, and they sang the Marseillaise with all the passionate ardour of their Latin temperament. It was epic. It was the last occasion on which Russia was to feel supremely confident about the outcome of the war.

The capture of Lemberg had softened the grim defeat of Tannenberg. But the Tannenbergs were to be repeated, and, although the Russians were to hold their own against the Austrians almost to the end, it was already clear that they were no match for the Germans. Tannenberg, in fact, was the prelude to the Russian revolution. It was a message of hope to Lenin. It gave a handle to the hidden army of agitators in the factories and in the villages and, by destroying the pick of the Russian officers, it undermined the war-spirit of a people who by nature and by the exigencies of the Russian climate have always been incapable of any sustained effort.

Certainly, the transition from optimism to pessimism was not accomplished in one stage and, if on the Russian front there never was the same immobility as in France, there were long periods of monotonous inactivity.

The decline in morale was, in fact, gradual, and, as it became clear that the war was to be a long one, life stabilised itself. In Moscow, which was far removed from the front, the spirit of the bourgeoisie was by no means discouraging. There was, it is true, little attempt to economise or to make sacrifices. There was no sentiment of public opinion against shirkers, and "embusqués" could find security in a Red Cross organisation without fear of being handed a white feather. Theatres and places of amusement flourished as in peace time, and, although the proletariat and the peasantry were deprived of their alcohol, no such restrictions were imposed on the well-to-do classes. To replenish their private stock of wine they required a permit, but, as the cost of living rose and since Russian officials were badly paid, permits were easily obtainable. In restaurants the only difference was that one drank one's alcohol from a teapot instead of from a bottle. As control became more lax, even the pretence of the teapot disappeared.

On the other hand, an immense and extremely valuable work was done by the so-called public organisations, represented by the Union of Cities and by the Union of Zemstvos, in providing the army with a whole network of hospitals and factories. Without this aid, the Russian military machine would have broken down far sooner than it did. Yet, instead of stimulating this patriotic effort and encouraging the public organisations in every way it could, the Russian Government did its best to hamper and curtail its activities. It may be said that the public organisations were politically ambitious, that they were honeycombed with Liberalism and therefore a menace to the autocracy. Admittedly, both the Cities Union and the Zemstvos Unions were controlled by Liberals, who had a deep suspicion of St. Petersburg. Admittedly, too, their headquarters were in Moscow, and Moscow was never popular with the Emperor. But, in the beginning at any rate, their enthusiasm for the war was single-minded, and the political aspirations, which came later, were the direct result of a policy of perpetual pin-pricks. It was the tragedy of Russia that the Tsar, dominated by a woman who was obsessed with the one ambition to hand down the autocracy unimpaired to her son, never took the public organisations into his confidence. The fact that gradually Moscow became more absorbed in the internal political struggle than in the war itself was mainly the result of the Tsar's fatal obtuseness. And, although his loyalty to his Allies remained unshaken to the last, it was his failure to harness the loyalty of his own people which eventually cost him his throne.

For me personally that first winter of 1914-1915 was a period of sadness relieved only by incessant hard work. My wife had made a slow recovery from her illness. Her nerves were shattered, and she was forced to enter a Russian sanatorium — an experience which did her little good and which, had I known more about Russian sanatoria, I should never have allowed her to undergo. We gave up our flat, and in the period of looking for a new one took over a furnished flat from some English friends who had gone to England. My days and frequently my nights were entirely absorbed by consular work, which the war had more than trebled. In particular, the blockade and the manifold regulations controlling imports and exports involved an immense amount of ciphering, most of which I had to do single-handed. Moscow, too, had become an all-important political centre, and, as Bayley relied almost entirely on me for his political intelligence, my time was fully occupied. Another difficulty in my own case was the want of money. My wife's confinement had been expensive. With the new impor-tance of our position our social obligations had increased. The business community—and Moscow was the chief commercial city of Russia—was prospering exceedingly from the lucrative war contracts, which were being handed out lavishly, and with the increased cost of living which this prosperity brought in its train we were left at a sore disadvantage both towards the Russians and towards our own English colony. Moreover, the war had put an automatic end to my earnings from journalism. I was not permitted to write about the war. The English news-papers were interested in nothing else.

A pleasant relief to the monotony of our existence at this time was the visit of Hugh Walpole, who arrived in Moscow shortly after the outbreak of the war, and who remained with us for some months. He was a frequent visitor to our flat, and his cheery optimism was a godsend to my wife. At that time he had written several books, including "Fortitude," and already had his feet well planted on the ladder of success. He was, however, entirely unspoilt, could still blush from an over-whelming self-consciousness, and impressed me more as a great, clumsy schoolboy, bubbling over with kindness and enthu-siasm, than as a dignified author, whose views were to be accepted with awe and respect. With the exception of Bayley we took him to our hearts, and he repaid our friendship with a sympathy and kindness which have never failed. With Bayley he was less successful. Bayley, who was then a sick man, was a cynic and an autocrat. He mistrusted enthusiasts. Still more did he dislike contradiction. Hugh, whose enthusiasm for everything Russian knew no bounds, liked argument and had views of his own. He irritated Bayley, and I fancy the irritation was mutual.

When Hugh left us, he went to the front as a Red Cross orderly. Later, he became head of the British propaganda bureau in St. Petersburg. From the first he had made up his mind to make the best of Russia. Certainly, Russia got the best out of him. His adventure at the front produced "The Dark Forest." His experiences in St. Petersburg inspired "The Secret City."

My diary shows that at this period I went out little and that such spare time as I had was spent in reading. In the last fortnight of January, 1915, I read and finished "War and Peace" in Russian. Occasionally I went with Walpole to the ballet and to the circus. It was with Hugh, too, that I first met Gorky —at Nikita Baleieff's "Bat." In those days the "Bat" was the favourite haunt of literary and artistic Moscow. Its performance did not begin until after the theatres had ended and many actors and actresses went there to sup as much as to see the performance. The "Bat," in fact, started as a kind of club of the Moscow Art Theatre, Baleieff himself having been a member of the company and failed to make good in that severe school. To-day, his troupe is as well-known in Paris, London and New York as ever it was in Russia, but to my mind the performances have lost much of the delicious intimacy of those early Moscow days, when there was no gulf between player and audience. Baleieff, incidentally, is an Armenian and belongs to what was once a rich family.

Gorky made a deep impression on me as much by his modesty as by his talent. His eyes are extraordinarily expressive, and in them one can read at once that sympathy with human suffering which is the dominating influence on his character and which in the end was to drive him, after a long period of opposition, into the arms of the Bolsheviks. To-day, Gorky writes more bitterly against the bourgeoisie and against the moderate Socialists than the most violent "Chekist" in Moscow, but in spite of these literary outbursts I refuse to believe that he has lost that fundamental kindness which in the past he never failed to show to any case which deserved his pity. No one who has ever seen Gorky with children, with animals, and with young authors, will ever credit him with the power to inflict harm or suffering on any of his fellow-creatures.

It was at the "Bat," too, that I first met Chaliapin. An hour

before I had seen him at the opera in "Boris," a part in which
he is and looks every inch a king with the manners of a great
aristocrat and with hands which seemed to belong to some
ancient Doge of Venice. The whole thing was a trick—a
marvellous example of that dramatic art which, as Stanislavsky
always used to say, could have made him the greatest actor in
the world, had he chosen to abandon his singing for the drama.
Off the stage the man was still a peasant, with a peasant's
appetite and the huge, strong hands of a son of the soil. In
those days Gorky used to tell a good story of Chaliapin. In
their youth the two men were tramping the Volga district in
search of work. At Kazan a travelling impresario was looking
for local talent to supplement his chorus. He wanted a tenor
and a bass. Two poorly clad applicants entered his ramshackle office and were given an audition. The impresario
took the tenor and rejected the bass. The tenor was Gorky.
The bass was Chaliapin.

Moscow, always much more anti-German than St. Petersburg, was a perfect cesspool of rumours of pro-German intrigues in high places. One entry in my diary in February,
1915, runs as follows: "To-day an officer telephoned to ask
when England was going to rid Russia of 'the German
woman'." This, of course, was a reference to the Empress,
and my own comment was: "This is the third time that this
kind of thing has happened this week." It was to happen still
more frequently as the months passed. To this period, too,
belongs the most popular Moscow story of the war. The
Tsarevitch is seen crying in the corridor of the Winter Palace.
A general, who is leaving the Palace after an audience, stops
and pats the boy's head.

"What is wrong, my little man?"

The Tsarevitch replies, half-smiling, half-crying:

"When the Russians are beaten, papa cries. When the
Germans are beaten, mama cries. When am I to cry?"

Stories of this kind were repeated all over the country and
did immense harm both among the industrial proletariat and
the peasantry. Moscow, in fact, lived on stories and rumours,

and, if the spy-hunting mania was never as bad as in England and in France, there was considerable persecution both of the Jews and of the Russians of German extraction. Not all the stories, however, were concerned with the shortcomings of the autocracy. The German Kaiser received a considerable share of the wit and sarcasm of the Muscovite humorists. Many of them are too coarse for print. Others have been told before. One, however, is, I think, new to English readers. In the winter of 1915 the Kaiser visited Lodz and with a view to placating the local population made a speech. His audience was, of course, mainly Jewish. As they listened to him, they heard him refer, first, to the Almighty and the All-Highest, then to God and himself, and finally to himself and God. When the speech was ended, the leading Jews withdrew into a corner to discuss the situation.

"This man will do for us," said the Chief Rabbi. "He's the first Christian I've met who denies the Holy Trinity."

How strange and unreal these stories sound to-day. Then, however, they were the stock-in-trade of every gossip and the staple entertainment of every salon.

CHAPTER TWO

I HAVE SAID that Bayley was a sick man. Lack of exercise—always the curse of the Moscow winter—and overwork had undermined his health, and in April, 1915, he made up his mind to return to England and to undergo the operation which for some time he had been told was necessary. With characteristic kindness he insisted on my taking a week's leave before his departure. It was the last real holiday I was ever to have in Russia and I enjoyed every minute of it. Leaving Moscow still bound in the grip of winter, I went to Kieff, the cradle of Russian history and the Holy City of the Orthodox Church. When I woke up after my night in the train, I looked out on green fields and delicious white cottages glistening in the warm sunshine. My travelling companion, an officer, who was returning to the front, greeted me with a smile. "You will like Kieff. You will find a better atmosphere here than in Moscow, let alone St. Petersburg." In the exuberance of my spirits I was prepared to believe anything. Actually, he spoke the plain truth. Although full of wounded, Kieff had far more war-spirit than Moscow. Indeed, right up to the revolution, the nearer one came to the front, the more optimistic was the prevailing sentiment. All the best of Russia (with, admittedly, some of the worst elements) was in the trenches. It was the rear and not the front, which let the country down.

As we drew near to Kieff, we stopped for some considerable time at a wayside station. A train, carrying Austrian prisoners, was stranded in a siding. The prisoners, apparently unguarded, had slipped out of their cattle trucks and were sprawling about on some wood-piles, enjoying the first warmth of the Southern sun before continuing their long "trek" to Siberia. Poor devils. They looked as underfed as they were wretchedly clad. In Moscow the news of the capture of so many thousands of prisoners had always filled me with a fierce exultation. Here, face to face with the unfortunates themselves, I had only one thought. Snodgrass, the American Consul-General, who was in charge of German interests in Russia, had given me a graphic account of the terrible conditions of the Russian prison-camps, and with a deep pity in my heart I wondered how many of these poor fellows, some, doubtless, happy to be captured and ignorant of the fate that lay ahead of them, would ever see their homes again. Then, as I stood at the open window looking at them much as a visitor studies a new animal in the Zoo, one of the prisoners began to sing the Intermezzo from *Cavalleria Rusticana*. He was a Croat, and the spring had warmed his heart, bringing him memories of his Dalmatian home. He was sublimely unconscious of our train-load of Russians. He was singing to please himself, and he sang as though his heart would burst. I do not know who he was. Probably he was a tenor from the Zagreb opera. But the effect of his voice in that tiny station with its background of green fields and orchards was magical. His fellow-prisoners stopped their pebble-throwing. The Russians in our train rose from their seats and stood in silent admiration at the windows. Then, when he had finished, Austrians and Russians combined in one spontaneous outburst of applause, while from the carriages a hail of cigarettes, apples and sweetmeats descended on the prisoners. The singer bowed gravely and turned his head away. Then the whistle went, and we passed on our way.

I arrived at Kieff about mid-day on Good Friday and spent the afternoon wandering about the town and looking at the churches, of which there are almost as many as in Moscow. Then, tired and rather lonely, I went to bed at nine o'clock. The next day I was up betimes. The sun was streaming into my room, and I was determined to make the best use of my temporary freedom. I am an American in my passion for sight-seeing, and I "did" Kieff with all the thoroughness of the typical American tourist. After Moscow it was a relief to find hills and a real river. The fine weather had brought the whole of the town into the streets, Russians doing their Easter shopping and Jew shopkeepers catering for their needs. For, in spite of its churches, Kieff is almost more Jewish than Christian. Everyone seemed to be smiling. The news from the Austrian front, for which Kieff was the base, was still good. Przemysl had fallen only a few weeks before, and in the prevailing optimism I felt happier than I had felt for months.

After luncheon I took a "droschke" and drove to the Vladimir Hill, where I left my driver and climbed up to look at the view. In England or in America private enterprise would have built a hotel or a sanatorium here. The Russians have put up a statue to St. Vladimir, who stands overlooking the Dnieper with a great cross in his hand. The Dnieper itself is a noble river—far more imposing than the Volga and totally unlike any river I had ever seen. After more than three years in a plain without hills and without sea I found it more soul-satisfying than perhaps I should to-day.

Then I drove down to the Suspension Bridge to have a look at the town from the plain. For, strangely enough, while Kieff itself is built on a cluster of hills, all around the country is as flat as the plain round Moscow. The white-roofed steam-boats were already plying on the river. The trees were just coming into bloom. The lilac was out, and by the roadside buttercups were growing in profusion. By its position over-looking the river Kieff reminded me of Quebec, and, if Quebec has perhaps the finer site, the picturesqueness of the Kieff architecture is more than sufficient compensation.

In the evening I went to Saint Sofia to attend the midnight service. In Moscow my visits to the Russian church had always been on such official occasions as the Emperor's birthday or name-day. Always I had been in uniform and had stood among the elect on a square shut off from more humble worshippers. Here at Kieff I was one of a crowd so dense that several people fainted. In spite of the discomfort, I remained to the end, took part in the procession, and shared in the emotional uplift of the vast congregation of peasants and pilgrims.

The pilgrims, pleasantly picturesque at a distance, were assembled in force, and on Easter Monday I went to see them at the famous Kieff Lavra, which with the Troitse-Sergievski Monastery near Moscow is the most celebrated holy place in Russia. So warm was the sun that I had to go back and take off my waistcoat. When I arrived at the monastery church, a service was going on, and thousands of soldiers were drawn up on the square outside. Pilgrims—bearded old men with limpid eyes and wizened-up old women—were picknicking everywhere. In the church itself I found an aged philosopher in a corner contentedly munching a loaf of black bread. He seemed supremely happy. From the church I went to the catacombs—cold and unimpressive subterranean passages containing the bones of forgotten saints. In front of each coffin was a collecting box by which sat a priest, and, as the footsore pilgrims clumsily inserted their copecks, the priest leant forward over the relics of the dead saint and chanted: "Pray to God for us." With a shudder I ascended into the sunshine and went out to a grassy plot on the cliff-edge. Here three blind beggars, sitting about three paces apart, were reading aloud the Gospel with varying degrees of success. One, a young man of not more than twenty-five, was wearing a soldier's uniform. If he had lost his sight in the war, how had he learnt the Braille system so quickly? If not, why was he wearing a soldier's uniform? I did not disturb his peace of mind by asking an indiscreet question, preferring to regard him as a living member of that holy Russia, which in those early days of the war had evoked the emotional sympathies of my own countrymen.

Farther along the bank a gipsy with a fortune-telling parrot was doing a lucrative trade with the soldiers. The parrot was a well-trained bird and could give its customers the correct change up to about thirty copecks. What with the necromancers and the priests, most of the soldiers and the pilgrims must have gone away with empty pockets. What was left went to an old harpist who, to his own accompaniment, sang Caucasian folk-songs in a wheezy voice. It was all very peaceful, very harmless and very orderly. Both pilgrims and soldiers had in a contented mind a full reward for their outlay.

In Kieff I had no adventures; yet the memory of the week I spent there remains more clearly fixed in my mind than any other incident in the war. Perhaps it was the spell of the sunshine, or perhaps the contrast with the excitement of my

Moscow life, which has left me with so lucid an impression of this episode. Certainly, prolonged excitement can become as monotonous as the most vegetable existence, and in the next three years exciting incidents were to tax my memory to its utmost capacity.

As I left Kieff, the weather broke, and the rain descended in torrents. The station was a desert of depression, and, as I looked back over the railway-bridge, I felt grateful that the town had put on its gayest colours for my special benefit. Yet my heart was weighed down with the thought that I was leaving the south, the sunshine, and the smiling, laughing Ukrainians for the cold and cruel north. I did Moscow and the Great Russians an injustice. When the collapse came, Kieff was to be the centre of the worst atrocities of the revolution and the Ukrainians the perpetrators of the most brutal outrages.

On the return journey I had one minor adventure, which was due to Russian carelessness or to Russian indifference to accepted Western conventions. I had to share a sleeper with a lady. She was charming and within the first hour had told me her life story. She had been a famous singer and, having amassed a considerable fortune, had married a Guards officer. After six years of married life he had shot her in a fit of jealousy. The bullet had penetrated her neck. Since then she had been unable to sing. In her company the hours passed unnoticed, and it was late before I retired to rest. There was, however, no romance about the meeting. Although she carried her years well, she must then have been over sixty.

Soon after my return to Moscow Bayley went to England on sick-leave, and at the age of twenty-seven I was left in charge of what was rapidly becoming one of our most important posts abroad.

His departure neither exalted nor depressed me. I had acted for him before when he was absent on tours of inspection. I expected him back within a month. I was merely carrying on during his temporary absence.

Events, however, were to prolong my period of responsibility. From Kieff I had returned to a Moscow full of rumours and depression. Things were going badly on the German front. The Russian advance into Austria had been checked. The heavy counter-attacks had already begun, and refugees were streaming into the city and taxing its housing resources to the utmost. From my Socialist acquaintances I had received disquieting reports regarding discontent and disorders among the new conscripts in the villages. The wounded did not like going back. The peasants objected to their sons being taken away from the fields. My English friends in the provincial textile factories had become increasingly anxious about the Socialist agitation among the workmen. It had become anti-war as well as anti-Government. In Moscow itself there had been bread riots, and the Assistant-Prefect had been stoned. Sandetsky, the commander-in-chief of the Moscow district and a gruff old patriot, who hated Germans, had been removed from his post, and Prince Yusupoff, the father of the young Prince who later was involved in the Rasputin murder, had been appointed Governor-General in his place. The only reason for Sandetsky's dismissal, it was rumoured, was an excess of patriotism. The Empress, whose work for the wounded was untiring, had given ikons to the Russian soldiers and money to the German and Austrian prisoners. True or untrue as this report may have been, Sandetsky had protested against the molly-coddling of prisoners in high quarters and had been disgraced. The atmosphere was unhealthy. Confidence in the Russian arms had given way to a conviction of German invincibility, and in every section of the Moscow population ruled bitter resentment against the alleged pro-German policy of the Russian Government. The famous Russian steam-roller, which English imagination had invented (incidentally, it was one of the stupidest comparisons ever coined), had broken down.

Obviously, the situation called for action, and I sat down and completed two tasks on which I had been working even before Bayley's departure. One was a long report on the industrial unrest with a first-hand account of the aims of the Socialists. The other was a political report on the situation in Moscow. It was pessimistic in tone and hinted at the probability of serious riots in the immediate future. Then, with some trepidation, I sent them off to the Ambassador. I received a personal letter of thanks with a request that political reports should become a regular feature of my work.

My prediction of trouble received startling confirmation within a fortnight. On June 10th vast anti-German riots broke out in Moscow, and for three days the city was in the hands of the mob. Every shop, every factory, every private house, owned by a German or bearing a German name, was sacked and looted. The country house of Knop, the great Russo-German millionaire, who more than any man had helped to build up the Russian cotton-industry by importing English machinery and English managers, was burnt to the ground. The mob, mad with drink, which it had procured from the wreckage of some German-named wine merchant, showed no mercy. It cared nothing that its victims were Russian subjects and in many cases men, who, in spite of their names, could speak no German. At Zündel's, a factory in the worst industrial area, the German-speaking manager, terrified into firing on the mob, was killed on the spot. I went out into the streets to see the rioting with my own eyes. For the first twenty-four hours the police could or would do nothing. Fires broke out in many quarters of the city, and, if there had been a wind, the disaster of 1812 might have repeated itself. On the Kuznetsky Most I stood and watched, while hooligans sacked the leading piano store of Moscow. Bechsteins, Blüthners, grand pianos, baby grands and uprights, were hurled one by one from the various stories to the ground, where a high bonfire completed the work of destruction. The crash of falling woodwork, the cruel tongues of flame, and the raucous yelling of the mob swelled into a terrifying discord, which even the troops, who had been called out, were at first unable to quell.

On the third day, after some shooting, the authorities were able to restore order. But, for the first time since 1905, the mob had felt its power. Its appetite for disorder had been whetted.

In this holocaust a considerable amount of British property had been damaged, and I therefore called immediately on the

Prefect and on Prince Yusupoff, the Governor-General, to make my official protest. I found the unfortunate Prefect in a state of collapse. He knew that he would be held responsible —as indeed he was. He was superseded within twenty-four hours. Prince Yusupoff, as one of the richest landowners in Russia, was in a different situation. He was bitterly opposed to what he called the pro-German "brakes" in St. Petersburg and he was inclined to take the view that the riots would have a salutary effect on a lukewarm Government.

Shortly afterwards Prince Yusupoff went on leave and never resumed his post. The account of his dismissal or, as he called it, his refusal to return is amusing. Soon after the riots he gave a dinner to General Klimovitch, the new Prefect, and to Count Muravieff, the Governor of the province of Moscow. Two days later Djunkowsky, the Assistant Minister of the Interior and the head of the secret police, rang up Muravieff from St. Petersburg and said to him:

"Two days ago you dined with Yusupoff."

"Yes."

"You had sterlet and chaud-froid of partridge."

"Yes."

"You discussed the merits of Moscow and Petersburg women."

"Yes."

"You drank a Mouton-Rothschild of 1884."

"Yes," said the astonished Muravieff, "but how the devil do you know all this."

"Why," replied Djunkowsky, "Klimovitch has just sent me in a full report."

Muravieff repeated the story to Yusupoff, who exploded angrily, said he was not going to be spied upon by his assistant, and swore he would not return to Moscow until Klimovitch was kicked out.

Klimovitch remained, and Yusupoff never returned.

The origin of the Moscow riots is still shrouded in mystery, but I have always held the view that the Moscow Governor-General was greatly to blame in that he first tolerated what he apparently thought was to be a healthy anti-German demonstration and did not intervene until the situation had become highly dangerous.

As a result of this deplorable affair I received a request from the Ambassador asking me to come to St. Petersburg to see him. Looking back across the years, I find it hard to recapture the thrill which this message gave me. Vice-Consuls, even acting Consuls-General, were not summoned every day to be consulted by Ambassadors. For one awkward moment I wondered if in any respect my handling of affairs had been remiss or if in any way I could be held responsible for what had happened. I decided the question in my own favour and consolidated my growing store of self-confidence. I took the precaution of calling on Michael Chelnokoff, the Moscow Mayor and my best friend in Russia, to collect the latest political information. Then, packing my bag, I set out for the station, where the indispensable Alexander had "wangled" me a sleeper to myself.

CHAPTER THREE

ALTHOUGH I HAD been three years in Russia, it was my first visit to St. Petersburg. It was also the first time I was to see Sir George Buchanan. Although to-day I have a hate of all towns, a city which is new to me rarely fails to touch some side of my emotions. In one sense St. Petersburg did not disappoint me. It is, in truth, a far more beautiful city than Moscow, and the view—especially the winter view—from the British Embassy, which has or had a noble site on the river opposite the fortress of Peter and Paul, is almost fairy-like in its beauty. But even in summer, in the season of the white nights, St. Petersburg always seemed to me cold and grey. Beneath its lovely exterior its heart was chill. Never at any time did it inspire me with the same friendly affection as Moscow.

On my arrival in the early morning I drove to the old Hotel de France, made a careful toilet, breakfasted, and then walked across through the Palace Square to the Embassy. I had a feeling of uncomfortable apprehension as if I was about to visit my dentist. As a Scot I sometimes try to cure my inferiority complex towards the English by a simulated contempt for their intellectual shortcomings. In the presence of foreigners I am a lion of self-confidence. The blustering swagger of the Americans only increases the sense of my own importance. Russians always make me feel that I am a "grand seigneur." But the meek arrogance of an Englishman's modesty reduces me to the level of an awkward gawk. I imagine that this inferiority complex, which now cramps me more securely than ever, dates from that day when I first entered the portals of the British Embassy.

As I made my way up one side of the broad double staircase, at the top of which the Ambassador used to receive his guests and on which three years later the unfortunate Cromie was to be shot down and trampled to death by Bolshevik soldiers, I felt like a schoolboy going to interview his headmaster. I turned to the left and was shown into a kind of ante-room which

opened out of the corridor. Here I was met by Havery, the
Chancery servant—a wonderful character, who had all the
Englishman's contempt for foreigners and whose penchant
for grumbling was equalled only by his kindness of heart.
I was given a chair and was told to wait. As the minutes passed,
the anticipated pleasure which my visit had aroused in me,
gave way to an increasing trepidation. The only member of
the Embassy staff whom I knew was Colonel Knox, the military attaché. He was out. The Ambassador had fixed no time
for my interview. Obviously, everyone was very busy. Perhaps
I should have telephoned to ascertain the hour of my appointment. I became nervous and ill-at-ease. An ultra-sensitive
nature has been my curse all through life. It—and it alone
—is responsible for that reputation for calculated insolence
which I acquired—most undeservedly—during my official
career and which, later, was to cause a very high official in the
Foreign Office to stigmatise me as an "impudent schoolboy."
Never has this sensitiveness frozen me into such unnatural
impotence as during that long drawn-out quarter of an hour
in Havery's ante-room.

At last, a large white door with an iron bar across it opened,
and a tall, athletic, and extremely good-looking man of about
thirty came out. It was "Benji" Bruce, the Head of the
Chancery and the inevitable and indispensable favourite of
every Ambassador under whom he has ever served. Telling me
that the Ambassador would see me in a few minutes, he took me
into the Chancery and introduced me to the other secretaries.
Later, I was to know them better and appreciate their merits,
but my first impression was of a typing and telegraph bureau
conducted by Old Etonians. At uncomfortably close quarters
in a large room, blocked with tables, sat half a dozen young
men busily engaged in typing and ciphering. That they did
their task well, that "Benji" Bruce could type as fast as any
professional typist and cipher and decipher with astonishing
speed is beside the point. Here was a collection of young men,
all of whom had had thousands of pounds spent on their education, who had passed a difficult examination, yet who, in the

middle of a great war in which their special knowledge might
have been used to their country's advantage, were occupied
for hours on end in work which could have been performed just
as efficiently by a second-division clerk. This system, now
fortunately abolished, was typical of the want of imagination,
which reigned in Whitehall during at any rate the first two
years of the war. Any side-show mission—and in Russia there
must have been a score—could command an almost unlimited
supply of money from the Treasury. The professional diplomatists, who, whatever their shortcomings may have been,
knew their job better than the amateurs, were left to carry on
as in peace time, not because of any danger of secrets being
divulged, but merely because this system had been in force for
generations and because, in the Chief Clerk's Department in
the Foreign Office, there was no one with sufficient elasticity
of mind or force of character to insist on its being altered. No
wonder that, after the war, many of the younger diplomatists,
weary of this senseless drudgery, sent in their resignations.
Bruce was a case in point. A man of strong and attractive
personality, an excellent linguist, and a firm disciplinarian
with a real genius for organisation, he ran his Chancery with
remarkable efficiency. If a trifle obstinate as becomes an
Ulsterman, he served his various chiefs with passionate loyalty.
When he resigned soon after the war, the Foreign Office lost
perhaps the best-equipped of its younger diplomatists.

After I had kicked my heels in the Chancery for twenty
minutes, Havery came in and announced that the Ambassador
was free. As I entered the long study, in which afterwards I was
to have so many interviews, a frail-looking man with a tired,
sad expression in his eyes came forward to meet me. His
monocle, his finely-chiselled features, and his beautiful
silver-grey hair gave him something of the appearance of a
stage-diplomat. But there was nothing artificial about his
manner, or, indeed, about the man himself—only a great
charm and a wonderful power of inspiring loyalty, to which I
yielded at once.

His whole manner was so gentle that my nervousness left me

instantaneously, and for an hour I talked to him, telling him my fears and my anxieties about the situation, the shortage of munitions, the subterranean propaganda against the war, the growing discontent of every class of the population with the Government, the murmurs against the throne itself. He showed some surprise. "I thought the atmosphere in Moscow was much healthier than in St. Petersburg," he said rather sadly. Indeed, it was, but I guessed that up to this point he had rated Moscow patriotism too highly. I had shaken a faith that perhaps was never very strong.

I was asked to luncheon and was introduced to Lady Georgina, the Ambassador's wife. She was a woman of strong likes and dislikes, which she made little attempt to conceal, and for some months she never failed to greet me, whenever I came to St. Petersburg, with the remark: "Here comes the pessimistic Mr. Lockhart." In every other respect, however, she showed me nothing but kindness, and, although I never quite overcame my original awe, I counted myself among the fortunates who enjoyed her favour. To Sir George himself she was everything that a wife should be, watching over his health with tireless zeal, running his house like clockwork and never failing in that passion for punctuality which in the Ambassador amounted almost to a mania. She was a big woman, and her heart was in proportion to her bulk.

This is no place in which to give an account of Sir George Buchanan's work in Russia, but I should like to pay my tribute to the man himself. Every British official, who was in Russia during the war years, has had inevitably to face the criticism which failure brings in its train. And in British eyes the collapse of Russia in 1917 was the greatest of all failures. The tendency, therefore, to seek scapegoats among their own countrymen is strong. Sir George Buchanan's name has not escaped the calumniators either in England or in Russia. I have heard ministers of the Crown declare that with a stronger British Ambassador the revolution might have been avoided. There are Russians, who with the basest ingratitude have accused Sir George Buchanan of having instigated the revolution.

Both criticisms can be dismissed as wholly ridiculous. Indeed, the Russian accusation is a particularly cruel and baseless slander, which, to the shame of London society, has been repeated without contradiction in London drawing-rooms by Russians who have enjoyed British hospitality in high places. It is a form of vilification which no personal sufferings can justify or ever excuse. Sir George Buchanan was a man whose every instinct was opposed to revolution. Until the revolution came he always refused to meet and, actually, never did meet any of the men, who were responsible for the overthrow of Tsardom, nor did he either personally or through his subordinates give any encouragement to their ambitions. Naturally he would have been lacking in perspicacity, if he had failed to foresee the catastrophe that was approaching, and in his duty if he had been afraid to warn the Russian autocracy of the dangers which he saw threatening it. This difficult task he undertook in a memorable conversation with the Emperor. I saw him just before he went to see the Tsar. He informed me that if the Emperor received him sitting down all would be well. The Tsar received him standing.

The Whitehall assertion that a stronger ambassador might have averted the final catastrophe is based on a fundamental ignorance of the traditions of the Russian autocracy. Contempt for foreigners is a characteristic of the English race, but in this respect the attitude of the most insular John Bull is tolerance itself compared with the arrogant indifference of St. Petersburg society to the stranger within its gates. With no long lineage and less real civilisation than one might expect from the luxury of its life, the Russian aristocracy lived in a world of its own. A foreign ambassador was not accepted merely because he was an ambassador. If he was liked for his own social qualities he was invited everywhere. If not, he was ignored. It was not actual snobbishness. The Russian aristocracy was as hospitable as the other sections of the Russian population. But it made its own selection of the recipients of its hospitality, and frequently its choice was startling in its indiscrimination. During the war years a junior lieutenant in the British Military Censor's office probably went to more parties in high places than all the members of the Embassy put together.

To the aristocracy the complete absolutism of the Tsar was something more than a religion. It was the rock on which its own sheltered existence was built. In its eyes the Emperor was the only real monarch in the world, and for its own sake it was always ready to regard any attempt by foreign diplomatists to influence him as an encroachment on the Imperial authority. The most efficient members of the bureaucracy were Baltic barons—a class hidebound even to-day in reaction. From the first they saw in the war a danger to the autocracy, and England as the home of constitutional monarchy they regarded with deep suspicion. Nor, for all his weakness, was the Emperor himself easily accessible or in any way, except the most tactful, amenable to foreign influence. He would have resented as much as his advisers any attempt by an English diplomatist to speak plainly to him.

Sir George Buchanan's task was therefore abnormally difficult. He had to overcome the political prejudice against England which still remained from past differences of policy. He had to take into consideration the peculiar susceptibilities of the ruling class. To suggest that because he walked warily he was a weak man is to underrate his whole character. He had been selected for the St. Petersburg Embassy because of the excellent work he had done at Sofia, and I doubt if there was anyone in the British diplomatic service who understood the Slav character better. If not a man of outstanding intellect (he had the Scot's mistrust of brilliance), he had remarkable powers of intuition and an abundant supply of common-sense. To Russian cleverness he opposed complete honesty and sincerity tempered with caution. He won the full confidence of Sazonoff, the most reliable of the Tsarist ministers, and by the vast bulk of the Russian population he was regarded as a man whose heart was in an Allied victory as distinct from a purely English victory, and who would countenance no intrigues at the expense of Russia. I say intentionally "the bulk of the Russian population," for it is a mistake to imagine that Sir George

Buchanan was an unpopular figure in Russian society. Except in pro-German circles his admirers among the aristocracy were numerous. It was only after the revolution that the nobility began to murmur against him, seeking in him a scapegoat for their own failure and a cloak for their own loose talk against the Emperor. More than all the resolutions of the Zemstvos and the Cities Unions, more than all the agitation of the Socialists, it was the openly expressed criticism by Grand Dukes and highly placed aristocrats which sapped the authority of the Imperial throne. When the history of Anglo-Russian relations during these fateful years is seen in perspective, future generations will recognise how great was the work accomplished by Sir George Buchanan in helping to keep Russia in the war for as long as she remained. Certainly, I can imagine no greater calamity to the English fortunes than an English Ambassador in St. Petersburg who had tried to play the little Napoleon of Whitehall before the Emperor.

As a chief Sir George Buchanan was delightful—a man in whom all thought of self was submerged in the highest conception of duty. He was worshipped by his staff, and, when he took his daily walk to the Russian Foreign Office, his hat cocked on one side, his tall, lean figure slightly drooping under his many cares, every Englishman felt that here as much as the diplomatic precincts of the Embassy itself was a piece of the soil of England.

If there was one aspect of his character, on which I should lay stress, it was his magnificent courage both physical and moral. Physically, he did not know the meaning of the word "fear." Morally, he triumphed completely over what I think was a natural inclination to the line of least resistance and faced without a moment's hesitation situations and interviews which were repugnant to him.

To me he was unfailingly kind. Through the insignificance of my own position I was able to see people, whom neither he nor other members of his staff could see. I was thus enabled to supply him with information which, provided it was correct, was of some value to him. Many an ambassador would have taken this information as a matter of course and incorporated what he required in his own despatches. This was not Sir George's way. He not only gave me every encouragement both by letter and in personal discussion, but he also sent my reports home to the Foreign Office—frequently with a covering despatch of approval. As a result, I was given full credit for my work in London and on several occasions received a personal letter of commendation from Sir Edward Grey. My head went a little higher in the air. I fought more fiercely with the Chief Clerk's department for increased office and personal allowances. But to Sir George I was full of gratitude and of that respectful submission which gratitude should always bring with it. Later, I was to forfeit his goodwill by the anti-intervention attitude I adopted after the Bolshevik revolution. But of all the men I have worked under in my career he was, with the single exception of Lord Milner, the one who inspired in me the greatest affection and hero-worship, and I am glad that, before he died, I was able to make my peace with him.

CHAPTER FOUR

I RETURNED to Moscow well pleased with my reception and greatly encouraged by the Ambassador's request that I was to keep in close touch with him and to come to St. Petersburg whenever there was anything important to discuss. Although I said nothing about my visit, the redoubtable Alexander was not so silent, and very soon I found that both with the officials and with the politicians my prestige was considerably enhanced. I expect that on Alexander's lips the story lost nothing in the telling and that in the Governor-General's office and in the headquarters of the Zemstvos and Cities Unions it was broadcast that His Excellency the Acting British Consul-General (Alexander always omitted the Acting) was now going regularly to St. Petersburg to consult if not actually to advise His Super-Excellency (in Russia ambassadors *were* Super-Excellencies) the British Ambassador.

During that summer of 1915 I consolidated my friendship with Michael Chelnokoff, the Moscow Mayor and a former vice-president of the Imperial Duma. Chelnokoff, a splendid type of Moscow merchant, grey-bearded, patriarchal, broad-shouldered and, in spite of a game leg, stout-hearted beyond most of his compatriots, was a grand fellow. Although he was twenty years older than myself, we became the closest friends, and through him not only did I come to know intimately all the Moscow political leaders like Prince Lvoff, Vasily Maklakoff, Manuiloff, Kokoshkin, and many others, but I also received copies of the numerous secret resolutions which were passed by such bodies as the Moscow Municipality, the Zemstvo Union, of which Prince Lvoff was head, and the Cities Union of which Chelnokoff himself was the moving spirit. Sometimes I was even able to obtain in Moscow through the same source copies of secret resolutions passed by the Cadet Party in St. Petersburg or of such documents as Rodzianko's letter to the Prime Minister and to send them to our Embassy in St. Petersburg before anyone else had brought them to its notice. These minor successes naturally added to my reputation as a "news-getter." Through the Zemstvos and Cities Unions, too, I was of some service to the War Office. The Zemstvos and the Cities Unions, though stupidly hampered by the Government, were the nearest Russian equivalent to our Ministry of Munitions, and from Lvoff and Chelnokoff I received regularly the latest figures regarding the output of every kind of war material.

During the two and a half months of Bayley's absence I had entrenched myself solidly in Moscow. I had received the thanks of the Foreign Secretary. I was *persona grata* with the war-leaders in Moscow. The Ambassador had sent for me. At the end of July Bayley would return. He would, I felt, be pleased and I should have the satisfaction of knowing that I had done my job well. There seemed nothing more to which I could look forward.

Then, however, came a new crisis. Things had gone from bad to worse on the Russian front. The retreat in Galicia and in the Carpathians did not affect Moscow so much except in the increase of wounded, but the advance on Warsaw was different. For some weeks Polish refugees had been pouring into Moscow. Now on July 19th came a telegram from Grove informing me that Warsaw was being evacuated and that he and the remaining members of the British colony were leaving for Moscow immediately. Three days later he arrived, and on the same day came a telegram from Bayley, informing me that he had been appointed Consul-General in New York and was returning to Moscow at once to pack up. I had no ill-will against the Groves. If I had any personal ambitions, I was unconscious of them. But I must confess that this double-barrelled shock filled me with consternation. If Bayley went to New York, Grove obviously would take his place in Moscow, and, quite candidly, after Bayley I did not relish a return to the Grove régime.

On July 30th Bayley arrived, carrying a surprise-packet in his pocket. All my apprehensions were ended. Grove was to be transferred to Helsingfors. I was to be left in charge of the Moscow Consulate-General. Bayley informed me that, on his appointment to New York, the Foreign Office had promptly appointed a new Consul-General to Moscow. Sir George Buchanan, however, had protested, saying that I had done invaluable work and that it would be a mistake to hamper my activities by imposing on me a chief who could not know the situation as well as I did. Bayley told me with genuine joy that the Foreign Office was very pleased with me. I tried to look unconcerned. Although I had done nothing to push my own claims, I was full of remorse about the Groves, who I knew would be bitterly disappointed. But deep down in my heart there was a quiet exultation: "Not yet twenty-eight and in charge on your own merits of one of the most important Consulates-General in the war." A certain amount of self-conceit is good in the young. Except in the case of the ambitious and the brigands it soon gets rubbed off.

For a week I waited hand and foot on Bayley, helping him to clear up, arranging farewell dinners for him, and taking over from him at the Consulate-General. The British Club gave him a splendid send-off, and we had our own formal parting at the Consulate-General, when everybody gave Bayley a gift and was given one in return. I received a massive cigarette case which I have to this day. Alexander wound up a rather trying performance with a speech which undid the last floodgates of even Bayley's emotions. (My lady secretaries were both crying, and only old Fritz, the Lett clerk, remained impassive.) In lyrical language he referred to Bayley and myself as shining examples to all Russians of what an official ought to be and declared his firm intention that, if I were to leave Moscow, he would leave with me. The bathos of Alexander's oratory just put the necessary brake on my own tear-glands. Yet I was full of sadness over Bayley's departure. He had been more like a father to me than a chief. He had been kindness itself to me during my wife's illness. That he was devoted to me and genuinely interested in my advancement, though pleasing to my vanity, did not deter me from listening to the excellent advice which he gave me from the store of his worldly knowledge. I was losing not only a friend but an ally—in a very real sense my only ally in a city of nearly two million inhabitants. Alas! I never saw him again.

His advice, which consisted mainly in an exhortation to observe the eleventh commandment so long as I remained an official, fell on stony ground.

The fall of Warsaw was the culminating tragedy of the disastrous summer campaign of 1915. It was a blow, which could not be hidden even from the masses, and naturally there was a great increase of pessimism and peace talk. Men like Chelnokoff and Lvoff were firm enough; their roots were in the soil. But the professional politicians were excited, and their nervousness spread like a wet fog until it enveloped half the population. Horrible rumours of Russians manning the trenches with nothing but sticks in their hands percolated through from the front to the countryside. Neither the old men nor the young recruits had any stomach for this slaughter, and at factory centres like Ivanovo-Voznesensk there were anti-government strikes attended in some cases by shooting.

As usual, the authorities devised a counter-irritant for this public excitement. On August 23rd, when the pessimism was at its worst, Moscow hummed with rumours, emanating apparently from official quarters, that the Allies had forced the Dardanelles. In the afternoon a Moscow newspaper came out with large headlines: "Official: Dardanelles Taken." Then followed a graphic account of the bombardment of the straits with casualty lists and names of ships complete. On receipt of this news vast crowds assembled in the streets. People knelt on the Tverskaia Square to thank God for this glorious victory. There was a manifestation before the Consulate-General. In vain I tried to tell the mob that the news was false. "Official communiqué" shouted the newsboys, and in the storm of cheering my voice was lost. Later in the evening the crowd got out of hand, and near the Skobolieff monument there was a demonstration against the police, which ended as usual with a charge of mounted gendarmes.

The next day there was general disappointment at the false report, and, together with my French colleague, I called on the Prefect to demand summary action against the editor and the publishers. He received us with the usual official unctuousness.

He had already anticipated our just indignation. He had closed down the newspaper for the rest of the war. We expressed our gratitude in proper terms. After this statement I was surprised to find the paper still continuing to appear, having changed its name from *Evening News* to *Evening Gazette*. In every other respect it was identical with its predecessor. The headlines and the type were the same. The erring editor of the day before had signed the leading article of to-day.

I fumed and gave the Prefect best. I discovered later that the victory stunt had been operated in connection with the police in order to let the public work off steam.

I do not profess ever to have mastered the psychology of the Tsarist police. I refuse, however, to believe either in its efficiency or in its honesty. The dreaded "Okhrana" of the Seton Merriman novel was a myth fearful more by its name than by its omniscience. It was an organisation run by bunglers and clever crooks, and in it the bunglers outnumbered the brains by nine to one.

As the autumn advanced, the approaching tragedy of Russia impressed itself more and more on my mind. Worse things were to happen than the fall of Warsaw. Yet the same defect of character, which made the Russian incapable of sustained effort, helped to take the edge off his pessimism. No Muscovite could continue for long to wring his hands. Actually, as blow succeeded blow, local patriotism reasserted itself, and, if in St. Petersburg there were few people who believed in a Russian victory, Moscow adopted the slogan that the war could not be won unless the dark influences in the capital were eliminated. From this moment dates the first of the many resolutions demanding a ministry of national defence or of public confidence. At first these demands were modest enough. Moscow was prepared to accept legitimate Tsarist ministers—that is, men like Krivoshein, Sazonoff, Samarin, Sherbatoff and others, who had no connection with the political parties in the Duma. It would at this stage have been simple enough for the Tsar to have formed a new Ministry, which would have satisfied public opinion, without going outside the usual circle from which he chose his advisers. By giving in time the six inches of reform, which were necessary, he might have saved the yards which a disillusioned country was to take by force afterwards. Those nearest him, however, saw the matter in another light. They told him that any concession now would be regarded as a fatal weakness and that the appetite of the reformers would only be whetted. This was an argument which never failed to convince the Empress, and in consequence the Tsar's reply to those who were working hardest for Russia's victory was to dissolve the Duma, to relieve the Grand Duke Nicholas of his command, and to dismiss Samarin, Sherbatoff and Djunkowsky, the three Ministers who at the moment were most popular in Moscow.

The dissolution of the Duma provoked the usual strikes and protests. But the assumption of the Supreme Command by the Tsar himself was the first milestone on the way to Golgotha. It was the most fatal of the many blunders of the unfortunate Nicholas II, for as Commander-in-Chief he became personally responsible in the eyes of the people for the long succession of defeats which owing to Russia's technical deficiencies were now inevitable.

The dismissal of Samarin and Djunkowsky was the indirect sequel of an episode of which I myself had been a silent witness. One summer evening I was at Yar, the most luxurious night-haunt of Moscow, with some English visitors. As we watched the music-hall performance in the main-hall, there was a violent fracas in one of the neighbouring "cabinets." Wild shrieks of women, a man's curses, broken glass and the banging of doors raised a discordant pandemonium. Head-waiters rushed up-stairs. The manager sent for the policeman who was always on duty at such establishments. But the row and the roaring continued. There was more coming and going of waiters and policemen, and scratching of heads and holding of councils. The cause of the disturbance was Rasputin—drunk and lecherous, and neither police nor management dared evict him. The policeman telephoned to his divisional inspector, the inspector telephoned to the Prefect. The Prefect telephoned to

Djunkowsky, who was Assistant Minister of the Interior and head of all the police. Djunkowsky, who was a former general and a man of high character, gave orders that Rasputin, who, after all, was only an ordinary citizen and not even a priest, should be arrested forthwith. Having disturbed everyone's enjoyment for two hours, he was led away, snarling and vowing vengeance, to the nearest police-station. He was released early next morning on instructions from the highest quarters. He left the same day for St. Petersburg, and within twenty-four hours Djunkowsky was relieved of his post. Samarin's dismissal, which followed later, made a very painful impression. A nobleman of splendid character, he was then Oberprokuror or Minister in Charge of Church Matters and one of the very best representatives of his class. No one but a madman could accuse him of anything but the most orthodox conservative opinions or of any lack of loyalty to the Emperor. Yet every Liberal and every Socialist respected him as an honest man, and the fact that the Emperor could thus sacrifice one of his most loyal advisers for a creature like Rasputin was accepted by nearly everyone in Moscow as a complete proof of the Tsar's incompetence. "Down with the autocracy!" cried the Liberals. But even among the reactionaries there were those who said: "If the autocracy is to flourish, give us a good autocrat."

This was the only occasion on which Rasputin came across my path. From time to time, however, I saw the mark of the beast at Chelnokoff's house, where the Mayor would show me a short typewritten note requesting him to fix up the bearer in a safe and comfortable job in the Cities Union. The note was signed in an illiterate scrawl "G.R."—Grigori Rasputin. The requests were invariably turned down by the sturdy Chelnokoff.

With the advent of winter—and in that year of 1915 it came early—a period of stagnation set in on the front and with it came a lull in the political discontent. Life went on.

My wife and I dined out six nights in the week. Most days we had people to luncheon—English officers, generals, admirals, colonels, captains, passing through Moscow on their way to the headquarters of the various Russian armies. Once a week my wife had a reception, and by some innate talent of her own succeeded in making the wolves lie down with the lambs. She was especially delighted when she could include a Socialist or two in her bag. Nevertheless, everybody came—from the Commandant of the Kremlin, the Governor, the Prefect and the Generals of the Moscow district (not all of the generals were well disposed either to the Government or to the local authorities) down to the rich Moscow millionaires, and the ballet dancers, the actors and writers, and the shy and rather awkward politicians of the Left. There were, as far as I remember, no contretemps, although on one occasion Sasha Kropotkina, the daughter of that fine old anarchist, Prince Kropotkin, nearly came to blows with Countess Kleinmichel over the lack of martial spirit in St. Petersburg. This mingling of the different sets of Russians in Moscow was as good for them as it was useful to us. It broke down barriers which had never been stormed before. It provided us with information of the most varying character.

That there were Russians whose hearts were still set on victory was brought home to me in a remarkable manner when my brother Norman was killed at Loos. I did not receive the news until early in October. We had been out in the country and were dining with some Russians at the Hermitage. My wife had gone home to change her shoes. There she found the telegram and telephoned to me at the restaurant. It was the first time that the death of someone I loved had come to me without warning, and in the telephone box I broke down and cried bitterly. I told my Russian friends what had happened and went home. The next morning nearly every Moscow newspaper had a very generous tribute to my brother and to the heavy losses of the Scottish troops, and for days to come I received letters of sympathy from Russians of every class and rank. Many came from people I did not know even by sight. Most of them ended with an expression of profound conviction of the ultimate triumph of the Allies.

It must not be thought, however, that my life was all tragedy. The strikes, the political discontent, the defeats, stand out to-day like landmarks in a great plain, but they were not everyday occurrences or even an important part of my daily life. I had my own problems to tackle: committees to attend (the British colony ran various enterprises for the wounded and the refugees; in addition, there were recruiting committees, war supply committees, etc.) and an immense routine work at the Consulate which, apart from my political work, was a whole time job in itself. Some of my troubles were humorous; others merely irritating. I could laugh when my wife rang me up at the Consulate to say that the servants had gone on strike or rather refused to enter the flat, because there was an evil spirit, a Poltergeist, whose chief offence seemed to be the breaking of valuable plates. Certainly, a rare and precious ikon had fallen by itself, and, as my wife took the servants' side, there was nothing for it but to enlist the services of the priest. He came and for the sum of five roubles gave the Poltergeist a liberal sprinkling of holy water. The flat was cleansed; the servants returned; and strangely enough, the queer noises and the breaking of plates ceased.

Less amusing were the frequent rows among my Consular staff, which had swollen considerably since the influx of the British refugees from Warsaw. Bayley had left me with a legacy in the person of Francis Greenep, a once well-known London lawyer. Always very neatly dressed, he was a fine-looking old man, and his silver hair and his monocle lent distinction to a staff of which I myself was almost the most youthful member. When in the right mood, he had charming manners. His work, too, was punctually and excellently done. But—and it was a big but—his temper was explosive and, as he was always on the look out for insults, there were many scenes. One day it would be Alexander who had ruffled his dignity. Another time it would be St. Clair, the Vice-Consul from Warsaw, who had been attached to me and who, although more Polish than Scottish, had all the pride of the ancient Scottish family to which he belonged. Strange, difficult fellows they were: responsive to emotional appeals, but not to be driven. I expect I tried them highly, and in any case living for months and indeed years on end at high tension in a small office, where one saw the same faces every day, was strain enough to break the strongest nerves, and neither Greenep's nor St. Clair's were up to standard. I could manage the rows between the various members of the staff. It was another matter when Greenep's wrath was unloosed on visitors to the office. For his own sake I kept him as much as possible in his own room, but obviously, I could not prevent him from entering the main office in the execution of his duties. In a long series of incidents two had serious results. One morning, as I was deciphering a telegram in my own room, I heard an angry altercation from the outer office. Above the general din, I could hear Greenep's voice, trembling with rage: "Do what you're told, sir, or leave the office."

I rushed out just in time to prevent my aged hot-head from doing physical violence to an English artillery major, who was purple with indignation.

"Are you in charge of this Consulate?" he stuttered to me. "Then you will give me satisfaction or I'll report you to the Foreign Office. This fellow here has insulted the King's uniform."

Greenep was standing by the side of the office counter, his finger pointing at the portrait of the King which adorned the wall.

"Take off your hat, sir, in His Majesty's presence."

He kept repeating his demand in a kind of eldritch refrain. With the help of Fritz, my Lettish clerk, who had been a witness of the whole scene, I sifted out the truth. The officer in uniform had come into the office with his cap on. Greenep, who was passing through, had pointed to the King's portrait and had said politely enough: "Don't you see the King's portrait, sir? This is not a station waiting-room." The officer had paid no attention. Greenep had then demanded more peremptorily that he should remove his hat. And then the fur had started to fly.

It was a difficult case. Actually, Greenep was in the wrong in losing his temper. The officer, however, had been tactless. He was inclined to stand on his rights and insisted that, when he came into an office, it was correct for him to keep his cap on. But for his pomposity I should have had no alternative but to dismiss the unfortunate Greenep—a course which I was loath to take, partly because the man was devoted to me and, secondly, because it meant putting him into the street. I tried to smooth down the officer without sacrificing Greenep, but he insisted on his pound of flesh. I refused to give it to him. He left me vowing vengeance. I reported the whole matter to the Ambassador, apportioning the blame equally between the two protagonists and representing the affair as a case of war nerves. I heard no more, and fortunately for me the incident was closed.

More serious was a similar episode in which Greenep affronted Baleieff, a rich Armenian and a brother of the famous Nikita. In his spare time Greenep supplemented his income by giving lessons to rich Russians. Baleieff was one of his pupils. Apparently there had been some trouble about payment. At any rate, Greenep nursed a grievance. It found its outlet, when one day Baleieff came into the Consulate to obtain a visa. Unfortunately, Greenep was again in the main office, and the sight of the rich man, who he alleged had done him out of his hard-earned roubles, maddened him. Once again I had to rush out and make peace. This time, however, the consequences were more serious. There had been witnesses of the incident, and Baleieff was determined to take his legal remedy. Luckily, his lawyer was a great friend of our own lawyer and was as anxious as I was to prevent a public scandal. Between us we worked out every possible compromise which would satisfy Baleieff's wounded feelings and at the same time save Greenep from dismissal. In the end Baleieff agreed to drop all proceedings in return for a public apology to be made in the presence of the Consular staff and of himself and his lawyer. The apology was to be drafted by him.

It was a long one. There were several references to gentlemen and gentlemanly behaviour. It was an unpleasant dose for anyone, and for twenty-four hours Greenep refused to swallow it. I pointed out to him that I could do no more and that if the matter came before the courts there could only be one result. He would have to go.

Finally, he agreed. The apology was typed out, and with the lawyers I arranged the formalities for its delivery. In the main office Fritz and the three lady typists sat like mummies at their desks. On the door side of the counter stood Baleieff and his lawyer. I took up my own stand on the office side of the counter. When all was ready, I walked to Greenep's room, brought him up before the counter, and put the apology into his hands. He was in his best suit. His hair was carefully brushed. His monocle was fixed firmly in his eye. His face was like a statue. Only from the trembling paper in his hands could one suspect the suppressed rage.

"Shall I begin?" he said in an ominous whisper. He read through the idiotic document, a rich flush suffusing his cheeks until they became the colour of a turkey's comb, while Baleieff, fat and sweating with fear, extracted what satisfaction he could from the Englishman's humiliation. When he had finished, Greenep turned one awful glare at his enemy, crumpled up the paper in his hand and with a "There, you may have your pound of flesh!" strode out of the room.

To-day, the scene seems comic enough and, indeed, a trifle undignified as far as my own participation is concerned. But at the time it was a serious business. Indeed, so great was Greenep's capacity for nursing a grievance, that he might very easily have involved the Consulate-General in a scandal or in expensive litigation and, certainly, in ridicule.

There were, however, compensations. In November, 1915, the Ambassador wrote me a letter informing me that the Foreign Office was so pleased with my work that I was to be left in charge of the Consulate-General until the end of the war. I used this letter with great effect in order to improve my financial position, which, with my increased responsibilities, was becoming precarious. For some time I had been conducting a bitter correspondence with the Foreign Office. We were in the middle of a great war. I was being involved in far greater expenditure than ever Bayley had had to face, and I was receiving neither increase of pay nor increase of office allowance. I enlisted the services of the Ambassador on my side. They were given whole-heartedly. Very early on, he wrote to the Foreign Office saying: "There is scarcely any Consular post of the same importance as Moscow at the present moment. It is the industrial and, in a certain broad sense, the political capital of Russia. . . . You will have seen from Mr. Lockhart's despatches the excellent work that has been done by that office since Mr. Clive Bayley's departure."

Even Ambassadors, however, cannot disturb the unimaginative routine of the Chief Clerk's Department or of the Treasury, and it was not in an obdurate Whitehall, but in the heart of my grandmother that Sir George Buchanan's letter was of service to me. The old lady, thrilled always by success, was delighted by the Ambassador's encomiums. I knew just exactly how to launch my appeal. My brother Norman had supplied the perfect form to all of us, when he was a small boy in his first term at Marlborough. As his birthday approached, he had written to his grandmother as follows:

"Dear Grannie,

I hope you are well. I am enjoying school very much. My birthday is next Tuesday. All the boys here have cameras and spend their time taking snap-shots. The weather has been very good, and we have played more hockey than 'rugger.' I am in the fourth form and my housemaster is called Taylor. His nickname is 'Trilby.' He is a parson and he says prayers faster than anyone I have ever heard. I hope you are well, dear Grannie, and that you are not finding Edinburgh too cold. I was first in scripture last week.

Your loving grandson,

NORMAN.

P.S.—I have no camera."

With the right bow in my hands—and this time I had it, I could play a still better tune on this fiddle. I gave the old lady a glowing account of the Scots in Russia and the part the Bruces, the Gordons, the Hamiltons, had played in building St. Petersburg and in winning Peter the Great's battles. Had not a Learmonth—the very name of her house—provided Russia with her greatest poet? I dwelt on all the famous people I had met. I described the dinners given by my colleagues and by my Russian friends. My P.S. assured her of my unfailing belief in ultimate victory provided the cost of living could be kept down.

Perhaps in her dreams (I have said she was ambitious) she already saw me rallying the spent Russians to the attack. Perhaps she was amused by my artfulness in the same way as she had been amused by my brother's hint about the camera. At any rate, just as he received his camera, so I received my cheques—cheques, too, for generous amounts—which relieved my financial embarrassments and enabled me at any rate to keep my end up.

May her soul rest in peace. She was a grand woman and even in the days of my failure she treated me better than I deserved. Without her I should have been completely lost in Moscow— a reflection which I feel sure will not make the members of the Chief Clerk's department sleep less comfortably in their beds. Let them not think I bear them a grudge, The Whitehall game of battledore and shuttlecock, of vouchers and vouchers for not producing a voucher, has been played ever since the gods were on Olympus. It will be played for all time. On the whole, too, it is played in good temper by both sides. My only complaint is that in war time the rules of the game should be relaxed.

AS 1915 DREW to its end, my political work increased. The Allies were now seriously anxious about the Russian situation, and to my other labours was added the task of entertaining and shepherding the various missions sent out by France and England to stimulate the Russians to fresh efforts. Hitherto we had had a small list of more or less regular visitors. They included men like Colonel Knox (now General Sir Alfred Knox), Sir Samuel Hoare, the head of a special intelligence mission, General Sir John Hanbury-Williams, and Admiral Sir Richard Phillimore, the two British representatives attached to the Tsar's military headquarters, and the various officers attached to the different armies on the Russian front. Of these officers, Colonel Knox, who had spent many years in Russia, was by far the best informed on military matters. Very early in the war he had seen the cracks in the Russian wall, and, if the Allies formed an exaggerated idea of the Russian strength, it was certainly not the fault of the English military attaché. Up to the revolution no man took a saner view of the military situation on the Eastern front and no foreign observer supplied his Government with more reliable information.

Of the others Sir John Hanbury-Williams was a charmer, who was popular with everyone. Admiral Phillimore maintained the highest traditions of the British Navy by persisting in rising daily at seven o'clock—or was it six?—in a country where nobody stirred before nine or ten. The impression on the Russians was immense and wholly beneficial. Sir Samuel Hoare triumphed over a whole field of obstacles by the same industry and persistence which to-day have elevated him to Cabinet rank. His appointment to St. Petersburg was not popular with the regular soldiers. It was hard to understand in what respect his mission could supplement the work which was being done by the other British organisations. He himself had no special qualifications for the task, and, when he arrived, I anticipated friction and failure. With a less tactful man the forebodings would have been justified. Sir Samuel, however, beset himself to his task with unflagging and unobtrusive enthusiasm. He learnt Russian. He worked indefatigably. He made it his business to meet every class of Russian. He gathered in his information from many fields, and, unlike most intelligence officers, he showed a fine discrimination in sifting the truth from the chaff of rumour. In short, he made good. If, at the time, anyone had asked me to lay the odds against Sir Samuel as a future leader of the Conservative Party or as a possible Prime Minister of England, I confess that I should have had no hesitation in going the limit. Now, however, I realise that the same qualities which he showed in Russia in circumstances of great difficulty have stood him in good stead in his subsequent political career. Behind Sir Samuel's small frame there is, combined with considerable ability, courage, and capacity for mastering his subject, a strong and very persistent will power. Where eighteen years ago I should have laid a thousand to one against, to-day I should not give more than two to one.

These, as I have said, were our regular visitors. Now they were to be supplemented by the various side-shows. The first of these to visit Moscow was the French political mission to Rumania. Its object was to counteract German influences in Bucharest and to bring Rumania into the war. It was composed of Charles Richet, the eminent scientist, Georges Lacour-Gayet, the historian, and M. Gavoty, the former proprietor of the "Revue Hebdomadaire." I saw much of all three men during their long stay in Moscow for, strangely enough, the mission was held up for weeks before it reached its destination. It was combated—and, for a long time, successfully—by the French Minister in Rumania.

This visit is very memorable to me for three reasons: the first, entirely creditable, the second purely vain, and the third slightly discreditable, for which, however, my wife must share the blame. The creditable reason is that in Richet I met the greatest genius and most attractive personality I have ever known. Few men who have seen anything of the politico-military administration of the war can have any faith left in the "great man" theory. Most of our geniuses die unrewarded, but it is quite certain that they are rarely, if ever, found in the unfertile field of politics or modern warfare. Richet, however, is a genius who has found honour in his own time. Absolutely unaffected and simple as a child, he is wholly charming in character. The first constructor of a modern aeroplane and a poet and a prose writer of distinction, he received the Nobel prize for medicine. The war took six of his seven sons, but it left no rancour in Richet's heart—no hate except of war itself. He is still living; still at the age of eighty almost alone among his countrymen in throwing his weight into the scale of international understanding against the balance of malicious self-interest and ignorant nationalism.

At that time Richet was of course a patriot—that is, he believed in an Allied victory as an essential condition to the defeat of militarism. How well, too, he pleaded the Allied case before the Russians. How quickly he understood the Russian character. After his first speech in Moscow—a wonderful performance with all the University professors on the platform—he took me aside.

"This is our war," he said, "your country's and mine. We must be strong in ourselves and count only on ourselves."

The second reason why this visit remains very vividly in my memory is that it was to have furnished the occasion for my first big public speech. It is true that a few weeks before I had made my first public speech in Russian at the opening of a hospital. It had been, however, very short. At the luncheon given by the British Club to the distinguished Frenchmen I was to have made my first attempt at war propaganda on a public platform. On the eve of the luncheon I was stricken with tonsilitis and influenza. I fainted at the telephone and cut my head on the receiver as I was in the act of summoning the doctor. It was perhaps a fortunate escape. The three Frenchmen were brilliant professional orators. It was better for me to make my début among my own countrymen who, in Parliament and outside it, are in my experience (and I have visited nearly every Parliament in Europe and have heard most of the great foreign orators) the worst speakers in the world.

The third and slightly discreditable reason was the procuring by my wife of a document of considerable importance. I have said that the French mission had not been allowed to proceed to Rumania owing to the protestations of M. Blondel, the French Minister of Bucharest. The three Frenchmen were very indignant and made little attempt to conceal their anger or their intention of demanding explanations when they returned to Paris. Their hands had been strengthened against their own diplomatic representative in Rumania by a report by Marshal Pau, the one-armed French general, who had just completed an extensive study of the whole situation in that country. Pau's report was known to be extraordinarily frank in its criticisms, and we were very desirous of seeing the original document. During the visit one of the Frenchmen (as all three are still living, it would be unfair to say which) stayed with us in our flat. Like most Frenchmen he was a courtier. In Paris the most severe and respected of professors, he thawed in the warm and rather licentious atmosphere of Moscow. He made my wife his confidante. He became indiscreet. One afternoon, to relieve her of a headache, he gave her the famous Pau report to read. With great presence of mind she committed it to writing, and in this manner I was able to send a complete copy to Sir George Buchanan. Soldiers have a reputation for bluntness, but the Marshal's report would have shocked even the bluntest fire-eater in our own War Office. In language more effective because it was unadorned by any extravagances of style, it gave a devastating picture of conditions at the Rumanian court in 1915. The Marshal had spared no one. There was a thumbnail sketch of the King with chapter and verse for the numerous weaknesses of a character in which there was little to admire. There was a complete dossier of romantic adventure in high places with a "Who's who" of the personalities involved and a record of their influence and political sympathies. There was an unflattering picture of the French, British and Russian ministers, who were accused of setting a bad example in war-time to

Rumanian society and of wasting their diplomatic effort by unseemly dissensions among themselves. The Marshal was frankly pessimistic. Rumania's subsequent entry into the war was to justify his gloominess. He thought nothing of the Rumanian army. He thought still less of Allied diplomacy in Rumania. The full force of his indignation was reserved for the French and Russian ministers, whose antipathy to each other enabled the pro-German party to drive a wedge between two influences which should have been paramount. England, said the old soldier, had no historical role to play in Rumania. The only influence she could usefully exert would be through the good looks of her men. She should send her best-looking military attaché to the Rumanian Court. As a result of the Pau report there were changes in Rumania. As her new military attaché, England sent Colonel C. B. Thomson, who was subsequently to become the personal friend of Mr. Ramsay MacDonald, to be made a Labour Peer and a Cabinet Minister, and to perish in the ill-fated initial voyage of the dirigible R.101.

I remember little about that second Christmas of the war except that it was gay. Russians, rightly or wrongly, never allowed depression to interfere with their festivals, nor did they try studiously to cultivate a war attitude. They were undisciplined and amoral. Their whole effort was individual and not co-operative.

On January 1st, 1916, my wife and I spent the whole day paying official visits—one of the few really irksome duties of officialdom in Russia. The beginning of the year must have inspired more people than myself with good resolutions, for as a result of my visits my diary notes for January are remarkably optimistic. Two factors were responsible for this healthier atmosphere. Our Russo-Greek friend, Lykiardopoulos, had just returned from an adventurous journey into Austria and Germany. He had gone to obtain information for the Allies, and, disguised as a Greek tobacco merchant, had visited the leading cities of both countries. "Lyki" had left Moscow as a profound pessimist who was convinced of the invincibility of the German arms. He returned full of optimism, quite certain that Germany was feeling the pinch more than Russia and that Russia could hold out far longer. As far as supplies were concerned he was, doubtless, right. What he had miscalculated was the difference in the resisting power of the two peoples.

His news, however, made Moscow cheerful, and for a few weeks he was a national hero. Still more encouraging was the reception of Prince Lvoff and Chelnokoff by the Emperor at his military headquarters in Moghilieff. The visit had been arranged by General Alexeieff, the Chief of the General Staff and a sturdy patriot, who had a soldier's contempt for the average Russian politician. When the Grand Duke Nicholas was commander-in-chief, the Cities and Zemstvos Unions had always addressed their petitions to him personally. Their relations with the Emperor had been less happy. Disliking the various political resolutions which they had passed, he had hitherto refused to see them. On this occasion, therefore, they came to Moghilieff to see General Alexeieff and not the Emperor. As Mayor of Moscow Chelnokoff brought with him the greetings of the "heart of Russia" to the army and an official resolution of the City Duma affirming that no peace must be made until complete victory had been attained. General Alexeieff, knowing the immense work these great public organisations were doing in equipping the army with every kind of supply, was determined to restore good relations between the Emperor and the two Unions.

"The Emperor's all right," he informed the two Muscovites bluntly. "The only trouble is the band of b—— who surround him. You wait here, and I'll take the resolution to him."

Presently he returned with the order that Chelnokoff was to enter the Imperial presence. When the broad-shouldered Mayor limped into the room, the resolution was lying on the Emperor's table.

"Why was this excellent resolution not sent to me direct?" asked the Tsar.

Chelnokoff stammered out some clumsy excuse about

etiquette and said that, if His Imperial Majesty would allow him, he would offer him the greeting there and then. He then stood up and in his best official manner conveyed Moscow's loyal greetings to the Emperor and read the resolution. The Tsar was greatly pleased.

"I agree with everything in this resolution," he said. "Peace will not be made until complete victory is attained. You are right, too, in expressing your gratitude to the army. We should go down on our knees before it."

The Tsar then questioned Chelnokoff about the situation in Moscow. The Mayor replied that there was no fuel, and not enough to eat because the railways were being run so badly and that, in these circumstances, rioting during the winter months was a possibility that could not be excluded. The Emperor replied that, if people were cold and had not enough to eat, one could not be too severe on them if they complained with violence. He asked rather suspiciously if the Mayor were not exaggerating.

Chelnokoff replied: "No."

The Tsar then said: "Everything I can do to alleviate this situation will be done."

I received a full account of this visit from Chelnokoff as soon as he returned to Moscow. Both Prince Lvoff and he—grave, bearded men with no frivolities in their lives—were as pleased as schoolboys. They had returned from the "Stavka" with a whole heartful of optimism. The Emperor had been splendid. Their own work was now to go forward unimpeded. The army was on their side. What, then, did St. Petersburg matter? The army was more important, more powerful, than any Government.

Alas! the high hopes raised by this visit were to be rudely shattered. Impending tragedy would not allow the Emperor to deviate from the fate which had been marked out for him. A little common-sense, a few words of praise, on the Emperor's part, would have been sufficient to strengthen the ties of personal loyalty, to chain to his throne the patriotic fervour of the vast bulk of the people of Russia. How small was the effort required I had seen in the enthusiasm of these two public leaders, who, considerably less revolutionary in temperament than Mr. Lloyd George, were to be driven unwillingly into revolution and to become its first victims. The effort, however, was beyond the Emperor's capacity of vision. The old system continued. The national effort was cramped in every way. Every minister who sympathised with it was sooner or later certain to be dismissed. And as, one by one, the patriots and the men of confidence disappeared, the allegiances of three hundred years were undermined by despair. In my own mind the feeling of inevitable disaster became stronger and stronger. Yet in public I had always to appear ultra-optimistic, calm and reso- lute, and unshakeably convinced of the ultimate victory of the Allies. If my real optimism was confined to the West, I had to simulate increasing confidence in the East. And after a time a smile which has no heart behind it becomes visibly artificial.

In February, 1916, I was summoned several times to St. Petersburg. We had a new scheme on foot: an official British propaganda office in St. Petersburg to be run by British journa- lists. Hugh Walpole and Harold Williams (greatest and most modest of all British experts on Russia) were its chief sponsors. There was to be a sub-office in Moscow. This was to be under my charge, and as my propaganda officer I engaged the versatile Lykiardopoulos. In St. Petersburg the propaganda bureau was a very official organisation with special offices and a proper staff. I ran my organisation in Moscow from the Consulate-General without any flourish of trumpets and without the knowledge of the outside world. In this way I was able to bring considerable influence to bear on the local newspapers without their feeling that they were being inundated with official propaganda. This part of my work I enjoyed, although here, too, great tact was necessary, especially when it came to the selection of Moscow journalists for the literary mission, which as part of the new policy we were sending to England. The bright idea was that, when these scribes had seen the tremendous efforts being made by England, they would write them up in the Russian Press, and we should then hear less about Britain keeping her navy in a glass case and about our willingness to fight to the last drop of Russian blood. One writer, whom I invited or was instructed to invite, was Count A. N. Tolstoy, a sleek, fat Bohemian with a great literary talent but a strong predilection for the creature comforts of life. To-day, in order to retain these comforts, Count Tolstoy has made his peace with the Bolsheviks and, at the expense of a play or two against the Romanoffs, has succeeded in remaining a bourgeois individualist in a country where even literature has been communised.

It was at this moment that I received a telegram from Sir George Buchanan requesting me to make arrangements for the reception of a British naval mission which, as part and parcel of the new propaganda policy, was being sent to Moscow. I received exactly two days' notice of this visit. No information was vouchsafed me regarding the source from which I was to draw the financial sinews for the entertainment of His Britannic Majesty's Senior Service. This conundrum is one of the rare problems which the British Government leaves invariably to the initiative and to the pocket of the man on the spot. All I knew was that the seven leading officers of our submarine flotilla in the Baltic—all very gallant gentlemen, who had sunk several German cruisers and innumerable smaller craft—would arrive on February 15th and would spend four days in Moscow. They had received instructions to put themselves unreservedly in my hands.

Both the British colony and my Russian friends rallied to my support with remarkable spontaneity and generosity. In one afternoon I completed my programme. My old friend Chelnokoff promised a "rout" at the Town Duma. Madame Nossova, the sister of the Riabushinski brothers, the richest millionaires in Moscow, undertook to provide a whole evening's entertainment at her house, with dinner for a hundred people and dancing afterwards. Princess Gagarina arranged a reception. The Intendant of the Imperial Theatre provided at the shortest notice a special gala performance at the opera. Baleieff, the owner of the "Bat," and the Moscow Artists' Club undertook to amuse the guests in their own exhilarating and invincible manner. The British Club, without whose aid my own efforts to entertain distinguished British visitors would have been unavailing, arranged the first of those sumptuous Anglo-Russian banquets which right up to the revolution provided the flesh and bones—not to mention the caviar and vodka—of Anglo-Russian friendship in Moscow.

The visit was a complete success. The Navy may now have fallen on evil days, but my own experience of British naval officers abroad has been of the happiest. Far better than Army officers do they understand the gentle art of placating and impressing the foreigner. They can relax without loss of dignity. There are few brass hats and few brass heads among them.

My seven submarine officers adapted themselves to their new role of public performers with remarkable skill. They had come to be "lionised," but they were tame and friendly lions. They allowed themselves to be stroked. They fraternised with the ballerinas and with the officials. And Cromie, their leader and an officer grave beyond his years, roared on one occasion with splendid effect. The occasion was the supper given by the Alatr—an artists' and actors' club—in honour of our youthful guests. The supper was accompanied by an impromptu entertainment during which the best dancers and singers Moscow could provide had danced and sung for the good of our digestion. When the evening was well advanced, nothing would satisfy the Russians but that Cromie should make a speech. He was taken up on to the small stage. A tall, dark Byronesque figure with heavy eyebrows and side-whiskers, he faced his audience without a tremor.

"Ladies and Gentlemen," he said. "You are all artists—musicians, poets, novelists, painters, composers. You are creators. What you create will live long after you. We are only simple sailors. We destroy. But we can say truthfully that in this war we destroy in order that your works may live."

It was the shortest and in the effect it produced the most impressive speech I ever heard in Russia.

The Russians were delighted. The visit of the submarine

officers coincided with the capture of Erzerum by the Russian army in the Caucasus, and for four days we lived in an atmosphere of jubilant optimism. As far as I was concerned, there was only one flaw in a programme which was carried out with harmonious smoothness. At the British Club dinner I made my first big speech. For two days I had rehearsed it before my wife and the faithful "Lyki," who as secretary of the Moscow Art Theatre was an expert in elocution. I delivered it with emotion and modesty. There was a touching reference to those who in the literal sense of the words go down to the sea in ships. My oratory drew tears from my audience and from myself. But to my chagrin my speech was not reported. The Russian naval staff, fearful of what might happen to the Baltic Fleet if the Germans were to know that the British submarine commanders were absent from their ships, had imposed the strictest censorship on the whole visit.

With the departure of the naval mission Moscow returned to its primordial pessimism—a depression distinct from the pessimism of St. Petersburg in that it was free from malevolent pacifism. Moscow was prepared to fight to the end. It could not help feeling that the end was likely to be disastrous.

At this particular moment these forebodings were aggravated by the German offensive against Verdun and by the influx of aristocratic Polish refugees into Moscow. These Poles were an unhealthy influence. Superficially, they were attractive. They added to the amenities of Moscow social life. Their passion for political discussion provided fresh material for my reports. But, much as I was inclined to sympathise with their sufferings, closer acquaintance changed my sympathy into mistrust and even dislike. I found it natural that they should hate Russia. I could not tolerate the manner in which they accepted the warm hospitality that was offered to them everywhere and which they repaid by sneering at their hosts and hostesses and by affecting to despise the good Moscow bourgeois. Still less could I stomach their self-centred vanity and their pessimism. The climax came when, one evening, during the most critical period of the Verdun offensive, a frivolous but vain princeling remarked in the presence of the head of the French military mission: "If Verdun is taken, Paris, too, will fall. What a terrible thing that will be for the Polish question." This is only one of many examples of Polish tactlessness. Yet these people, who have never been able to help themselves and who certainly contributed little to the Allied cause in the war, have been rewarded with the largest slice of territory granted to any nation under the Treaty of Versailles.

CHAPTER SIX

IN THAT SPRING of 1916 I had throat trouble again. This time it was accompanied by a bad attack of depression. Everything seemed to be going wrong. Even Chelnokoff had complained to me about the failure of English firms to fulfil their war contracts, and for the first time I began to question the ability of the Allies to win through. My gloom was only partly relieved by a surprise visit from Hugh Walpole, resplendent in a Red Cross uniform and as tremendously enthusiastic and as refreshingly sentimental as ever. He had just returned from England, where the first of his Russian books, "The Dark Forest," had had a great success. He brought me sugar and spice in the form of complimentary appreciation of my work from Lord Robert Cecil and other members of the Foreign Office. When he left, my depression returned, and with the arrival of Easter my wife induced me to take a few days rest.

In order that I might have a change from Moscow, we went down to Sergievo, to the famous Monastery. The indispensable Alexander had made the most elaborate preparations for our reception. Actually there was not much rest about our visit. We arrived on Thursday evening in Holy Week and were met at the station by a monk. By another monk we were driven straight from the station to a long service. The monastery itself, the most famous in Russia, was a miniature Kremlin, surrounded by a wall which was broad enough to allow two carriages to drive abreast along its cobbled stones. The place had stood a hundred sieges in the course of its history, and but for the presence of the monks was much more like a fortress than a place of worship.

After the service we had tea with the Abbot—a fine, simple old gentleman with a flaxen beard and soft, spongy hands which he washed incessantly. It was nearly seven o'clock before we were allowed to seek our quarters—a little monastery hotel attached to the Church of the Chernigoff Madonna about a mile from the Monastery. Fortunately, it was very clean and comfortable.

On Good Friday the rain came down in torrents, and I stayed indoors all day and read the Sir Roger de Coverley papers from the "Spectator." On the Saturday, however, we were plunged again into a round of sight-seeing and religious services. Early in the morning a monk waited on us to drive us to the Bethlehem Monastery—a beautiful little place beside a lake about three miles away. Then in the evening we drove through the birch woods to attend the midnight service at the Lavra itself. The whole Monastery was illuminated by electric light, and against the deep purple background of the sky the huge belfry stood out like a giant skyscraper. The service was impressive. For over an hour we stood in an evil-smelling crowd of soldiers and peasants all holding candles and tapers and sprinkling themselves and us liberally with candle-grease. So ineffable, however, was the singing that we never felt the fatigue.

The next two days were sheer joy. There was a warmth in the sun which banished all my fears and all my pessimism. The whole countryside was a mass of primroses and cowslips. White churches nestled peacefully in a background of birch trees. Above all, there were lakes with perch and carp as old as time itself. After Moscow the peacefulness of it all was wonderful.

On Easter Monday we attended another service and took part in a procession round the great wall of the Lavra, walking in the place of honour just behind the Archimandrites. We had, too, a stupendous luncheon, consisting of some six or seven courses of different fish, with the Abbot, and while we ate, he spoke good words to us. In his conversation there was nothing martial, no "God with us" boastfulness. He spoke of miracles, in which he was a firm believer—and, indeed, if Russia was to win the war, a belief in miracles was necessary—and of the virtues of Christian submission and of a contrite and holy spirit.

For the most part, however, we made long trips into the country, extracting the maximum of enjoyment from our stolen leisure and reaping the full benefit from the glorious

sunshine. One drive, in particular, I remember very vividly—
a long, rambling adventure along a narrow, disused track to a
lake beyond the St. Paraclete Monastery. Our way ran through
a narrow gorge covered with gorse and brambles, and neither
coming nor going did we pass a living soul. It was almost
the most perfect hour of complete contentment that I can
remember.

I returned to Moscow full of energy and fresh hope and better
able to battle with the irritations of my daily life. For, much
as I loved my Russian friends, they *were* irritating. They were
a charming people to know, a hopeless people to work with,
and, fatalistic as I became, I never quite mastered the nuances
of a language in which "at once" means "to-morrow," and
"to-morrow," "never."

I cannot illustrate better the difference between the Russian
and the English attitudes towards life than by a reference to a
Russian trial which took place at this time. In some of its
aspects it bears a certain resemblance to the famous Malcolm
trial in England. In Warsaw a Russian police officer called
Zlatoustovsky had fallen in love with a certain Madame
Marchevsky, the wife of an officer who was fighting for his
country at the front. When Warsaw was evacuated, Zlatoustovsky (his name in Russian means golden-mouthed!) brought
the woman to Moscow and took her to live with him in his
own flat. Warned by a letter from the police officer's wife,
Marchevsky came back from the front and tried to break into
Zlatoustovsky's flat. Zlatoustovsky then emptied his revolver
through the door and killed Marchevsky, who was unarmed.
In spite of the bad conduct of the police officer in the whole
case, he was acquitted. Public opinion made no protest against
the verdict, nor did Zlatoustovsky lose his job.

Renewing my contact with Chelnokoff and the other
Moscow leaders, I found them more depressed than usual.
The resignation of Polivanoff, the War Minister, who had
been dismissed for his too friendly co-operation with the public
organisations, had made them down-hearted. The fall of Kut,
following on our failure in Gallipoli, and the Easter rising in

Dublin had been a severe blow to British prestige. Chelnokoff and I laid our heads together. What could we do to stimulate public confidence? How could we checkmate defeatism and lack of faith in the Western Allies? The Mayor, whose Anglophilism was proof against all shocks, suggested an official visit of the British Ambassador to Moscow. I said I was sure he would come if the visit would do good.

"We might give him the freedom of the city of Moscow," said Chelnokoff.

"Excellent," I replied, "it is in the best English tradition."

There was, however, one drawback. Only one foreigner had ever been made a freeman of Moscow. The honour had never been conferred on an Englishman. It was a rare and precious gift, and it could be conferred only by a unanimous vote of the Town Council. Now the Town Duma was a replica of the State Duma. It was composed of representatives of all the political parties, including the extreme Right, which was not very pro-English and definitely opposed to the Liberal Parties. It was quite impossible for Chelnokoff, even as Mayor, to obtain a unanimous decision. He stroked his long, patriarchal beard. Then, in his fine, deep voice, he gave me his considered opinion.

"I know my colleagues," he said. "They are like children. They will never accept a suggestion coming from me. But if you go to see the various leaders separately, tell them that Sir George Buchanan is coming to Moscow, and let them think that the suggestion of the freedom comes from them—well, if you do your work cleverly, they will jump at it."

I carried out the plan exactly as he prescribed. I saw Nikolai Guchkoff, Victor Briansky, and the other refractory leaders, and with the unanimous decision of the Duma in my pocket I went to see the Ambassador.

The visit, on my suggestion, took place on Empire Day. It was, I believe, the first occasion on which Empire Day was celebrated officially in Russia, and it was from first to last an immense success. The whole city showed a united front in welcoming the Ambassador. "Black Hundred" lions lay down with "Cadet" lambs. Octobrists and Social-Revolutionaries vied with one another in the vehemence of their protestations of friendship and of their determination to fight to a victorious end. The generals and officials fell over each other in their eagerness to contribute their share to the festivities. I wrote an Empire leader for the leading Moscow newspaper. Obviously, even at that moment, I was qualifying for my Empire Crusader's badge. I wrote an appreciation of Sir George Buchanan for the second most important Moscow newspaper. I persuaded the Ambassador to write his speech beforehand, enlisted the services of Lykiardopoulos to translate it, and had a beautifully printed Russian translation served with the caviare to our distinguished Russian guests. At the Empire banquet that evening I proposed the Ambassador's health in a speech, which a Moscow reporter described as a masterpiece of dignified eloquence and self-confidence. Alas! that was sixteen years ago.

The Ambassador himself, as the main arch in this glorious edifice, was splendid. He was the most elegant figure that Moscow had seen for several generations, and his gentle manner and his obvious sincerity went straight to every Russian heart. The happiest omens were augured from his Christian name. Was not St. George the patron Saint of Moscow? In that hour the tide of Anglo-Russian friendship was at the flood.

There was, in fact, only one slight hitch to mar the perfection of the setting. On the next night the City Fathers in solemn sitting, surrounded by all that was best and brightest in Moscow Society, formally conferred on his Super-Excellency Sir George Buchanan, Ambassador Extraordinary and Plenipotentiary of His Britannic Majesty to the Emperor of all the Russias, the title of honorary hereditary citizen of the city of Moscow. With the scroll of honour were conferred other more substantial gifts: a priceless ikon and a loving cup. In the heart of Russia it was necessary for our man to say at least a word or two in Russian. Alas! Sir George was no Russian scholar. "Benji" Bruce and I had reduced the formula to the least common denominator and we had carefully rehearsed the Ambassador to say, when he received the loving cup, "spasibo," which is the shortest and most colloquial Russian term for "thank you." When the fateful moment came, the Comptroller of tongues intervened, and in a firm but low voice Sir George was heard to say: "za pivo," which, being interpreted, means " for beer!"

No philological inexactitude, however, could mar the whirlwind success of those two triumphant days. Chelnokoff was elated. I was elated. We felt we had scotched the German in our midst. Sir George himself was quietly emotional and grateful. As I said good-bye to him on the station platform, he took my hand in his.

"Lockhart," he said, "this is the happiest day in my life, and I owe it all to you."

Sir George Buchanan's visit, as I see it now, was the turning point in my official career. It marked the zenith of my own influence with the Ambassador. It was the last occasion on which I was conscious of the youthful enthusiasm of heroworship. True it is that it gave me a new confidence in my own ability. In the future I was to face the Foreign Office with the aggressiveness of a bumptious lion. But with increased confidence came a falling-away in my own character. I had become an oracle, and oracles are apt to be too cocksure. Perhaps at the time I was unconscious of my shortcomings. Perhaps I scarcely realised the wearing effect of months of excessive work on a highly-strung temperament. Be this as it may, many of my ideals of 1914 had disappeared in the welter of inefficiency which surrounded me, and with their departure came a relaxation of my own self-discipline. The highest form of vanity is fame. I do not say that I have never had it, but it has never been able to compete with my passion for self-indulgence. The romance of the war had gone and with it all hope of a Russian victory. From now on there were to be no illuminating intervals to dispel the gloom which had settled like a pall over the prostrate body of Russia.

As far as my personal feelings were concerned, the first shock came within a few days of the Ambassador's departure. During his visit he had told me in strictest confidence—a confidence not to be broken even in the case of my wife—that Lord Kitchener was coming to Russia. The great man would visit Moscow. I was to hold myself in readiness to attend to all his desires. Even now I might begin discreetly to mark down in the antique shops any genuine examples of old china, in which Lord Kitchener was greatly interested.

Within the next few days half a dozen Russian journalists must have telephoned to ask me if the news were true. At my wife's weekly reception General Wogak, a charming, cultured soldier, who had at one time been military attaché in Peking and Washington, announced the visit, with its date and object, as if no secrecy were needed. Long before Kitchener had sailed from Scotland the news of his mission was common property in both St. Petersburg and Moscow.

I quote these indiscretions merely as an instance of the leakages that were so frequent in the Russia of these war days. I do not suggest that they bore any relation to the fate of the ill-starred *Hampshire*.

I never met Lord Kitchener. I am, therefore, not in a position to say authoritatively what he might or might not have done in Russia. I venture, however, to doubt the opinion, so frequently expressed by English writers on Russia, that, if he had come face to face with the Tsar, the whole course of the war would have been changed. I have little faith in the great man theory— perhaps because I have the valet mind. The strength of nations is in their collective force. Strong nations produce strong men. Weak nations go to the wall. But, even admitting that Kitchener was a superman, I do not believe that his influence on the Tsar would have been more than ephemeral. Even strong men cannot compete with nature. In any case, his visit would have been too late. The inexorable hand of Fate was already stretched out over the ruling class of Russia.

Nevertheless, the tragedy of Kitchener was a disaster which aggravated the sickness of the Russian body and the faintness of the Russian heart.

It was followed by another shock which had even more serious repercussions on the Russian situation. Early in August,

Sazonoff, the pro-Ally Russian Minister of Foreign Affairs, resigned or, to be accurate, was forced to resign. The circumstances of his dismissal were similar to those in which other loyal and pro-war ministers had been dismissed. For some time he had felt insecure. He had, therefore, been to the Stavka (Russian headquarters) to see the Emperor. He had been delighted with his reception. On his return to St. Petersburg his train had crossed the train bearing M. Stürmer, the most unpopular of all the Tsar's Prime Ministers, to headquarters. Almost before M. Sazonoff reached St. Petersburg the Emperor had reversed his plans. M. Sazonoff was requested to take a holiday in Finland. His dismissal followed soon afterwards. The forces of darkness had triumphed once again.

M. Sazonoff was an honest, if not a great, man. He had been most loyal in his co-operation with Sir George Buchanan and M. Paléologue, the French Ambassador. He had sought to work with the Duma and was trusted by the public organisations. His name figured in every list of "cabinets of public confidence" which were the favourite pastime of the Liberals and the maxima of their demands at that time. A firm supporter of the monarchy, he was one of the few men whose advice, if it had been listened to, might have kept the last Romanoff on his throne. His place in the Russian Foreign Office was taken by Stürmer himself, and even in the drawing-rooms of the Grand Dukes the new appointment was received with scowls and bitterness. Under the strain of so much madness the last props of Tsardom were falling away. Amongst the patriots depression assumed the proportions of hopelessness.

Sazonoff has embellished the history of diplomacy with one imperishable anecdote. I did not hear him tell it. When I saw him again in Prague some years after the revolution, he neither admitted nor denied its authenticity. I am assured, however, that the story is true in substance, if not in detail. This is the generally accepted version:

There had been a dinner-party at the British Embassy at which both Sazonoff and the French Ambassador were present. After dinner the three "big shots"—Sazonoff, Sir George

Buchanan and M. Paléologue—had retired to the Ambassador's study to discuss the situation over their cigars. The conversation had turned to diplomacy. What nation supplied the finest diplomatists? M. Paléologue, who was a Frenchman and therefore a flatterer, was loud in his praise of the Russians. Sir George, who was a Scot and, therefore, strictly honest, gave his vote to the Germans. They argued the point without being able to agree and finally appealed to Sazonoff. The Russian smiled.

"Your Excellencies," he said, "are both wrong. In my opinion there can be no question of dispute. The palm belongs surely to the English."

M. Paléologue, already sufficiently jealous of Sir George, made a sour face. Sir George's eyes registered an innocent astonishment.

Again Sazonoff smiled.

"You would like my explanation. When I have given it, you will admit that my argument is irresistible. We Russians—and I thank M. Paléologue for his compliment—are a talented race. We are admirable linguists. Our sources of knowledge are unlimited. Unfortunately, however, we cannot trust ourselves. There is no continuity about our work. We never know what our most trusted Ambassadors are going to do next. They may fall a hopeless victim to the first unscrupulous woman, and in that condition they are capable of selling the ciphers to the enemy.

"Now the Germans are just the reverse. They are admirable workers. They are all continuity. But they begin laying their plans so many years beforehand that, long before the plot is hatched, the whole world knows what they intend to do.

"The whole art of diplomacy is to mask one's intentions. And that is where the English excel. No one ever knows what *they* intend to do"—here the Russian stroked his beard and smiled affectionately at Sir George—"because they never know themselves."

Assuredly, the dismissal of a man who knew the Allies so well was a heavy loss to the Allied cause.

THE STORY OF the next few months leading up to the first revolution is a chronicle of almost unrelieved pessimism: failures on the front (the Brusiloff offensive against Austria had flattered only to deceive), boredom and ennui in official circles in the rear, bewildering changes of ministers, impotent protestations by the Duma, increasing discontent and murmurs not only in the villages, but also in the trenches.

In St. Petersburg and even in Moscow the war had become of secondary importance. The approaching cataclysm was already in every mind, and on everybody's lips. The ruling class, awakened at last to the impending disaster, sought to warn the Emperor. Political resolutions, passed now, not only by the Liberals, but by the nobility, were showered like autumn leaves upon the Emperor. There was no disloyalty in these addresses. They merely begged the Tsar to change his counsellors, to replace them with men enjoying the confidence of the country. The Emperor made changes with the rapidity of a card-trick expert, but very rarely did they satisfy public opinion. On no occasion were they ever made in response to the demand, however discreetly made, of a public body. For this man of all the domestic virtues, this man of no vices and no will-power, was an autocrat by divine right. He could change his mind four times in as many minutes, but he could never forget his inheritance.

"What is all this talk about the people's confidence?" he said. "Let the people merit *my* confidence."

During these last six months of the monarchy my Consulate-General became a kind of post-box for complaints. My time was occupied in translating resolutions—to-day I still have scores of them among my private papers—and lampoons. At this time there was a salon poet called Miatlieff, a cavalry officer with a knack for versification, which he employed to attack the more unpopular members of the government. I translated the resolutions into prose. I paraphrased Miatlieff into English doggerel. I sent both prose and verse to the

Embassy. In the end it must have been wearied by my wasted energy.

The tragedy was that both the resolutions and the lampoons were written by men who had no thought of revolution in their hearts, who earnestly desired a more efficient prosecution of the war, and who to-day, if they were alive, would give their right hand to replace the Emperor or, at least *an* Emperor on the throne of Russia.

As far as Moscow is concerned, I do not exaggerate. I was in almost daily contact with the men who, sorely against their wish, formed the first provisional government after the abdication of the Tsar: Prince Lvoff, Chelnokoff, Manuiloff, Avinoff, Maklakoff, Novikoff, Kokoshkin. From intimate personal intercourse I knew that they were appalled by the problem which confronted them as Russian patriots. The problem itself was very succinctly put by Maklakoff, the famous Russian orator and subsequent ambassador of the Provisional Government in Paris, in one of those parables in which, owing to the censor, Russians were experts. A motor-car is going down a steep hill. At the bottom there is a yawning precipice. Your mother is seated in the front seat next to the driver. You yourself are in the back seat. Suddenly you realise that the driver has lost control. What are you to do?

As one of those quandaries set as a competition in the popular Press, it would have been an interesting conundrum, which would have evoked entirely satisfactory answers from Mr. Lansbury, Sir Malcolm Campbell, Miss Ethel Mannin, Lord Castlerosse, and Lady Inverclyde ; in the life of a nation, plunged in the vortex of a world war, it was a matter of life or death. In this case there was no attempt at a solution. The driver was left to run his car over the precipice.

During that torrid summer visitors came to Moscow and went—English generals, Locker-Lampson's armoured car unit, English journalists, the Grand Duke Michael, the brother of the Tsar. I entertained the English visitors and listened to their views. I had a long and rather futile conversation with the Grand Duke Michael when he came to a private show of some

French war films. In his Cossack uniform he made a pleasant impression. A tall, handsome figure of a man with charming manners and an easy-going disposition, he struck me as a prince who might have made an excellent constitutional monarch. He talked quite freely about the war, about the lack of munitions and the need for an improved transport system, but he made only one remark which could be interpreted as political. "Thank God," he said, "the atmosphere at the front is far better than the atmosphere of St. Petersburg." He was the quietest and perhaps the least confident of all the Grand Dukes.

When summer passed into winter there were more visits to the Embassy. There was one gala dinner given by Sir George Buchanan to Chelnokoff and a small deputation of the Moscow Duma—a return for the hospitality lavished on the Ambassador during his Moscow visit. Chelnokoff and I travelled to St. Petersburg together. At the dinner he singled me out for special praise, greeting me in his speech as a true friend of Russia.

I was invited to luncheon by the French Ambassador. I had a one-sided conversation with Sazonoff, who asked many questions and vouchsafed no information. The young man from Moscow was an object of interest.

But—and it was a big but—I found the atmosphere of St. Petersburg more depressing than ever. Champagne flowed like water. The Astoria and the Europe—the two best hotels in the capital—were thronged with officers who should have been at the front. There was no disgrace in being a "shirker" or in finding a sinecure in the rear. I had an impression of senseless ennui and *fin de siècle*. And in the streets were the long queues of ill-clad men and garrulous women, waiting for the bread that never came. Even in the Embassy hope had sunk to a low ebb. Sir George himself looked tired and ill. He still wore his hat at the same rakish angle. Never for one moment did he relax his optimism in the presence of the Russians. But, when he walked, his shoulders drooped as though his burdens were more than he could bear. In the Chancery there were signs of frayed nerves—the inevitable result of long months of monotonous and profitless work. My own conduct was puerile and reprehensible. I protracted my visits longer than was necessary, making bogus excuses of work in order to go to Russian parties and to be entertained by those whom I had entertained in Moscow. I drank the champagne—more than was good for me —of those I criticised, and I returned to Moscow ashamed and unhappy. My life at this moment gave me no satisfaction.

With the advent of December the tone of the various anti-government resolutions became bolder. In the factories the Social-Democrats and the Social Revolutionaries were now conducting an active revolutionary propaganda. Goaded to fury by the inanities of Protopopoff—a former Liberal member of the Duma, who as Minister of the Interior revealed himself as more reactionary than any member of the Black Hundred— the Zemstvo and Cities Unions defied his action in forbidding their Congress by passing a secret resolution which in the violence of its language exceeded all their previous political demands. There was, it is true, no word against the Emperor, but after a long preamble, in which full emphasis was laid on the ills from which Russia was suffering, the resolution declared that "the government, now become an instrument of the dark forces, is driving Russia to her ruin and is shattering the Imperial throne. In this grave hour in its history the country requires a government worthy of a great people. Let the Duma, in the decisive struggle which it is waging, justify the expectations of the people. There is not a day to lose!"

This document was only secret in so far as it was forbidden to be published. It was circulated in roneoscript in thousands of copies, both at the front and in the rear.

This resolution was passed just before Christmas. Two days before the end of the year Rasputin was assassinated. The story has been told too often to bear retelling. Of the three participants in this perhaps mistaken act of patriotism only the Grand Duke Dmitri was known to me personally at the time. All three—the two others were Prince Felix Yussupoff and M. Purishkewitch—were supporters of the old régime. Their act was intended to save the old régime. Although for a moment it raised the hopes of the patriots, its only effect, viewed to-day in the light of history, was to assist the anti-war elements and to hasten the revolution, which unbiased observers had long realised was sooner or later inevitable.

The only person to benefit from this assassination was the Grand Duke Dmitri—the best-intentioned and most pro-English of the Grand Dukes. The banishment to the Caucasus which his complicity in the murder brought down upon his head enabled him to escape through Persia, when the revolution broke out, and to avoid the terrible fate which was meted out by the Bolsheviks to so many of his relations.

Before the lamp of Tsardom was finally extinguished, it was to flicker up in one last feeble flame of hope. Towards the end of January, 1917, an inter-Allied delegation arrived in St. Petersburg. The object of this visit was to secure a more efficient co-operation between the Allies to put the final dots on the "i's" of the peace terms, and to consecrate the victory which was always on the lips of the French and English and in which so few Russians now believed. Rarely in the history of great wars can so many important ministers and generals have left their respective countries on so useless an errand. The British Mission was the largest. It was headed by Lord Milner, who had with him as his political advisers Lord Revelstoke and George Clerk[1], and as his military advisers Sir Henry Wilson and five other generals. The French were more economical. They sent only one politician—M. Doumergue—and two generals, one of whom, however, was the gallant Castelnau. The Italian mission was headed by Signor Scialoja, who was supported by General Ruggieri.

In the presence of so much magnificence my own little star sank into insignificance. Nevertheless, I had my part in the proceedings. The mission was to visit Moscow, and I was summoned to St. Petersburg to discuss the situation and arrange the programme with Lord Milner. Moscow, as usual, had set high store by the arrival of the delegation, hoping for some last-minute action by the Allies, which would restore the fallen fortunes of Russia. Such hopes as may have been raised

[1] Now Sir George Clerk, H.M. Ambassador to Turkey.

in my own breast were shattered as soon as I arrived in St. Petersburg. I lunched with Lord Milner at the British Embassy. I had a long talk with him in the afternoon, and in the evening I dined alone with him in his rooms at the "Europe." I think he was glad to escape at least for one night from the interminable round of festivity to which he and the other delegates were being subjected. Of all the great figures in public life with whom I have come into contact I found him the most understanding and sympathetic. He was, too, extraordinarily well informed about facts and figures, which he seemed to carry in his head without effort. I doubt if his intuition was as remarkable as his knowledge. But from the first day of his arrival he had realised the inefficiency of the Russians, and he made no attempt to conceal his opinion that he was wasting his time. He looked tired and overworked, but he listened to me with infinite patience. He was, I believe, at his best with young men, and I, like most other young men, fell at once before his charm. He asked me several questions, and I gave him my opinion candidly: that if some concession was not made to public opinion trouble was inevitable. He sighed.

"I do not say you are wrong," he said gently. "But I am bound to tell you two things. First, the general consensus of informed opinion, both Allied and Russian, in St. Petereburg, so far as I can gather, is that there will be no revolution until after the war. And, secondly, I see no means of enforcing the concessions to which you refer."

The next day I returned to Moscow, and Lord Milner resumed his place at the conference table. And, while the delegates were discussing Constantinople, Alsace-Lorraine, and the spoils of war, there were riots round the bread-shops, workmen were being arrested by the Ochrana, and in the entourage of the Imperial family frightened women were repeating the prophecy of Rasputin: "If I die or you abandon me, you will lose your son and your throne within six months."

A week later Lord Milner, accompanied by Lord Revelstoke and George Clerk, came to Moscow. (Sir Henry Wilson and the other British generals had gone to the front. Their visit was to come later.) To the end of his life Lord Milner never forgot those two days in Moscow. They were the last nail in the coffin of his discomfort. There was a reception at the Town Duma at which he had to make a speech and to present Chelnokoff with the K.C.M.G., which the King had conferred upon him as a reward for his services to the Anglo-Russian entente. (Poor Chelnokoff. This was the final hour of his reign as Mayor. When the revolution came, he had to flee the country, leaving his precious K.C.M.G. behind. To-day, he is dying of cancer in the Belgrade Russian hospital. When I saw him there a few years ago, he expressed the wish that fresh insignia might be given to him. I tried to obtain a new Order for him through the Foreign Office and was informed that he would have to purchase it himself!) There was an Anglo-Russian luncheon, which lasted five hours, and at which various members of the Imperial Duma were determined to deliver their set speeches even at the risk of prolonging luncheon into dinner. The unfortunate Englishman, who understood no Russian and who, doubtless, would have liked to see something of the Kremlin and the ancient city, was chained to his duty from early morning to late night. I cannot congratulate myself on my staff work on this occasion.

And yet the visit was the occasion of one historical meeting. I arranged a private interview between Prince Lvoff and Chelnokoff on the one side and Lord Milner and George Clerk on the other. I acted as interpreter. Prince Lvoff, a quiet, grey-bearded man, tired out with overwork, spoke with great moderation. But lest there should be any doubt as to his views he brought a written memorandum with him. It was a long document, but the gist of it was that, if there was no change in the attitude of the Emperor, there would be a revolution within three weeks.

My duties were not ended when I had put Lord Milner to bed. I had my report to send to the Embassy. There was George Clerk, determined to see something of Moscow by night, and still young enough to sacrifice his sleep to his determination.

Enlisting the services of a young Russian millionaire, we took him to a gipsy party—doubtless one of the last of the great gipsy parties celebrated under the monarchy. Goodness knows what it cost. I could not have paid. There were eight of us: four English and four Russians, and as the guest of honour George Clerk had to bear the brunt of the champagne bombardment. My young Russian millionaire did his best. Maria Nikolaievna sang countless " charochki," and with her own hands offered countless bumpers to George Clerk. As a diplomatist he has had many triumphs, but never has he borne himself more bravely than on that last evening in Moscow. He never refused a toast. He drank each one down in the approved Russian manner, and his monocle never moved. Not a hair of his head was ruffled. There was neither flush nor pallor on his cheeks.

In the early hours of the morning Prochoroff, my young millionaire officer, signed the bill and distributed the necessary largesse, and we set off home; my wife, George Clerk, "Jimmie" Valentine and I in one car; Prochoroff and his Russian friends showing the way in another. A quarter of a mile down the road we passed him. He had pulled up beside a policeman and was standing in the road. For George Clerk's edification we stopped to watch. Prochoroff was fumbling in his pockets. He pulled out his purse and handed a rouble to the policeman, who clicked his heels together and saluted. His hand on his sword, Prochoroff drew himself up to his full height. There was a sparkle in his eye, and he looked as though he were about to lead a charge.

"Boje Tsaria Khranee!" he thundered. "God save the Tsar," repeated the policeman. And "bey Jidoff!" (beat the Jews).

We drove on. Prochoroff did not hate the Jews. In so far as he had any political views he was a Liberal. But he would go on with his "God save the Tsar and beat the Jews" refrain all the way home. It was the prescribed ritual. It was the prerevolutionary tradition.

Lord Milner and George Clerk having returned to St. Petersburg, we were promptly inflicted with the military invasion of Sir Henry Wilson and his brother officers. There was no political significance attached to this visit. Yet it nearly ruined my relations with my Russian friends and involved me in one of the most uncomfortable incidents in my official life.

The generals had come to Moscow, not for business but for relaxation. They had had their bellyful of official entertaining. In any case they were not interested in the political views of Moscow malcontents or, for that matter, of a beardless Consular officer. What could I do to amuse them? Could I arrange a small dinner and a dance for them? And, as they were fifteen strong, need I invite the husbands? This was the burden of my conversation with Sir Henry Wilson on his arrival, and, anxious to please so great a soldier, I rushed away to fulfil his commands.

I sought the assistance of my wife. She rang up the wives of the Russians who throughout the war had done most to help us to entertain the various English missions which had visited Moscow. With delicious zest they entered into the spirit of the adventure, and before luncheon time we had arranged an almost perfect party. Need I say that our invitations had been extended only to the young and pretty wives and that their husbands had not been taken into their confidence. Oh, egregious, over-zealous youth!

The party was held in a private room in the Hermitage Restaurant. The food, the wines, were the best that Moscow could provide. The orchestra was Korsch, and in honour of the English guests Krysh played "Love Me and the World is Mine" with even more than his usual feeling. The party was a complete success. It was friendly. It was decorous. In the presence of such pillars of respectability as General Clive, Lord Duncannon (to-day Lord Bessborough), and Sir Henry Wilson himself how could it have been otherwise? And yet in this fold of innocents there was one black sheep. Lord Brook asked if he might bring a friend to the dinner. She was unknown to my Moscow friends. She was an aristocrat. She had been divorced. Worst of all, she came from St. Petersburg.

Let me hasten to say that both she and Lord Brook behaved

even more decorously than the most decorous member of this decorous gathering. But the mischief was done. And at an early hour next morning my telephone buzzed incessantly with calls from irate husbands demanding apologies for my conduct. The final blow came when my richest, most influential Russian friend called at the Consulate-General and asked to speak to me. He was shown into my room. He walked up to my desk and clicked his heels. There was a look of steel in his eyes.

"Roman Romanovitch," he said, "You were my friend. I consider it my duty to inform you that your conduct in inviting my wife without me last night was ungentlemanly. Good-bye."

And, righteously indignant, he strode out of the room.

It took me weeks of arduous attention to gather up the fragments of my broken friendships.

A FEW DAYS later the assembled delegations left for England, France and Italy. There were no bands to play them off, no official farewells. They travelled via Murmansk, where the *Kildonan Castle* was waiting to pick them up, and, mindful of the fate of Kitchener, they kept the day and the hour of their departure secret. And, in order that the secret might be better guarded, they sacrificed their shoes, which, at the request of those responsible for their safety, were left outside their bedroom doors long after the occupants had stolen away.

There is a story current that on his return to England Lord Milner wrote a Cabinet report in which he expressed his firm conviction that there would be no revolution, and that before the ink on it was dry the revolution had already started.

I have been unable to verify the authenticity of this account, which was given to me by a Cabinet Minister. But for the respect in which I hold Lord Milner's memory I should like to believe that it were true. It is an ending which flatters my complacency as much as it appeals to my sense of the dramatic. After all, I had given an accurate forecast, and it had been disregarded.

Truth, however, compels me to doubt if Lord Milner ever wrote such a report or made such a categorical expression of his opinion. The Foreign Office, it is true, was furnished with a report which began: "It may seem presumptuous in one who has spent only a fortnight in Russia," and which ended with a bold prophecy that there would be no revolution. But that report was not signed by Lord Milner.

Nor was there anything in Lord Milner's attitude during his Russian visit, or in the numerous conversations which I had with him, to give the impression that he had any confidence in the permanence of the Tsarist régime. What advice he gave to Mr. Lloyd George I do not know, but I cannot believe that it was optimistic. Sir Samuel Hoare, who accompanied the Milner Mission on its return journey to England and whose evidence cannot be lightly disregarded, is emphatic in his statement that all the members of the Mission were mistaken in almost all their conclusions and that their reports, written on the *Kildonan Castle*, were absurdly over-confident.

In spite of Sir Samuel's evidence I still maintain that Lord Milner's optimism must have been qualified. His Russian visit cast a gloom over him which could not have been dispelled by the exuberance of his subordinates. Certainly, there was no evidence of optimism in his subsequent letters to those British officials who remained in Russia. One quotation will suffice—an extract from a letter written to "Benji" Bruce, the head of the Embassy Chancery, a few weeks after Lord Milner had returned to London. It runs as follows: "Alas! alas! I fear all the Missions of British Labour leaders and all the compliments we have showered on the Russian revolution—'triumph of democracy,' 'the union of free peoples against the tyrants,' etc., etc., are perfectly futile. It is evident to me that, intentionally or not, Russia is going out of the war. It must be heartbreaking for your Chief, who has done so much in the past to cement the friendship between Russia and England, and who would have averted the catastrophe which has actually occurred if his advice had been listened to. Even now he seems to be managing wonderfully in a very difficult situation, but I fear no steering is of much avail in the teeth of such a typhoon."

This does not read much like optimism. One thing is certain. If this Mission did not open the eyes of its members to the state of Russia, it was useless even as an object-lesson to the Western Allies. As far as Russia was concerned, it might just as well have remained in London, Rome and Paris.

On March 12th, less than three weeks after the departure of the Allied delegates the storm broke, and in a night a bread-riot, similar to hundreds which had taken place during the previous twelve months, had become a revolution. In Moscow there was no bloodshed. There was no one left to defend the old régime. It was a bitterly cold day. Our house, which was central-heated, had been short of fuel for nearly a week, and I went out into the crowds in the street. My most vivid memory of that afternoon was the warmth of the surging mob before the Town Duma. There was no hooliganism. The crowd was willing enough to let me through, but before I reached the door I was roasting with heat and glad to take off my fur cap. I was the first foreigner to enter the Moscow headquarters of the revolution. Inside, the rooms and passages of the huge Town Hall were thronged with bands of students and soldiers —the soldiers hot, greasy and officious; the students raucous and exultant. Nor was only youth in the ascendant. There were grey-bearded men, bent with years—men who had suffered exile, who had lived in mouse-holes, and who, with trembling knees and a strange light in their eyes, were now rejoicing over the hour of their triumph. The enthusiasm was compelling, almost infectious, but it was more impressive in the masses outside than in the delegates inside the building. I sought out Chelnokoff. He came out of the Council room to see me. Beads of sweat were standing on his brow. His limp was more pronounced than ever. His voice had gone.

"I'm fighting for my life, Roman Romanovitch," he said. "The Social-Revolutionaries and the Social-Democrats don't want me as Mayor. But, never fear, I'll master them yet. But it's a bad business—and not good for the war."

And with that he left me and returned to the battle of tongues which had now been unloosed. The man who yesterday had been too revolutionary for the Emperor was already too reactionary for the revolution.

On my way out I met Gruzinoff, the President of the Moscow Provincial Zemstvo. He had just been appointed to the command of the revolutionary troops. He, too, seemed embarrassed by the enthusiasm and hero-worship of the band of women students and high-school girls who surrounded him. The fire was travelling fast.

One other scene in that first day of good-tempered confusion remains clear-cut before my eyes. On my way home I met Harry Charnock in the street. For months he had been negotiating for the sale of the great Vicoul Morozoff textile works to a rich American group. As far as the Americans were concerned the contract would have been signed months before and the purchase money paid over. Charnock himself, who was general manager and stood to make a small fortune by the deal, had been in favour of signing, but the Morozoffs with peasant obstinacy had haggled and haggled until now it was too late. Laconically Charnock handed me a paper. It was a telegram from the Americans saying the deal was off. Big capital had taken fright.

As I passed through the Theatre Square Socialist agitators, mostly students and schoolgirls, were distributing anti-war pamphlets to the troops. Opposite the National Hotel someone in the crowd recognised me. "Long Live England," cried a student voice. "Long Live England and the Revolution," answered the greasy mob. It was a disturbing and confusing day.

The story of the revolution has been told by many pens. It will be a theme for historians for all time. I do not propose to discuss it in detail except in so far as I myself was concerned in it. Nor do I intend to analyse its causes or speculate on what might have happened if Kerensky had done this on this date, and General Ivanoff that on that date. My own views on the revolution can be given in a single paragraph.

The revolution took place because the patience of the Russian people broke down under a system of unparalleled inefficiency and corruption. No other nation would have stood the privations which Russia stood, for anything like the same length of time. As instances of the inefficiency, I give the disgraceful mishandling of food-supplies, the complete break-down of transport, and the senseless mobilisation of millions of unwanted and unemployable troops. As an example of the corruption, I quote the shameless profiteering of nearly everyone engaged in the giving and taking of war contracts. Obviously, the Emperor himself, as a supreme autocrat, must bear the responsibility for a system which failed mainly because of the men (Stürmer, Protopopoff, Rasputin) whom he appointed to control it. If he had acted differently, if he had been a different man. . . . These arguments are childish.

What it is important to realise is that from the first the

revolution was a revolution of the people. From the first moment neither the Duma nor the intelligentzia had any control of the situation. Secondly, the revolution was a revolution for land, bread and peace—but, above all, for peace. There was only one way to save Russia from going Bolshevik. That was to allow her to make peace. It was because he would not make peace that Kerensky went under. It was solely because he promised to stop the war that Lenin came to the top. It will be objected that Kerensky ought to have shot both Lenin and Trotsky. The soldiers, who argue in this way, always ignore the psychological premises. The old régime having broken down, the type of leader (i.e. a Kerensky) whom the first revolution threw up was bound to be a man who would not shoot his opponents. It was the first state of a natural process. Secondly, even if Kerensky had shot Lenin and Trotsky, some other anti-war leader would have taken their place and would have won through on his anti-war programme.

This was so fundamentally true of the Russian situation that only the gravity of our own situation in the West can excuse us for the folly of the various schemes (from the futile feebleness of the Archangel expedition to the greater, but, fortunately, unfulfilled stupidity of Japanese intervention) which we advocated for the reconstruction of the Eastern front. Among the foolish and the egregious I include myself. And among the soldiers General Macready stood alone in his sane commonsense.

My own contact with the first revolution lasted for eight months. It was a period of depression and disintegration, of a new activity from which all hope and faith had gone. I had been no admirer of the old régime, but I had little difficulty in realising what the effect of the new must be on the war. Three days after the outbreak of the first rioting I sent off a long analysis of the revolutionary movement to the Embassy. The précis of this despatch entered in my Diary at the time runs as follows: "The position is so unclear and so uncertain that any attempt at prophecy is difficult. It seems impossible that the struggle between the bourgeoisie and the proletariat can be liquidated without further bloodshed. When this will come no one knows, but the outlook for the war is full of foreboding."

The revolution had begun on a Monday. On the Saturday I took part in my official capacity in a grand review of the revolutionary troops on the Red Square. It was an inspiring sight—40,000 troops celebrating a newly-won freedom by a march-past executed with perfect precision and order. And yet in spite of the cloudless sky and sparkling air I had a feeling as though I were in a prison. That vast Red Square, which has witnessed so much repression of freedom from the time of the executions of Ivan the Terrible to the May Day parades of the Bolsheviks, that grim background of high red wall furnished by the Kremlin—these are no symbols of liberty. Russians, as I was to learn later in even more disturbed times, have a genius for pageantry and processions. And if there was any tendency to over-enthuse on my part (and I am a romanticist who hates all governments by instinct), there were the generals—Liberal patriots like Obolesheff, who had just returned from the front —to supply the necessary correction. Discipline had disappeared. Men no longer saluted their officers. Deserters were seeking the villages in their thousands. The floodgates of three hundred years had been swept away. The tide was not to be stemmed by any individual effort until it had spent itself. Guided skilfully into less dangerous channels it might have been. But that was not the method of the Allies, who had greeted the revolution first with feigned enthusiasm and then with increasing alarm. They wanted—and on the part of the military advisers the wish was natural—things to be put back where they were before. And, unfortunately, there is no "as you were" either in time or in revolution.

A fortnight after the revolution I went to St. Petersburg to see the members of the new Provisional Government. Prince Lvoff, the Prime Minister, was my intimate friend. With most of the others I had been in close contact for the past two years. Men like Shingareff, a St. Petersburg doctor, Kokoshkin, the great Moscow expert on international law, and Manuiloff, the rector of Moscow University, were men of the highest integrity and ability. To the English Liberal Cabinet of 1906 they would have been an addition of strength and an ornament of distinction. They were too gentle to deal with the turbulent elements in the Soviets, which had made the revolution and which now virtually controlled the Duma.

Before catching my train, I dined with Chelnokoff, who had been appointed Commissar for Moscow. He gave me a forecast of what I might expect to find. His own position was becoming unbearable. He confessed that he had no chance of surviving the new elections, which now of course had been proscribed on a basis of universal suffrage for every municipality and every Zemstvo in Russia. Lvoff's reign, he said, would be no longer than his own.

The most phlegmatic of men, he spoke without anger or prejudice. I felt that he was right. Already "a free and unfettered democracy" (how later the Bolsheviks were to sneer at these slogans of the first revolution!) had no use for the Liberal leaders whose cry for years had been "trust the people."

I found Prince Lvoff at the Taurid Palace amid a scene of indescribable confusion. He had been presiding at a Cabinet meeting. Secretaries kept rushing into his room with papers to sign, decisions to be taken. He would start to talk to me, and then the telephone would ring. In the corridor outside, deputations from the front, from the villages, from goodness knows where, were waiting to see him. And in this restless, bustling turmoil there was not one man or woman who seemed capable of protecting the Prime Minister or relieving the burden on his shoulders. Everyone seemed to be playing a game of general post to escape from responsibility. I longed for a Miss Stevenson to send the whole pack of delegations about their business and to put some order into this warren of chaos.

Our conversation was conducted in snatches. Finally he gave it up.

"You see how it is," he said. "We are doing our best, but there is so much to do. Come and see me to-night at my flat at twelve o'clock."

He ran his hand through his grey beard and looked at me with a flickering smile. He looked tired and wan, and his eyes, small at all times, had almost vanished behind his eyelids. In two weeks he had aged ten years. A man of great charm, he would have made an excellent chairman of the London County Council. He was an ideal President of the Zemstvo Unions, but he was not the stuff of which revolutionary Prime Ministers are made. And yet I doubt if at this period any member of his class could have "held down" his post. Nature brooks no interference with her processes, and the time for dictators had not yet come or had already passed.

I went to see Lvoff at his flat—a modest two-roomed affair, where he had remained ever since the night he had arrived from Moscow to take over the reins of the Government. He was still in the same suit. The carpet bag, in which he had packed his clothes for the night, still stood in the hall. My heart went out to him. He seemed so forlorn and alone. As always, he spoke in his rather jerky little monotones. He was a shy man and, although he bore an aristocratic name, more like a country doctor than an aristocrat. To those who knew him slightly he gave an impression of cunning—due actually to his timidity. To those whom he trusted he was open and without restraint. He made no concealment of his fears and anxieties. Russia would come through, but . . . Russia would carry on with the war, but . . . His whole conversation was a confession of the weakness of his own position.

When I went to see my other Moscow friends in the Government I found the same helplessness, the same apprehensions. There was only one man in the Cabinet who had any power. That was the nominee of the Soviets—Kerensky, the Minister of Justice. The revolution had destroyed my old Liberal friends. Now I had to seek new gods.

IT WAS PRINCE LVOFF who arranged my first meeting with Kerensky. I could not have had a better introduction. Like most Socialists Kerensky admired and respected Lvoff as much for the integrity of his character as for the work he had done for the Russian people. I received an invitation to luncheon.

At the appointed hour my sleigh drew up before the Ministry of Justice, and I climbed up the long steps of the official staircase, where only three weeks before had reigned all the rigid ceremonial of the ancient régime, into an ante-chamber filled with a crowd of soldiers, sailors, legal functionaries, students, schoolgirls, workmen and peasants, all waiting patiently like one of the bread queues in the Liteinaia or the Nevsky. I pushed my way through the throng to a tired and much-harassed secretary.

"You wish to see Alexander Feodorovitch Kerensky? Quite impossible. You must come to-morrow."

I explain patiently that I am invited to luncheon. Again the machine-like voice breaks in: "Alexander Feodorovitch has gone to the Duma. I have no idea when he will be back. In these days you know. . . ."

He shrugs his shoulders. Then, almost before I have time to allow the disappointment to show on my face, the crowd surges forward. "Stand back, stand back," shout the soldiers. Two nervous and very young adjutants clear a passage, and in half a dozen energetic strides Kerensky is beside me. His face has a sallow and almost deathly pallor. His eyes, narrow and Mongolian, are tired. He looks as if he were in pain, but the mouth is firm, and the hair, cropped close and worn *en brosse*, gives a general impression of energy. He speaks in quick, jerky sentences with little sharp nods of the head by way of emphasis. He wears a dark suit, not unlike ski-ing kit, over a black Russian workman's blouse. He takes me by the arm and leads me into his private apartments, and we sit down to luncheon at a long table with almost thirty places. Madame Kerensky is already lunching. By her side are

The author in
Malaya, 1910

The author

The Charnock brothers and the author in the Morozovsti football team, Gold Medal winners in 1912

Pages from the author's passport

Lord Milner (*above*)
Arthur Henderson (*right*)

Sir George Buchanan,
British Ambassador in Moscow

S. D. Sazonoff Tsarist Foreign Minister

Prince George Lvoff

Alexander Kerensky

Boris Savinkoff

Lenin (*right*)

Trotsky (*below*)

N. I. Bucharin (*above left*)
Karl Radek (*above*)
Felix Derjinsky (*left*)

Opposite: Leaders of the October
Revolution: Trotsky, Lenin,
Lunacharsky, Spiridonova, Kollontai,
Raskolnikoff, Kameneff, Zinovieff

G. V. Chicherin and Maxim Litvinoff

Лев Троцкій. В.И. Ульяновъ (Н. Ленинъ). А.В. Луначарскій. М.А. Спиридоно

А.М. Коллонтай. Ѳ.Ѳ. Раскольниковъ. А.Б. Каменевъ. Зиновьевъ.

Память Второй Революціи 24/X 1917г.

Moura Budberg (*left*)

Sidney Reilly (*below left*)

Captain Cromie (*below*)

Breshkovskaia, the grandmother of the Russian Revolution, and a great brawny-armed sailor from the Baltic Fleet. People drift in and out at will. Luncheon is a floating meal and it seems to be free to all. And all the while Kerensky talks. In spite of the Government prohibition order there is wine on the table, but the host himself is on a strict diet and drinks nothing but milk. Only a few months previously he has had a tubercular kidney removed. But his energy is undiminished. He is tasting the first fruits of power. Already he resents a little the pressure that is being put on him by the Allies. "How would Lloyd George like it if a Russian were to come to him to tell him how to manage the English people?" He is, however, good-natured. His enthusiasm is infectious, his pride in the revolution unbounded. "We are only doing what you have done centuries ago, but we are trying to do it better—without the Napoleon and without the Cromwell. People call me a mad idealist, but thank God for the idealists in this world." And at the moment I was prepared to thank God with him.

Since that first luncheon I have had many meetings with Alexander Feodorovitch. In Russia I suppose I knew him better—far better indeed—that any other British official. I interpreted for him on several occasions in his negotiations with Sir George Buchanan. I saw him frequently alone. It was to me that he came when he was in hiding from the Bolsheviks. It was I who was instrumental in getting him out of Russia. And to-day, when thousands of anti-Bolshevik Russians—and English, too—revile him; when the men and women who once sought his favour and leant upon his words curse his name; I have remained his friend.

Kerensky was the victim of the bourgeois hopes which his short-lived success aroused. He was an honest, if not a great, man—sincere in spite of his oratorical talents, and, for a man who for four months was worshipped as a god, comparatively modest. From the start he was fighting a hopeless battle, trying to drive back into the trenches a nation which had already finished with the war. Caught between the cross-fires of the Bolshevik Left, which was screaming peace at every street-corner and in every trench, and of the Right and of the Allies, who were demanding the restoration of discipline by Tsarist methods, he had no chance. And he fell, because whoever had tried to do what he did was bound to fall.

Yet for a few weeks it seemed that his oratory might work a miracle and that his ridiculous belief (shared by all the Social-revolutionaries and most of the Liberals) in the common-sense of the Russian people might justify itself. For, in his own peculiar way, Kerensky must be regarded as one of the great orators of history. There was nothing attractive about his delivery. His voice was raucous from much shouting. He had few gestures—for a Slav amazingly few. But he had words at his command and he spoke with a conviction that was all-compelling. How well I remember his first visit to Moscow. It was, I think, soon after he had been made Minister for War. He had just returned from a visit to the front. He spoke in the Big Theatre—the platform on which, later, the Bolsheviks ratified the Peace of Brest-Litovsk. Kerensky, however, was the first politician to speak from that famous stage, which has given to the world Chaliapin, Sobinoff, Geltzer, Mordkin, and scores of other famous dancers and singers. On this occasion the huge amphitheatre was packed from top to bottom. In Moscow the embers of Russian patriotism were still warm, and Kerensky had come to stir them into flame again. Generals, high officials, bankers, great industrialists, merchants, accompanied by their wives, occupied the parterre and first balcony boxes. On the stage were the representatives of the Soldiers' Councils. A small pulpit had been erected in the foreground of the stage just above the prompter's trap-door. There was the usual ten minutes' delay, the customary rumours among the audience. Alexander Feodorovitch was ill. A new crisis had recalled him to St. Petersburg. Then the buzz of conversation gave place to a burst of clapping, and from the wings the pale figure of the War Minister made its way to the central dais. The audience rose to him. Kerensky held up his hand and plunged straight into his speech. He looked ill and tired. He drew himself up to his full height, as if calling up his last reserves of energy. Then, with an ever-increasing flow of words, he began to expound his gospel of suffering. Nothing that was worth having could be achieved without suffering. Man himself was born into this world in suffering. The greatest of all revolutions in history had begun on the Cross of Calvary. Was it to be supposed that their own revolution was to be consolidated without suffering? They had a legacy of appalling difficulties left to them by the Tsarist régime: disorganised transport, lack of bread, lack of fuel. Yet the Russian people knew how to suffer. He had just returned from the trenches. He had seen men who had been living for months on end with mud and water up to their knees. Lice crawled over them. For days they had had nothing but a crust of black bread for sustenance. They were without the proper equipment for their self-defence. They had not seen their women-folk for months. Yet they made no complaint. They had promised to do their duty to the end. It was only in St. Petersburg and in Moscow that he heard grumbling. And from whom? From the rich, from those who, in their silks and ornaments of gold, came here to-day to listen to him in comfort. He raised his eyes to the balcony boxes, while with fierce staccato sentences he lashed himself into a passion. Were they to bring Russia down in ruins, to be guilty of the most shameful betrayal in history, while the poor and the humble, who had every reason to complain, were still holding out? He was ashamed at the apathy of the big cities. What had they done to be tired! Could they not watch a little longer? He had come to Moscow for a message for the men in the trenches. Was he to go back and say that their effort was in vain because "the heart of Russia" was now peopled by men of little faith?

As he finished his peroration, he sank back exhausted into the arms of his aide-de-camp. In the limelight his face had the pallor of death. Soldiers assisted him off the stage, while in a frenzy of hysteria the whole audience rose and cheered itself hoarse. The man with one kidney—the man who had only six weeks to live—would save Russia yet. A millionaire's wife threw her pearl necklace on to the stage. Every woman present followed her example, and a hail of jewellery descended from every tier of the huge house. In the box next to me, General Wogak, a man who had served the Tsar all his life and who hated the revolution as the pest, wept like a child. It was an epic performance—more impressive in its emotional reactions than any speech of Hitler or of any orator I have ever heard. The speech had lasted for two hours. Its effect on Moscow and on the rest of Russia lasted exactly two days.

To-day the reactionaries and imperialists, who once fawned on him, have no good word to say of Kerensky. More even than the Bolsheviks, he is made the scapegoat of their short-comings.

In 1923 two young scions of the Russian nobility came to see me in Prague. They were in high spirits. They informed me that they had spent the afternoon reviling Kerensky. They had discovered that he was living in the Hotel Paris in Prague. They had hired the room next to his and had spent the after-noon shouting "dirty dog" and other abuse through the thin partitions. That is typical of the attitude of most Russians to-wards the man whose chief sin was that he had disappointed impossible hopes.

Kerensky was the symbol of a necessary interlude between the Tsarist war and the Bolshevik peace. His failure was inevitable. In the eyes of the Russia which supported him, it would have been a greater failure if he had died at his post.

In June, 1931, he was lunching with me in the Carlton Grill Room in London, when Lord Beaverbrook came over and joined our table. With his keen interest in human psychology he began at once to ply Kerensky with questions.

"What was the reason of your collapse?"

Kerensky's reply was that the Germans forced on the Bolshe-vik rising because Austria, Bulgaria and Turkey were on the verge of making a separate peace with Russia. The Austrians had decided to ask for a separate peace less than a fortnight before the October revolution.

"Would you have mastered the Bolsheviks if you had made a separate peace?" asked Lord Beaverbrook.

"Of course," said Kerensky, "we should be in Moscow now."

"Then why," said Lord Beaverbrook, "didn't you do it?"

"We were too naïve," was the reply.

Naïvety is Kerensky's proper epitaph.

To-day, he is fifty. He looks marvellously well. Since the removal of his tubercular kidney he has never had a day's illness. He lives in Paris and still dreams of the day when Russia will come back to him. He is still an idealist. He lacks, as he has always lacked, the ruthlessness of the successful revolutionary. He has two sons. Both are engineers and both are working in England.

By a strange coincidence Kerensky, Lenin, and Protopopoff (craziest of all the Tsarist ministers) all came from the same Volga town of Simbirsk. Kerensky comes of a family of orthodox priests. His father was a State official and was Lenin's trustee. In spite of this connection Kerensky never met Lenin and only saw him once or twice from a distance.

Other new revolutionary acquaintances with whom I came into contact during this period were Boris Savinkoff, Filonenko, Chernoff, Zenzinoff, Rudnieff, the new Moscow Mayor, Urnoff, the President of the Soldiers' Soviet, Minor, the venerable social-revolutionary editor, Prokopovitch and his wife Ekaterina Kuskova, a remarkable couple, who both in their personal appearance and in their work may be aptly described as the Russian counterpart of Mr. and Mrs. Sidney Webb. Some day, when the story of the Russian revolution fades into the same background of time as the French revolution, their names will figure in the Russian history books. To the foreign reader they are, with the exception of Savinkoff, of no significance.

For some reason, which I have never been able to understand, Boris Savinkoff has always been regarded by Englishmen as a man of action and therefore as a hero. More even than most Russians, Savinkoff was a schemer—a man who could sit up all night drinking brandy and discussing what he was going to do the next day. And, when the morrow came, he left the action to others. His talents cannot be denied. He wrote several excellent novels. He understood the revolutionary temperament better almost than anyone, and knew how to play on it for his own ends. He had mingled so much with spies and agents-provocateurs that, like the hero in his own novel, he hardly knew whether he was deceiving himself or those whom he meant to deceive. Like most Russians, too, he was a forcible speaker who could impress his personality on his listeners. At one time he entirely captivated Mr. Churchill, who saw in him a Russian Bonaparte. There were, however, fatal defects in his character. He liked luxury, and, although he was ambitious, was not prepared to sacrifice his self-indulgence to his ambition. His chief weakness was my own—a fatal capacity for short spells of frenzied work followed by long periods of indolence. Him, too, I saw frequently after the collapse of the Kerensky régime. He came to see me in Moscow in 1918 at a moment when a price was on his head. The danger to himself—and, incidentally, to me—was considerable. His only disguise was a pair of huge horn-rimmed spectacles with darkened glasses. His conversation was mostly recriminations against the Allies and against the Russian counter-revolutionaries, with whom he was supposed to be co-operating. The last time I saw him was in a night-haunt in Prague in 1923. He was a pathetic figure for whom one could not help feeling the deepest sympathy. He had exhausted all his friends, and, when later he returned to Moscow and offered his services to the Bolsheviks, I was not surprised. Doubtless behind that tortured brain there was some grandiose scheme of striking a last blow for Russia and of carrying out a spectacular *coup d'état*. It was a gambler's throw (all his life he had played a lone hand), and, although anti-Bolsheviks maintain that he was murdered—poisoned and thrown out of a window—I have little doubt that he went to his own end.

The period of the Kerensky régime was the most unhappy in my official career. I had lost hope and with it my own balance. I sought relaxations from the stress of over-work in material pleasures. I was restless and uncontrolled. The war, which has branded so many of my generation, had destroyed all the former zest of my life. I longed for the peace of the country and the calm of the cooling fields, and, unable to obtain them, I abandoned myself to the temptations of the town. I was definitely on the down-grade.

As the dangers of the Russian revolution came home to the British ministers at home, strenuous efforts were made to bring the Russians to their senses and to recall them sternly to the obligations of their alliance. Some genius hit on the idea of sending out a Franco-British Socialist delegation to persuade the Russian comrades to continue fighting. And in the middle of April, MM. Moutet, Cachin and Lafont, representing French Socialism, and Messrs. Jim O'Grady, Will Thorne, and W. W. Sanders, as stalwarts of British Labour, arrived in St. Petersburg to preach wisdom and patriotism to the Soviets. The three Frenchmen were intellectuals. Moutet was a lawyer. Cachin and Lafont were professors of philosophy. On the British side Sanders was then secretary of the Fabian Society. To the British public O'Grady and Thorne require no introduction.

From the first the visit was a farce. The delegates fulfilled their task honourably. But, as anyone might have foreseen, they were completely lost in the wilderness of Russian revolutionary phraseology. They were bewildered by the endless discussions on peace terms. They understood the jargon of the Russian Socialists far less than I did. They were handicapped by their ignorance of the language. Worst of all, they never succeeded in winning the confidence even of the moderate Socialists, who from the first regarded them as lackeys of their respective governments.

If the effect on the Russians was less than nothing, the reaction of the delegates themselves to the revolution was amusing. O'Grady and Thorne—especially Thorne—were splendid. Never shall I forget that luncheon at the Embassy, when this honest giant regaled us with stories of his adventures. He had all the Englishman's contempt for verbiage, and the babel of foreign tongues had disgusted him. He longed to use his strong arms and to knock the heads of the garrulous comrades together.

The Allied delegates came to Moscow. They visited the front. They delivered—through the aid of their interpreter—innumerable patriotic speeches, and in the end they went away, sadder and wiser men. The sequel to this visit is amusing. O'Grady has become Sir James O'Grady and a Colonial Governor. Will Thorne is to-day the Labour doyen of the House of Commons and remains what he has always been—a Trades Union leader. Mr. Sanders was a member of the 1929 Labour Administration. He, too, is the mildest of pinks. Of the Frenchmen Lafont has passed through and out of Communism. Moutet is still a moderate Socialist. And Cachin—the most perfervid patriot of the six, the man, who, with tears of emotion in his eyes, implored the Soviets not to go out of the war until the triumph of the Allies was complete—has given himself body and soul to Moscow and to-day holds the fort of Bolshevism in France.

Events now began to move rapidly. A few days after the arrival of the Franco-British Labour delegation, and almost simultaneously with the return to Russia of Lenin, came M. Albert Thomas, the French Socialist Minister of Munitions. He, too, had been sent out by a French Government, claiming by its traditions to possess a special knowledge of revolutions and anxious to secure the co-operation of revolutionary Russia with the Allied cause. Thomas, whose Socialism was a shade less pink than the Conservatism of Mr. Baldwin, was accompanied by a host of secretaries and officers. Moreover, he carried in his pocket the recall of M. Paléologue, the French Ambassador and a cynic who never struck me as really serious, but who understood Russia much better than most people suspected. The recall was part of the new policy.

I saw a certain amount of Thomas—a jovial, bearded man with a sense of humour and a healthy, bourgeois appetite. He made friends with Sir George Buchanan. He stimulated the war loyalty of Kerensky. He visited the front and harangued the troops with patriotic speeches well larded with revolutionary sentiment. And he argued with the Soviet. One service, which seemed important at the time, he rendered to the Allies. The Soviets, at this moment, were engaged in abstract discussions about peace terms. They had invented the formula of "peace without annexations and contributions," and this phrase, adopted at thousands of meetings in the trenches and in the villages, had spread like wildfire throughout the country. It was a formula which caused considerable annoyance and even anxiety to the English and French Governments, which had already divided up the spoils of a victory not yet won, in the form of both annexations and contributions. And both the French Ambassador and Sir George Buchanan had been requested to circumvent this new and highly dangerous form of pacifism. Their task was delicate and difficult. There seemed no way out of the impasse, and in despair they sought the advice of Thomas. The genial Socialist laughed.

"I know my Socialists," he said. "They will shed their blood for a formula. You must accept it and alter its interpretation."

So annexations became restitution and contributions reparations. It was, I imagine, the first time the word reparations was used officially, and Thomas certainly succeeded in persuading the Soviets to accept a clause in their formula for the restitution of Alsace-Lorraine. At the time it seemed an important achievement. Actually, as the Mensheviks and Social-Revolutionaries, who had yielded to the Thomas subtlety, were so soon to be swept away, it made no difference whatsoever.

M. Thomas was the most entertaining of the French and English Socialists who visited Russia during this period of the first revolution. He spoke well. He was adaptable. And he had courage. But the results were insignificant. His speeches were no more effective than those of our military attachés, Colonel Knox and Colonel Thornhill, who with more sincerity besought the Russian soldier not to abandon his allies, who were fighting his battle on the other side of Europe. To the Bolsheviks he was of course a renegade, a Socialist traitor, who had sold himself to the bourgeoisie, and as such he was denounced in all the highways and byways of the revolution.

The position of the Allied Missions in Russia was, in fact, rapidly becoming impossible. Everyone was engaged in trying to persuade the Russian to continue fighting when he had just overthrown a régime because it refused to give him peace. A little plain thinking should have made anyone see that in these circumstances the success of the Bolsheviks was merely a question of time.

Hot on the heels of M. Thomas came Mr. Arthur Henderson, despatched on a similar mission of fraternal goodwill by Mr. Lloyd George. Mr. Henderson, too, carried a letter of recall in his pocket. To be strictly accurate, the letter of recall was not actually included in the Henderson baggage-train. What had happened was this: When the British Labour Minister— and Mr. Henderson was the first Labour representative in the history of England to achieve Cabinet rank—was actually on his way to St. Petersburg, the Foreign Office sent a telegram to Sir George Buchanan extolling his work and suggesting that he should take a rest. In other words, he was to be recalled and his post given to Mr. Henderson.

On deciphering the telegram and without consulting the Ambassador, "Benji" Bruce, head of the Chancery, rushed off to see Sazonoff, ascertained from him that Tereschenko, the Foreign Minister of the Provisional Government, would be very sorry to see Sir George Buchanan replaced, and then went back to the Embassy and sent off a long private telegram in cipher to George Clerk at the Foreign Office, saying that Henderson's appointment would be a disaster.

As it turned out, this bold initiative on the part of a subordinate proved to be unnecessary. Mr. Henderson has been described by one of his Labour colleagues as the greatest Foreign Secretary England has ever had. True it is that Dr. Dalton, the colleague who made this remarkable statement, was Mr. Henderson's trusted lieutenant and assistant during his conduct of the foreign affairs of Great Britain and that, in praising his chief, he is casting reflected glory on himself. Nevertheless, on the occasion of his Russian visit, Mr. Henderson certainly showed an admirable discretion. Accompanied by

George Young, he took up his quarters at the Europe—the same hotel which had provided such luxurious shelter for Lord Milner, George Clerk, Sir Henry Wilson, and numerous other distinguished visitors to Russia. There, at the Ambassador's request, I came to see him. I dined with him in his private room. Throughout one long summer evening I walked with him down the Nevsky, across the Winter Square, past the Palace Quay. Beneath the gold reflection of the Admiralty Arch I heard the whole legend of the Hendersonian career. I accompanied him to Moscow. I took him to a full-dress meeting of the Moscow Soviet. And in the inner chamber of his Moscow hotel I arranged for him a private conversation (with myself as interpreter) with Urnoff, the then all-powerful President of the Soldiers' Soviet.

Mr. Henderson has the reputation—doubtless well deserved —of being a first-class organiser. He is a great man at Party meetings, which he succeeds in dominating by concealing his own intentions to the last moment. He is a man who is slow to commit himself. He does not give himself away.

On this occasion, however, I looked into Mr. Henderson's soul. His geography was a little weak. He was not quite sure where he was, but he was speedily convinced that the locality was unhealthy. The comrades in the Soviets bewildered him. He did not understand their language. He did not like their manners. Doubtless he would have liked to be the first Labour Ambassador. But after all, a Cabinet Minister is a more powerful person than the greatest of modern Ambassadors. Moreover, Sir George Buchanan was not the failure he had been painted. Sir George, as Mr. Henderson soon discovered, understood the wild men much better than did Mr. Henderson himself. Further, Sir George had been kind, and Mr. Henderson is susceptible to kindness and to flattery. The great sacrifice was therefore easily made. Mr. Henderson explained that, while the Embassy was his for the asking, he had come to the conclusion that no good purpose would be served by the removal of a man who understood Russia far better than he did and who had shown himself remarkably free from all party bias. Sir George was not even opposed to the Stockholm Conference, and Mr. Henderson, whose undoubted patriotism was tempered by the common-sense of internationalism, saw a glimmer of hope in the Stockholm meeting. So, shaking the dust of St. Petersburg off his feet, he returned to London to make the great renunciation and to recommend that Sir George Buchanan be retained as His Britannic Majesty's Ambassador and Envoy Extraordinary to the Revolutionary Government of Russia. On his return he had his historic wait on Mr. Lloyd George's doormat—a wait which ended with his resignation. In this manner he lost both his Embassy and his place in the Cabinet. It was a bitter reward for a mission which had been honestly if somewhat timorously fulfilled, and which, whatever its effect on the Russians, had the advantage of curing Mr. Henderson of any revolutionary tendencies for the rest of his life. As for the Stockholm Conference, the advocacy of which had caused Mr. Henderson's downfall, the proposal had the support of several British diplomatists, including Sir Esmé Howard, and, in turning it down, Mr. Lloyd George, who had blown hot and then cold on the idea, probably made a great mistake. At Stockholm we should have had everything to gain and almost nothing to risk.

During that disastrous summer of 1917 I had one novel experience which I must chronicle, if only for the serio-comic light it throws on the Russian character. As part of our propaganda baggage-train we had a travelling film mission, of which the able chief was Colonel Bromhead, the subsequent chairman of the British Gaumont. He, too, was enlisted to coax the Russians into fighting by showing them war films of the fighting on the Western front. The effect of these war pictures on the mind of the now undisciplined Russian army can be imagined. Not unnaturally, they served merely to increase the number of deserters.

It was not Bromhead's fault. He was a splendid fellow, who realised the futility of showing war pictures to men whose sole thought was peace. Still, he had his duty to do. Films were part of the Whitehall scheme for the regeneration of Russia, and shown they had to be.

To Moscow, then, came Bromhead for a monster demonstration of the British effort. Would I help to make his show a success? Could I enlist the services of patriotic speakers? Nothing seemed easier. Moscow, alas! had more orators than fighters.

We secured a theatre. We arranged a programme. And then the Soldiers' Soviet, infinitely more powerful than the Provisional Government, intervened. The show was for the Moscow troops. The soldiers might see the films. They were not to be exposed to the harangues of Imperialist jingoes. There must be no speeches.

In vain I went to see the Presidium of the Soldiers' Soviet. In vain I argued the merits of free speech. The utmost concession I could wring from them was that Lockhart himself— Lockhart who sympathised with the revolution and knew the views of revolutionary Russia regarding the peace terms— might speak. But there were to be no other orators. On these conditions the Presidium would guarantee the success of the show. They would be present in full force to see that the conditions were carried out.

Bromhead accepted the situation with unfeigned delight. My own consent was given with reluctance. An after-dinner speech before an audience rendered innocuous by good food and champagne was one thing. I saw nothing attractive in addressing twelve hundred sceptical and severely critical revolutionaries in their own language.

I took pains over that speech. I wrote it out very carefully in English and had it translated into mellifluous Russian by a Russian poet. I learnt it off by heart. Indeed, I made myself something more than word perfect. I rehearsed my effects even down to the place where my voice was to break. Not in vain had I gone the rounds with Kerensky.

My appeal was frankly sentimental. There is no other reason I know that will compel large bodies of men to fight. But my sentiment was Russian. I made no reference to the crime of deserting their Western Allies. I discussed quite frankly

Russia's desire and even need of a separate peace, and then I drew a picture of a better world created by the glorious revolution. But neither the better world nor the revolution itself could stand, if discipline was to be thrown to the winds and the road to Moscow opened to the enemy. Lenin would have demolished the argument with one sentence. But Lenin, fortunately, was still in hiding in St. Petersburg.

On the day of the ordeal I made my way to the theatre, secretly hoping that I might have no audience to address. But the Soldiers' Council had kept its word. The house was packed. Moreover, seated beside the Presidium in the balcony were the Assistant Minister of Marine and Kishkin, the High Commissar for Moscow. Our films were of two kinds: naval and military. Very wisely we showed the naval films last. They were impressive and free from all horrors. My speech came at the end. There was no applause when I stood up on the narrow stage before the curtain, and I began nervously. The silence, however, was respectful. I was to be given a hearing. I forgot all the tricks I had practised. I almost forgot my words. I spoke with a quivering anguish in my voice which the Russians mistook for genuine emotion. For twenty minutes I strove to master my nervousness, my voice now raucous, now breaking queerly at the oddest moments. To the end I was listened to in deathly silence. When I had finished my peroration, my knees shook and the sweat streamed like tears down my face.

Then pandemonium broke loose. A soldier jumped on to the stage and kissed me on both cheeks. In the box of the Presidium Kishkin stood up, and in stentorian tones declared that Russia would never desert her Allies. That afternoon he had received official news that the Russian Fleet had sailed out into the Baltic in full fighting trim. More cheers. More pandemonium. In every corner of the house soldiers were standing up and clamouring to be heard. The scene was almost like the opening of the war. I had unloosed the strings of Russian hysteria. It was a short-lived triumph. The next day the account of the meeting was severely censored. The Socialists had repented of their emotion.

This was my last public appearance as Acting Consul-General in Moscow. Just as the old Russia was advancing inevitably to her final tragedy, so, too, there was a minor tragedy in my own life. I relate it frankly and without excuses. Some months before I had formed an attachment to a Russian Jewess—whom I had met casually at the theatre. I had made myself talked about.

The matter came finally to the ears of the Ambassador. He sent for me, and we went for a walk together. No man could have been kinder. No man could have made a more successful appeal to my better nature. He told me the story of his own life. When he was young, he had undergone a similar temptation. Real happiness consisted in resisting temptations which one was bound to regret later. He referred to the good work I was doing. It was a pity to wreck what might be a wonderful career for what was merely a passing infatuation due to war strain. Convention might be the first cousin to hypocrisy, but in government service it had to be observed. Besides, there was the question of duty and of the war. I should put my country before my self-indulgence.

I was deeply moved. We shook hands emotionally—my emotion being due to genuine affection for this splendid old man, who had treated me with so much understanding, and his, I believe, to an equally genuine regret for his lost youth—and I returned to Moscow, having pledged myself to make the grand renunciation. I made it, and it lasted exactly three weeks. Then one day the telephone rang, and I went back.

This was the end. I had broken my word, and this time the Ambassador sorrowfully but firmly decided that I was on the verge of a nervous breakdown and that I must go home to England for a rest. Perhaps he was right.

There was no scandal. I do not suppose that even the Private Secretary at the Foreign Office was informed of the real reasons for my sudden return. It was said that I had broken down from overwork, and in this manner I received much sympathy. For the same reason I was able to avoid all the publicity of an official farewell. My friends in Moscow were kindness itself.

They were told I was ill and not to be worried. They all expected me to be back within six weeks, and in any case the approaching collapse of Russia was now so apparent that everyone was fully occupied with the salvage of his own affairs. To such of the public as thought about me I was a martyr to duty. But, knowing that my enforced sick leave was really a recall and that I should never come back, I felt my position keenly, and it was as a culprit rather than as a martyr that I slunk out of Moscow in those early days of September, 1917. I left St. Petersburg just as the Kerensky-Korniloff duel was starting. I arrived in London six weeks before the Bolshevik revolution.

BOOK IV

"HISTORY FROM THE INSIDE"

"HISTORY IS generally only the register of the crimes, the follies, and the mistakes of mankind."

Gibbon

CHAPTER ONE

OF THAT VOYAGE home to England I remember very little. I had to travel via Finland and Scandinavia and was seeing Stockholm for the first time. On this occasion it made no impression on me. I do not remember where we stayed. As far as I can recollect, I avoided our Legation. I kept no diary during this period. My mental anguish was extreme, and I wanted to forget.

All that remains in my mind is the memory of the railway journey from Christiania to Bergen. The scenery, wilder, more picturesque than the Canadian Rockies, provided the proper background for my own melancholy. The wild stretches of moor, the lofty peaks and tortuous ravines, the lochs and turbulent trout-streams, above all, the firs and the birches, their leaves golden with the first tints of autumn, reminded me of Scotland. At Bergen I met Wardrop, who was to take my place in Moscow. He was an elderly, scholarly man, and the personification of caution. Obviously, the Foreign Office were taking no more chances with youth. Mechanically I gave him the information he required about Moscow. I cannot say I enjoyed the interview. I could not bear the thought of having to talk about Russia. All I wanted was to go to my own country and fish.

I assume that I made the dreary journey—exciting only because of the danger from submarines—from Bergen to Aberdeen and that I crossed in the *Vulture*. In a court of law I could not swear either to the 1 ame of the ship or to the port of landing. I know that I arrived in London on the morning of the day on which Korniloff's troops were marching on St. Petersburg. I went straight to the Foreign Office to report myself. I was received with the greatest kindness. I was a man who had accomplished great things at the expense of his health. I was to take a long rest and not to think about the war or work or Russia until I had made a complete recovery. With disgust in my heart I accepted the rôle which had been forced on me, and that same day I made arrangements to go to the Highlands to stay with my uncle. Before I left I had one more ordeal to face. Within a few hours of my arrival in London the *Daily Mail* succeeded in tracking me down. They wanted information about the outcome of the Kerensky-Korniloff clash. Opinion in London favoured Korniloff's chances. I held definite views regarding the inevitability of Korniloff's failure. Would I write an article? It would have to be done at once. The *Mail* would pay handsomely for it.

There and then, with the sacrifice of my dinner, I scribbled out the article with the *Mail's* representative looking over my shoulder. I threw in some new photographs of Kerensky and Savinkoff and I received a cheque for twenty-five guineas. I showed my customary lack of business instinct. I sold my article for probably less than half the sum a more astute journalist might have received. On the other hand, the article had to be anonymous (as a Government servant I could not use my name), and the cheque paid for my return fare to Scotland. It was my first experience of frenzied journalism.

The ways of Providence are not only incalculable. They are on occasions highly diverting. Greatly refreshed in mind and body, I returned from Scotland to London fourteen days after the Bolshevik revolution. I was to start work again. I had been temporarily attached to Sir Arthur Steel-Maitland as his Russian expert in the new Department of Overseas Trade. I owe much to Sir Arthur. He overwhelmed me with kindness and insisted on my staying with him at his house in Cadogan Square. What was more important, he plunged me again into the very heart of Russian affairs. The Bolshevik *coup d'état* had completely nullified the value of my services to the Department of Overseas Trade. Sir Arthur helped me or rather pushed me into finding a new outlet for my activities.

During a hectic period of three weeks I lunched and dined with the politicians. Russia, of course, was the one topic of conversation, and in the prevailing ignorance I regained my self-confidence. I had long foreseen the inevitability of the Bolshevik revolution. I could not share the general belief, stimulated by the opinion of nearly all the Russian experts in

London, that the Lenin régime could not last more than a few weeks and that then Russia would revert to Tsarism or a military dictatorship. Still less could I believe that the Russian peasant would return to the trenches. Russia was out of the war. Bolshevism would last—certainly as long as the war lasted. I deprecated as sheer folly our militarist propaganda, because it took no account of the war-weariness which had raised the Bolsheviks to the supreme power. In my opinion, we had to take the Bolshevik peace proposals seriously. Our policy should now aim at achieving an anti-German peace in Russia.

Rather futilely I sought to combat the firmly-rooted conviction that Lenin and Trotsky were German staff officers in disguise or at least servile agents of German policy. I was more successful when I argued that it was madness not to establish some contact with the men who at that moment were controlling Russia's destinies.

The reactions to my pleading were varied. At that moment the general atmosphere in political circles was pessimistic. I think that in their hearts the Cabinet realised that Russia was out of the war for good, but with an obstinate lack of logic they refused to accept the implications of their secret beliefs. Hate of the revolution and fear of its consequences in England were the dominant reactions of Conservatives, who at that moment had an unnatural and to-day inexplicable dread of the machinations of Mr. Arthur Henderson. I found the same fears among the Labour patriots. At Cadogan Square I renewed my acquaintance with Jim O'Grady and Will Thorne. They, too, were critical of Mr. Henderson, who, they said, had gone over to the Snowdenites and was playing for revolution and the Labour Premiership. I saw Mr. Henderson himself at 1, Victoria Place. I found the same man as I had met in Russia seven months before. He was as God-fearing, as conventionally Methodist, as petit-bourgeois, and as scared of revolution as he always has been and always will be. He talked to me very frankly about his own position. He was bitter about his treatment by Lloyd George which, he said, had only strengthened his own standing in Labour circles. His views on the Russian situation were not very different from my own. He was entirely in favour of establishing contact with the Bolsheviks. He went further. He was in favour of a Conference—a form of negotiation which would have been infinitely more dangerous than the original proposal of the Stockholm Conference. In those days, however, Mr. Henderson, like Mr. Lloyd George, was convinced that he had only to meet Lenin face to face in order to vanquish him in the ensuing battle of wits.

During these three weeks from November 27th to December 18th, 1917, I must have met scores of politicians and experts. The endless conversations seemed to lead no further. One lesson that period should have taught me: that the man in London has a thousand advantages over the man on the spot. Then I was too young to profit by it. During the next year I was to acquire it by the bitter experience of being myself the man on the spot.

One exciting adventure I had at this time. On December 18th I was to dine at Cadogan Square to meet Bonar Law. It was a night of fog, and to the inconvenience of the fog was added the unpleasantness of an air raid. I dressed to the accompaniment of gun-fire and the crash of bombs. To the same discords I forced my way through the huddled crowds in the Piccadilly tube station, and after long delays and some trepidation I reached Sir Arthur Steel-Maitland's house an hour late. The table was set for eight people. Sir Arthur was in his day-clothes. There was no Bonar Law. I was the only guest who had succeeded in reaching his destination.

The next day, however, the weeks of talk were translated into action. Sir Arthur gave another dinner party. This time there were only two guests in addition to myself: H. W. C. Davis, the Oxford historian, and Lord Milner. We talked until late in the night, and I repeated all my arguments about the necessity of establishing contact. Lord Milner was very sympathetic. When he went away, he told me that I should hear from him very soon. The next morning I was summoned to Downing Street. I met Lord Carson and Lord

Curzon, both of whom referred very flatteringly to my work, and we had a long discussion on Russia. That same afternoon we had another meeting at the War Cabinet offices in White- hall Gardens. Several Russian experts were present, including Rex Leeper and Colonel Byrne. The Ministers who listened to our words of wisdom were General Smuts, Lord Carson, and Lord Milner. The discussions were rather futile. Lord Milner was the only Minister who seemed to have even an elementary knowledge of Russian geography, and Lord Carson nearly upset my unnatural solemnity by asking me seriously if I could explain to him the difference between a Maximalist and a Bolshevik. At the end of the meeting Lord Milner told me that the Cabinet approved in principle the necessity of establishing contact with the Bolsheviks, but that they were unable to find the right man for the task.

On the morning of December 21st I was again summoned to 10 Downing Street. I was kept waiting about ten minutes. Then I was ushered into a long, narrow room which seemed to me all table. A Cabinet meeting had just ended. Mr. Lloyd George, his pince-nez in his hand, was standing by the window, talking and gesticulating to Lord Curzon. My sponsor, Lord Milner, was not present, and for what seemed an eternity I stood waiting. Then Lord Milner came in, rescued me and took me up to Mr. Lloyd George.

"Mr. Lockhart?" he said. He shook hands and stepped back in order to scrutinise me more carefully. "*The* Mr. Lockhart?" I looked foolish. Then, having made me the centre of attraction, he continued very slowly, so that everyone could hear: "From the wisdom of your reports I expected to see an elderly gentle- man with a grey beard." He patted me on the back, asked me my age, muttered something about youth and Pitt being Prime Minister at twenty-four, and we sat down to business. Another meeting was started, this time with Mr. Lloyd George presiding. My diary tells me that at the time I thought he looked tired and old. He was, however, remarkably active and adroit in his handling of the meeting. He asked me a few questions about Lenin and Trotsky. A fresh question followed almost before I had time to answer the previous one. I saw that his own mind was made up. He had been greatly impressed, as Lord Milner told me afterwards, by an interview with Colonel Thompson of the American Red Cross, who had just returned from Russia and who had denounced in blunt language the folly of the Allies in not opening up negotiations with the Bolsheviks. The questions ended, Mr. Lloyd George stood up, referred briefly to the chaotic conditions in Russia and to the necessity of getting into touch with Lenin and Trotsky, emphasised the need for tact, knowledge and understanding, and finished up by stating that Mr. Lockhart was obviously a man whose right place at that moment was in St. Petersburg and not in London. I was then told I could go.

That afternoon I had another meeting with Lord Milner and Lord Carson. This time Viscount Cecil (then Lord Robert Cecil) was present, and I had a very difficult quarter of an hour. Lord Robert was then Under-Secretary for Foreign Affairs. He was supremely sceptical of the usefulness of establishing any kind of relations with the Bolsheviks, and, as a sidelight on his subsequent development as an internationalist, it is worth putting on record that the man, who since the war has sat so often round the same table in Geneva as Litvinoff and Lunacharsky, was at that time the most convinced of all responsible English statesmen that Lenin and Trotsky were paid agents of Germany, working deliberately for German ends, with no policy and no ambitions of their own. I was still in the dark regarding my fate.

That night Lord Milner and Lord Robert left for Paris, and I went home to spend Christmas with my father and mother, having been told to leave my telephone number and to hold myself in readiness in case I might be required to go on my travels again.

On New Year's Day I was back at the offices of the War Cabinet. A scheme was being evolved. It was certain that I was to return to Russia almost at once. In what capacity I was not told.

Three days later all my doubts were put at rest. I was to

go to Russia as head of a special mission to establish unofficial relations with the Bolsheviks. Sir George Buchanan was returning home. I was to leave on the cruiser which was to fetch him from Bergen. My instructions were of the vaguest. I was to have the responsibility of establishing relations. I was to have no authority. If the Bolsheviks would give me the necessary diplomatic privileges without being recognised by the British Government, we would make a similar concession to Litvinoff, whom the Bolsheviks had already appointed Soviet Ambassador in London.

The situation bristled with difficulties, but I accepted it without hesitation. The first essential was to acquire a suitable introduction to Lenin and Trotsky and to establish a *modus vivendi* with Litvinoff. Thanks to Rex Leeper, both tasks succeeded beyond my expectations. Leeper was on friendly terms with Rothstein, subsequently Bolshevik Minister in Teheran and then an official translator in our own War Office. I had a long talk with Rothstein, the substance of which I carefully noted in my diary. Rothstein, who had lived for years in England, was an intellectual arm-chair revolutionary. He said Trotsky's ambition was not a separate peace but a general peace. He pointed out that if he were Lloyd George he would accept Trotsky's offer of a conference unconditionally. England would be the chief beneficiary. The Russian stipulations about self-determination would fall through with an ineffective protest from Trotsky, and England and Germany could arrange the colonial questions between them. Germany would agree to almost all other terms—that is, no annexations and no contributions. She might even be prepared to compromise on the Alsace-Lorraine question. In any case, it was absurd for England to prolong the war for the sake of Alsace-Lorraine. There was nothing easier to destroy than sentimental causes which are not rooted in a people itself, and we should have to consider very seriously whether we should get a better peace nine months hence.

At the time such proposals would have been regarded as treason. To-day, to a world which is groaning under the burden of the Peace Treaties, they do not seem so unreasonable. (Incidentally, it is interesting to note that Rothstein was only six weeks out in his prediction of the end of the war.)

I avoided any discussions of a general peace, brought the subject back to Russia herself, and elaborated my proposals for opening up negotiations with his friends. I expressed a genuine sympathy with Russia's desire for peace, pointing out that she might have great difficulty in concluding a separate peace with Germany and that even unofficial contact between the English and Russian Governments would be as useful to the Bolsheviks as to us.

We parted on good terms, Rothstein promising to use his influence with Litvinoff to provide me with the necessary recommendation to Trotsky. A few days later the whole affair was arranged over the luncheon table at a Lyons' shop in the Strand. The two contracting parties were represented by Litvinoff and Rothstein on the Russian side and Leeper and myself on the English side. There was to be no recognition— at any rate for the present. Unofficially, both Litvinoff and I were to have certain diplomatic privileges, including the use of ciphers and the right to a diplomatic courier.

It was an amazing meal. Outside, the January sky was like lead and the room, poorly lit at the best of times, was grey and sombre. Leeper and I were just thirty. Litvinoff was eleven years our senior. Rothstein was a year or two older than Litvinoff. Both men were Jews. Both had suffered persecution and imprisonment for their political convictions. Yet Litvinoff, whose real name was Wallach, was married to an English-woman. Rothstein had a son—a British subject—in the British Army.

The success of that luncheon was made by Rothstein, who supplied to the conversation the necessary mixture of banter and seriousness which afterwards I was to find so useful in my negotiations with the Bolsheviks in Russia. Small, bearded, with dark lively eyes, he was a kind of intellectual cricket, whose dialectical jumps were as bewildering to us as they were amusing to himself. There was certainly nothing bloodthirsty in his revolutionary make-up. If the British Government had only left him in peace, I believe he would be living quietly in England to this day. Litvinoff, heavily built, with broad forehead, was more sluggish and slower witted. My impression of him was not unfavourable. In so far as a Bolshevik can be said to differentiate in his degrees of hate of bourgeois institutions, he certainly regarded German militarism as a greater danger than English capitalism.

After a nervous beginning the course of our negotiations ran smoothly, and there and then, on the rough linen of a standard Lyons' table, Litvinoff wrote out my letter of recommendation to Trotsky. I give it herewith in Rothstein's translation:

Citizen Trotsky,
    People's Commissary for Foreign Affairs.

DEAR COMRADE,—

The bearer of this, Mr. Lockhart, is going to Russia with an official mission with the exact character of which I am not acquainted. I know him personally as a thoroughly honest man who understands our position and sympathises with us. I should consider his sojourn in Russia useful from the point of view of our interests.

My position here remains indefinite. I learnt of my appointment only from the newspapers. I hope a courier is bringing me the necessary documents without which the difficulties of my position are greatly increased. The Embassy, Consulate, and Russian Government Committee have not yet surrendered. Their relations to me will be determined by the relations of the British Government.

I wrote the other day to the Ministry for Foreign Affairs, asking for a meeting in order to regulate certain practical questions (the viséing of passports, use of ciphers, military convention, etc.), but have not received any reply. I presume the question of my recognition will not be settled until the arrival of Buchanan.

The reception accorded me by the Press is quite satisfactory. I am making the acquaintance of the representatives of the Labour movement. I have issued an appeal to the English working-men in all the Socialist papers. Even the bourgeois Press readily accords me its pages to explain our position.

I shall write more fully by the first courier. I have not received an answer from you to my telegram of January 4th, new style, No. 1. I request you very much to confirm the receipt of all telegrams and to number your telegrams.

The ciphers will, I trust, be delivered to me by the courier. Greetings to Lenin and all friends. I press your hand warmly.

Yours (signed) M. Litvinoff.

Rothstein begs me to greet you.

London, January 11th (new style), 1918.

The luncheon closed on a humorous note. As we were ordering a sweet, Litvinoff noticed on the menu the magic words: "pouding diplomate." The idea appealed to him. The new diplomatist would eat the diplomatic pudding. The Lyons "Nippy" took his order and returned a minute later to say there was no more. Litvinoff shrugged his shoulders and smiled blandly. "Not recognised even by Lyons," he said.

My last days in England were not solely occupied by Litvinoff and Rothstein. There was the personnel of my mission to engage. I was given almost a free hand. As my chief assistant I wanted Rex Leeper, whose knowledge of Bolshevism would have been invaluable. Almost at the last moment, however, he decided to remain at home, where he thought he could serve a more useful purpose by maintaining contact with Litvinoff, and by interpreting the peculiar mentality of the Bolsheviks to the mandarins in Whitehall. Subsequent events were to prove the wisdom of his action. Although at the time I regretted his decision, I was to be grateful later for his presence in England, when I ran my neck into the noose in Moscow. As a substitute for Leeper I took Captain Hicks, who had recently returned from Russia, where he had done useful work as a poison gas expert. A man of great personal charm, he was popular with Russians and understood their mentality. He was, too, a good linguist with a first-class knowledge of German and a working acquaintance with Russian. His views on the situation were in tune with my own. I never regretted my decision. He was a most loyal colleague and devoted friend. As my commercial expert I took with me Edward Birse, a Moscow business man, who had talked Russian from his cradle. Edward Phelan, a brilliant young official of the Ministry of Labour and to-day a prominent figure in the International Labour Office in Geneva, made up the full complement of my mission. As I was taking ciphers with me, I was also recommended to engage the services of a reliable orderly. This necessitated a letter from the War Cabinet and an interview with General Macready, the Adjutant-General. The interview was invigorating. General Macready had views on Russia. Standing before the fire-place of his room in the War Office, he delivered them in a series of snorts. An orderly for Russia! What the devil was the use of taking soldiers to Russia! Did the boys in the Foreign Office never read history? Couldn't they realise that when an army of ten millions had once broken it could not be reformed inside a generation? All military propaganda in Russia was useless and a sheer waste of money and man-power.

The General's views were eminently sensible. They would have saved unnecessary bloodshed and millions of money, if they had prevailed in Whitehall during 1918. I agreed with them and between the snorts endeavoured to tell him so. I explained to him that my mission was diplomatic and not military and that my object was to establish contact with the men who at that moment were negotiating a separate peace with Germany. I obtained my orderly—a six-foot-two ex-Irish guardsman, who was drunk when he joined me at the station, slept himself sober during the journey to Edinburgh, drank himself drunk again the next morning, offered to fight me for half a crown in Princes Street, and lost himself on the way to Queensferry. We never saw him again.

I had, too, a long round of interviews with the various

officials at the Foreign Office: Lord Hardinge, Eric Drummond, George Clerk, Don Gregory, John Buchan, Ronnie Campbell and Lord Robert Cecil—the last-named still supremely sceptical and still convinced that Trotsky was a German in disguise. During these first eleven days of January I derived a minor thrill from the English Press. My mission was vested with a certain amount of secrecy. There had been, however, the usual leakage. There were paragraphs, facetious or flattering according to the views of the particular newspaper, about the young man from Moscow. One evening paper excelled itself by declaring that I had been appointed Ambassador to Russia, that the choice had lain between Mr. Arthur Henderson and myself, and that my knowledge of Russia had turned the scales in my favour.

Lord Milner I saw almost daily. Five days before my departure I dined alone with him at Brooks's. He was in his most inspiring mood. He talked to me with a charming frankness about the war, about the future of England, about his own career, and about the opportunities of youth. He was bitter about the Foreign Office, called Mr. Balfour a harmless old gentleman, and castigated other prominent permanent officials who are still living. Before he died, he said, he would like to have six months at the Foreign Office. He would begin with a broom—no, he would start with a fire. He would have liked to see Lord Robert Cecil as Foreign Secretary, with Sir Eyre Crowe as his assistant.

About the war he was inclined to be pessimistic. As he gave me my final instructions about my mission, he pointed out the gravity of the situation. If the submarine menace were not speedily averted, a decision could not be long delayed. He envisaged the possibility and even the probability of a peace by negotiation. As far as Russia was concerned, things were so bad that it did not matter very much what I did. My main task must be to do as much harm to the Germans as possible, to put a spoke in the wheels of the separate peace negotiations, and to stiffen by whatever means I could the Bolshevik resistance to German demands. All the information I could obtain as to the real nature and strength of the Bolshevik movement would be extremely valuable. If I was in any difficulty, I was to telegraph to him direct.

I find it hard to write of Lord Milner in anything but super-latives. He never shone in the market-place of politics. He had none of the tricks of the politician. Certainly, he was no orator as Mr. Lloyd George is. But in a Cabinet, most of whose members were profoundly ignorant of everything outside England, his wide range of knowledge, his capacity for real work, and his comprehensive grasp of administrative detail made him invaluable. To Mr. Lloyd George he was the indispensable collaborator, who could be relied upon to read every paper, to sift every scheme, and to form an unbiased and detached view of every problem that was put before him. His nobleness of mind, his entirely natural charm of manner, his lofty idealism, the complete absence of ambitious scheming or of anything approaching self-conceit in his character, and his broad and vigorous patriotism made him the ideal inspirer of youth. With young men, too, he was at his best. He liked to surround himself with them. He believed they should be given their chance. For to the end of his life this man, so gentle and under-standing in manner and so tenacious in purpose, was deeply concerned with the future of England. He was, too, very far from being the Jingo and the Conservative reactionary whom popular opinion at one time represented him to be. On the contrary, many of his views on society were startlingly modern. He believed in the highly organised state, in which service, efficiency, and hard work were more important than titles or money-bags. He had little respect for the aristocrat, who was effete, and none at all for the financier, who had made his money not by production but by manipulation of the market.

I must have been one of the last of the young men to worship at his feet, and there I have remained. I see no Milners in our public life at present—men who are prepared to serve the State disinterestedly and with no other ambition than to serve it well, and to this day, far more than the politicians or the millionaires, he stands out as an example to the country of the ideal public servant. In the life of every nation it is character which counts in the end, and among all the so-called great men of the world whom I have met there has been none who in this respect is fit to hold a candle to Lord Milner. My own conduct must have tried him highly. He had arranged my Russian mission, not because he had anything but a profound abhorrence of Bolshevism, but because he believed that I understood the Russian situation better than most Englishmen. He was probably disappointed when I seemed to go over body and soul to the Bolsheviks. He may have regarded my subsequent failure in Russia as a reflection on his judgment. But his attitude to me underwent no change. He was as kind to me when I returned as when I set out. I dined alone again at Brooks's with him on several occasions. I was a frequent visitor at his house in Little College Street. When I went abroad again, I kept in touch with him. He took an interest in my career, and it was on his advice (taken, unfortunately, too late) that I left the Foreign Office.

In one respect Lord Milner's promotion of my interests was detrimental to my prospects. I had been selected for this Russian mission not by the Foreign Secretary but by the War Cabinet—actually, by Lord Milner and Mr. Lloyd George. The decision had been taken over the heads of the permanent officials, who chafed under the Lloyd George method of handling affairs and who resented having stray missions, headed by a junior Vice-Consul, foisted upon them.

I should have realised this at the time—indeed, I received a broad hint from Lord Robert Cecil—and with a proper humility should have placated the higher permanent officials. The Cecils and the Milners would depart with the end of the war. The Hardinges and the Tyrrells or their equivalents would remain. I did see Lord Hardinge, before I left, and was, I hope, properly humble. But I confess that I gave this aspect of my new position little thought. Adventure tugs at the heart-strings of youth. I had been given the opportunity for a great adventure, and my one thought was to start on it at once. During the month which had just passed I had seen and met, and even been listened to, by the men who were in the very heart of affairs in London. I had been selected from among God knows what weird choice of candidates for a difficult and exciting mission. I had had a colossal stroke of luck. If my head had not been turned a little—and I do not think it was—there were sure to be kind friends who would say that it had been.

My departure was in the grand manner. With Litvinoff's letter in my pocket and Lord Milner's blessing on my head, I travelled up to Edinburgh on January 12th and stayed the night with my grandmother, who cried affectionately over me. The next day, accompanied by the other members of my mission and by my wife, who had come to see us off, I made my way to Queensferry. It was a glorious, sunny day, and, as we passed the tenth mile stone, suddenly the Forth Bridge came into view and drawn up in two long rows behind it the assembled might of the British battle fleet.

We arrived at the Hawes Inn in time for luncheon. The Navy had now taken charge of us, and very little information was vouchsafed to us. Some time that afternoon we were to go on board the cruiser which was to take us to Bergen. Till dusk time lay heavy on our hands. I walked along the shore, looking at the great ships and wondering when I should be home again. I had been brought up on "Kidnapped." It was in this same salty old-fashioned Hawes Inn that Uncle Ebenezer and Captain Hoseason had made their plot to entice David Balfour on to the brig *Covenant* and to sell him into slavery on the American plantations. It did not seem a very happy omen. The day, too, was the thirteenth of the month. Action, however, soon banished the gloom from my thoughts. As the dusk grew into darkness, a young lieutenant came ashore and in a whisper informed us that we were to go aboard. There was a delicious secrecy and sense of mystery about the whole business. Soft-footed sailors spirited our luggage away. Then, silently, in single file, we crept down the steps of the jetty to the pinnace which was to convey us to the *Yarmouth*. At six p.m. we were on board. But it was not until dawn the next day that we raised anchor.

Then, headed by the two destroyers which were to be our escort, we steamed slowly between the towering lines of the great battle-cruisers, down past the massive cylinders of the Forth Bridge, and out into the open sea.

The Great Adventure had begun.

CHAPTER TWO

IF I HAD conveniently forgotten my sick leave voyage from Moscow to London, the return journey remains as clearly stamped on my mind as if it were yesterday. There was neither monotony nor much tranquillity about it. I had become someone—or, at least, something—of minor importance, and the change in my status was reflected in the different attitude towards me of those two great barometers of worldly significance: the Press and our own Legations abroad. On my first night on board the *Yarmouth* I dined alone in solemn state with the captain, a tall, well-built man with a strong face and a quiet, self-reliant manner. He was a grandson of W. G. Grace, the famous cricketer, and is to-day an admiral. The rest of my mission dined in the ward-room. For many of us that was the last meal we had on board. As soon as we had passed May Island we ran into terrible weather with heavy seas and a raging wind. The cold, too, was bitter, and every half-hour or so we encountered a fresh blizzard. It was, in fact, the North Sea at its worst, and a light crusier, cleared for action, was not the kind of ship best suited to face it. We could not go on deck. A goodly number of the crew and at least one officer were violently sea-sick. Hicks, Phelan and Birse were in extremis.

The next morning we arrived off the Norwegian Coast, but the seas were too stormy and the blizzards too blinding to permit our making the entry into the fjord. During the night one of our destroyers, unable to keep head with the weather, had been forced to return home. For some time we had lost touch with the other owing to the wireless freezing.

I have never been sea-sick in my life, but I confess frankly that I was relieved both of discomfort and of a certain amount of fear when, after twenty-four hours of cruising off the Norwegian Coast, we entered the Bergen fjord. Here we were met by Commodore Gade, the Commander-in-Chief of the Norwegian Fleet. He had on board his steam yacht Sir George Buchanan, General Knox, Admiral Stanley, Captain Scale and Captain Neilson, who were returning to England. I had half an hour's conversation with the Ambassador, who was his usual charming self. This time, however, he looked ill and tired. The first ten months of the revolution had added ten years to his life.

Having said good-bye to the Ambassador and his suite, we had an excellent luncheon with Gade and at four o'clock were glad to stretch our legs on the firm ground of Bergen. The next morning we made the railway trip—the most wonderful in the world—from Bergen to Christiania. It was not to my mind so impressive in winter as in the autumn.

Christiania, whose merchants had grown fat on supplying ships and fish to the Allies, was very expensive and almost gay. Champagne began to flow at eleven o'clock in the morning and never ceased. The inhabitants, too, were very pro-British and, owing to the Norwegian loss of life from German submarines, violently anti-German. A few days before we arrived a German music-hall artist, who had been hissed by his Norwegian audience and who had expressed resentment, had been torn almost to pieces.

We had twenty-four hours at Christiania, and, although owing to the Russo-German peace negotiations I was anxious to push on as quickly as possible, the time passed pleasantly enough. I dined at our Legation and met Sir Mansfeldt Findlay, one of the tallest Englishmen in the world and certainly the tallest man in diplomacy. He was a good organiser and, aided by Charles Brudenell-Bruce, ran his huge Legation (Christiania, in peace time a diplomatic backwater, had, owing to the blockade, the largest staff of any Legation or Embassy during the war) with great efficiency. In his political views he was an extreme Conservative, who would rather have lost the war than run the risk of social upheaval in England.

In Christiania, too, we met the first of the English refugees from Russia, members of our prosperous colonies in St. Petersburg and Moscow, who in a night had seen their comfortable existence swept away before their eyes in the maelstrom of revolution. One conversation, in particular, I noted in my diary. It was with Reynolds, a well-to-do timber-merchant, who had been very intimate with members of the Embassy staff. He had lost everything, was very nervous, and was obsessed with only one idea: that we should make peace as soon as possible in order, in alliance with Germany, to restore order in Rusisa.

I recall this conversation because it was typical of the point of view we were to find among the Russian bourgeois in Moscow and St. Petersburg during 1918. Yet in the face of these facts, all through this period our military experts were writing memoranda about the loyal Russians and about the restoration of the Eastern front. As if there were any Russians who thought of any other interests than their own or of any other front than the civil war front, once the Bolshevik revolution had started. This is not anti-Russian prejudice. It is plain common sense. An Englishman or a German, situated in similar circumstances, would have had the same thoughts and the same mental reactions. If there were Russians who accepted the English formula of restoring the Eastern front and who talked of the sanctity of their oath to fight until victory was assured, they did so, consciously or sub-consciously, with their tongues in their cheeks. The one aim of every Russian bourgeois (and 99 per cent of the so-called "loyal" Russians were bourgeois) was to secure the intervention of British troops (and, failing British, German troops) to re-establish order in Russia, suppress Bolshevism and restore to the bourgeois his property.

On our arrival at Stockholm we received news that civil war had broken out in Finland and that the chances of our getting through to St. Petersburg were very small. I was determined, however, to push on, and, while Sir Esmé Howard (to-day Lord Howard and ex-Ambassador to the United States, then our Minister in Stockholm) telegraphed to the British authorities at Haparanda and Helsingfors to make all possible arrangements for our journey, I went off to see Vorovsky, the Bolshevik Minister, to arrange for a Russian train to meet us at the Finnish frontier.

I rather liked Vorovsky. He had a fine intellectual face with wistful grey eyes and a brown beard. He was thin, looked ascetic, and gave me the impression of a man of taste and refinement. He had beautiful hands and in Paris would have been taken immediately for an artist or a writer. I showed him my letter to Trotsky, and he promised to do everything he could to help me. He also gave me the latest news of the Russo-German peace negotiations at Brest-Litovsk. From my point of view they were encouraging. At first the Germans had wanted to conclude peace with the greatest possible despatch, but now, encouraged by the defection of the Ukrainians, who had gone over body and soul to them, they were trying to force the most impossible terms upon the Bolsheviks. The negotiations, Vorovsky said, were likely to be prolonged. If it were humanly possible, he would get us to St. Petersburg in three days.

We arrived in Stockholm on Saturday, January 19th. It was Friday, January 25th, before we left for Haparanda and Finland. Although the delay was irksome, our sojourn in Stockholm was not uninteresting. The town itself looked its best in its winter mantle of snow and clear blue sky. The weather was wonderful and the air like champagne. My hotel was besieged with visitors—mostly English and Russian refugees from Moscow and St. Petersburg, who wanted me to protect their property or to take a message to their relatives. I lunched and dined with Sir Esmé Howard and through him met M. Branting, the Swedish Socialist Prime Minister. Branting, a massive and impressive figure of a man, was the convenor of the ill-fated Stockholm Socialist Conference, which had been frowned on by Mr. Lloyd George and which had failed through the refusal of the British seamen to convey Mr. Ramsay MacDonald and Mr. Henderson across the North Sea. Branting still wanted to have his Conference and to include the Bolsheviks in his general invitation. Sir Esmé Howard, who in Stockholm probably had a better objective view of both sides in the war than any other diplomatist elsewhere, rightly concluded that we had something to gain and nothing to lose from such a Conference, and supported Mr. Branting's proposals. Like every other proposal which seemed to hint at peace, they came to nothing.

In Stockholm, too, I found some old friends—the volatile Lykiardopoulos, Guy Colebrooke, and that fine old Russian gentleman, General Wogak—and made some new ones, including Clifford Sharp, the brilliant editor of the *New Statesman*. "Lyki," formerly a Liberal, had now, like other Russian Liberals, become very reactionary. He tried to strike terror into our hearts with tales of horror from Russia: how in Turkestan the population was killing off the old men and women and children because there was not enough to eat; how in Petrograd people were bartering a suit of clothes for a loaf of black bread. It was madness for us to proceed on our journey. England should reverse her policy and put her money on the monarchists. The Bolsheviks would not last another month!

More interesting was my dinner with Nobel—a member of the famous Swedish family. He had spent years of his life in St. Petersburg and had large interests all over Russia. He had formed a more accurate estimate of the situation and was convinced that Bolshevism had not yet reached its apogee. Like all foreigners who had property in Russia he was anxious for a general peace and for an Allied-cum-German intervention against the Bolsheviks. He was one of the few people who at that time had visualised Bolshevism as a world-danger. With other Swedes he had joined a rifle club in order that he might take his place behind the bourgeois barricades in the event of a proletarian rising in Sweden.

Not all my time was passed in such serious and lugubrious conversations. More frivolous entertainment was provided by Sir Coleridge Kennard, who was the Legation secretary in charge of British propaganda in Sweden. Sir Coleridge is an Orientalist, a poet, and a romanticist. Obviously, he would have imaginative ideas on propaganda. The Swedish upper-classses were pro-German. They were also sentimental and fond of late hours. Sir Coleridge conceived the fantastic but inherently sound plan of making them pro-ally by providing Stockholm with a first-class British variety entertainment. He won over the benevolent Sir Esmé Howard to his scheme. He convinced Whitehall that English beauty and English talent were more potent political factors than subsidised leading articles in the Swedish Press. And he was given almost a free hand.

He was as proud of his cabaret as Mussolini is of his dramas, and we were not allowed to leave Stockholm without seeing it. It was a great experience. We dined in the magnificent Moorish hall of the Grand Hotel, and then, beneath a star-lit sky with the moon shining on the icy waters of the fjords, we made our way to Rolf's, where Sir Coleridge held his court. Here for the first time I heard Miss Irene Browne sing "Hello, my dearie." Here, too, Miss Betty Chester made her contribution to the Allied victory by a vivacity which drew roars of applause from the sentimental, punch-drinking Swedes. It was an excellent and most successful form of propaganda, for it paid its own way. For me it was to be the last link with Western civilisation for nine months.

The next day I received a message from Vorovsky requesting me to come to see him. He had received a telegram from St. Petersburg. All arrangements had been made for our safe conduct from the Finnish frontier. He also gave me the latest news from Russia. It was disturbing. Shingarieff and Kokoshkin, two ex-ministers of the Kerensky Government, had been brutally murdered in their beds by sailors in the Marine Hospital in St. Petersburg, to which they had been taken from the Petropavlosk Fortress. I had known both men intimately—more especially Kokoshkin, who was an old Moscow friend. Each belonged to the very best type of Russian. Their whole lives had been spent in disinterested public service. They were Liberals, who had worked incessantly to help the down-trodden and oppressed, and it would have been hard to find two men in public life more free from personal ambition or self-seeking. The news of this butchery filled me with a sickening horror. The revolution was working out to pattern. Its chief victims were to be amongst those democrats who had trusted most in the common sense of the people. Even Vorovsky was shocked and seemed ashamed. Five years later he himself was to be shot down by the pistol of a Russian monarchist in the dining-room of the Beau Rivage Hotel in Lausanne.

That same evening, after a series of hurried farewells, we left for Haparanda, the Swedish frontier town on the Northern extremity of the Gulf of Bothnia. The journey was tedious, lasting more than twenty-six hours. There were many delays, the engine puffing and snorting as though unwilling that we should go farther. And, indeed, there would have been every justification for our turning back. Civil war had broken out in Finland between the Whites and the Reds. The Whites held the North. The Reds had seized control of Helsingfors. We should have to cross the line of fire between the opposing forces. The conductors and Swedish passengers on the train told us we should never get through.

On the morning of Saturday, January 26th, we arrived at Haparanda and, after some discussion and much uncertainty, we crossed over to Tornea on the Finnish side, where we spent the whole day debating our next decision. Having come so far, I was determined to push on. Thanks to the energy of Greener, the British Passport Control officer, we succeeded in persuading the Finns to run a train, and at ten in the evening we set out into the unknown. Our fellow passengers were mainly Russian emigrants—former exiles of the Tsarist régime—who were returning to the new Paradise. Most of them were in a state of abject terror. Doubtless, they were afraid of the Finnish Whites, who at this stage of our journey were in complete control.

At eight o'clock the next night we arrived at Ruhimaki, where we were told that the bridge at Kuovala had been destroyed by White Guards and that we could not proceed farther. We had a choice between returning to Stockholm or persuading the guard to make a detour and take his train to Helsingfors. We spent the night in the station and the next morning came on to Helsingfors to find the capital in a state of revolution. Desultory firing was going on in the square outside the station. On the platform we met Lednitski, a leading Polish lawyer, whom I had known in Moscow. He informed me that the hotels were crowded with refugees, that people were sleeping in threes and fours even in the bathrooms, and that we had no chance of obtaining accommodation. He offered to try to find rooms for us at the house of a Polish priest. When the firing seemed to have died down, I left Birse and Phelan in charge of our luggage and wandered off with Hicks and Lednitski to find the priest. The priest had no available accommodation. We left Lednitski with him and, armed with a map, set out on our long tramp back to the station. The weather was vile. There had been a thaw, and the snow, dirty and yellow, was soft and slushy. The firing in the side-streets sounded unpleasantly close. Then suddenly, as we mounted a hill and turned into a broad boulevard, we ran into a fleeing mob pursued by a detachment of sailors with a machine-gun. The sailors were spraying the street with bullets. The pursued had sought the shelter of the pavements. Some were rushing helter-skelter as fast as their legs could carry them. Others were trying to break open the locked doors of the shops and houses. Several corpses lay face downwards in the snow. The whole rush lasted only a few seconds, and Hicks and I, who were a fine mark in the middle of the road, had not time to turn back. We flopped on our faces in the snow. Very gingerly I held up a white handkerchief, while Hicks waved his British passport. The next few seconds seemed like eternity. The sailors, equally cautious, advanced very slowly with their machine-gun and pointed rifles. Fortunately, they were Russians, and my letter to Trotsky worked wonders.

The sailors, in fact, turned out to be a God-send. Satisfied regarding our bona fides, they took us to the station, where they gave strict orders for the safe custody of our baggage. Then they conducted us to the British Consulate. Here we met Grove and Fawcett, his Vice-Consul. They succeeded in fixing us up for the night in a small pension, and the next day Fawcett, who knew everyone in Helsingfors, persuaded the Red Finnish Government to give us a train and a safe conduct to the broken bridge on the other side of which we hoped to find a Russian train.

At seven o'clock the same evening we set out once more on our Odyssey. Thanks to our Red safe conduct, we travelled very comfortably. Our train, at least, was heated, and the accommodation, if rough, was ample. We were favoured, too, by circumstances. The Finnish Reds were especially kind to us, because at that moment the White Finns were negotiating for German assistance.

When we came to the bridge we had a moment of trepidation. Rumour, however, had exaggerated, as usual, the extent of the destruction. The line, it is true, had been torn up. The arch of the bridge had been buckled. But the bridge itself was still standing and still passable on foot. At midnight we got out of our warm train into the freezing night. Then, with the aid of a lantern, we crept our way across the bridge. It was another eerie performance, but once again it was safely accomplished. The Red Finns who accompanied us—we had been provided with an armed escort—were both kind and efficient. In two shifts they carried our heavy luggage across the bridge for us. This was no mean feat, for we had provided ourselves with an abundance of stores, and our packing cases were both heavy and cumbersome. Not as much as a parcel was missing when the task was completed.

What was more, thanks to the intervention of the Finnish Reds, a train with steam up was waiting for us on the other side. We entrained at once and at seven on the following evening we arrived in St. Petersburg without further incident or delay. We were the last British passengers to get through—the last British officials to make the journey from London to St. Petersburg via Scandinavia until the end of the war.

CHAPTER THREE

IT WAS A VERY different St. Petersburg to which I had returned. The streets were in an appalling state. The snow had not been swept away for weeks, and the sleigh-drive from the Finland station on the north side of the river to the Embassy was like a ride on a scenic railway—without the security. The people in the streets were depressed and unhappy. Very dreadful, too, was the condition of the horses. They looked as if they had not had a square meal for weeks. Just before we came to the Troitski Bridge, we passed a dead horse. It was frozen into the snow and had obviously been there for some days.

At the Embassy there was some confusion of thought and much division of opinion. Trotsky was at Brest-Litovsk endeavouring to make peace with the Germans, and no one seemed to know quite what was happening. The Embassy staff was split up into recognitionists and anti-recognitionists, and Lindley (now Sir Francis Lindley and H.B.M.'s Ambassador to Japan), who was in charge, steered an indecisive course between the two conflicting groups. Until we could find a suitable house, the members of my mission were quartered on different members of the other British missions in St. Petersburg. My own good Samaritan was Rex Hoare, now British Minister in Teheran and then second secretary at the Embassy. A charming companion with a slow drawl, which belied an extremely active intelligence, Hoare was one of the few Englishmen who could take an objective view of the revolution. He was in favour of recognising the Bolshevik Government, and his views were in close accordance with my own. That night, as I sought to read myself to sleep, I found beside my bed a copy of Lord Cromer's "Modern Egypt." In it I came across an aphorism, which had guided Cromer's conduct in Egypt: "*Il faut s'accomoder aux circonstances et en tirer parti même de ce qui nous deplaît.*" It seemed an excellent guide for my own conduct in the difficult situation in which I now found myself.

The next day I had my first interview with Chicherin, who in Trotsky's absence at Brest-Litovsk was in charge of the

Foreign Office. He received me in the same building in which Sazonoff had formerly held sway. Petroff, a swarthy Jew, was present during our interview, and the serio-comic nature of the situation may best be illustrated by the fact that both men had been released from an English prison in order to return to Russia.

A Russian of good family, who long before the revolution had sacrificed a fortune for his Socialist convictions, Chicherin was a man of great culture. In his youth he had begun his career as an official of the Tsarist Foreign Office, and he spoke French, English and German with fluency and accuracy. He was dressed in a hideous yellow-brown tweed suit, which he had brought with him from England, and during the six months of our almost daily contact I never saw him in any other. With his sandy-coloured beard and hair and his sandy-coloured suit he looked like one of those grotesque figures made by children on the sea-shore. Only his eyes, small and red-rimmed like a ferret's, gave any sign of life. His narrow shoulders were bent with much toiling over his desk. Among a group of men who worked for sixteen hours out of the twenty-four, he was the most indefatigable and relentless in his attention to his duties. An idealist, whose loyalty to his own Party was unshakable, he was extraordinarily mistrustful of everyone outside it.

Our first interview was satisfactory, but vague. Later, when I knew my Chicherin better, I learnt that he never took a decision without reference to Lenin. On this occasion, however, he had evidently received instructions to be friendly. Indeed, the Bolsheviks, whose obvious policy was to play off the Germans against the Allies and the Allies against the Germans, welcomed my arrival. In the Bolshevik Press the importance of my mission and of my own position was wilfully exaggerated, and I was described, not only as the man of confidence of Mr. Lloyd George, but also as an influential politician, whose sympathies were entirely with the Bolsheviks! This description of my standing caused some misunderstanding among the other Allied missions in St. Petersburg. In particular, one American intelligence officer, whose chief contribution to the war was the purchase of a stack of documents, so palpably forged that even our own secret service would have nothing to do with them, reported to his Government that a dangerous English revolutionary had arrived in St. Petersburg and was hob-nobbing with the Bolsheviks.

Chicherin was honest enough in his account of what was happening at Brest. He told me that the negotiations were going badly and that now was the great opportunity for England to make a friendly gesture towards Russia. Almost in the same breath he informed me that the Bolsheviks were now busily engaged in organising a new International, in which there would be no room for moderate Socialists like Branting and Henderson. This, in fact, was the beginning of the notorious Third International.

Another new acquaintance of these first days in the Bolshevised St. Petersburg was Raymond Robins, the head of the American Red Cross Mission, and brother of Elizabeth Robins, the well-known authoress. On the third evening of my arrival Rex Hoare invited him to dine with us, and we had a good talk. Robins, who was a philanthropist and a humanitarian rather than a politician, was a wonderful orator. His conversation, like Mr. Churchill's, was always a monologue, but it was never dull, and his gift of allegory was as remarkable as it was original. With his black hair and his aquiline features, he had a most striking appearance. He was an Indian chief with a Bible for his tomahawk. He had stood as Roosevelt's Vice-President in the "Bull Moose's" campaign for the American Presidency in 1912. Although a rich man himself, he was an anti-capitalist. Yet, in spite of his sympathies for the underdog, he was a worshipper of great men. Hitherto, his two heroes had been Roosevelt and Cecil Rhodes. Now Lenin had captured his imagination. Strangely enough, Lenin was amused by the hero-worship, and of all foreigners Robins was the only man whom Lenin was always willing to see and who ever succeeded in imposing his own personality on the unemotional Bolshevik leader.

In a less official sense Robins had a similar mission to my own. He was the intermediary between the Bolsheviks and the American Government and had set himself the task of persuading President Wilson to recognise the Soviet régime. He knew no Russian and very little about Russia. But in Gumberg, a Russo-American Jew, who for years had been in close touch with the Bolshevik movement, he had an assistant who supplied him with the necessary knowledge and arguments. And Gumberg's arguments in Robins's mouth made a most convincing case for recognition. I liked Robins. For the next four months we were to be in daily and almost hourly contact.

My first twelve days in St. Petersburg were spent in an endless round of discussions with Chicherin and our own officials. My relations with Lindley, who as Chargé d'Affaires might reasonably have resented my intrusion into the political arena (as the official representative of the British Government he had, of course, no dealings with the Bolsheviks), were of the friendliest. I co-operated with him to the fullest extent, reporting everything to him, and consulted him about every step I took, and in this way what might have been an awkward and unpleasant situation was averted.

I made, however, little progress, and most of my telegrams to London remained unanswered. We were still completely ignorant of the true course of the negotiations at Brest, and Chicherin did little to enlighten our darkness. All that he would admit was that, while German militarism and British capitalism were equally hateful to the Bolsheviks, German militarism was for the moment the greater danger. Germany was now the centre of an anti-Bolshevik league. She was supporting the bourgeois cause in Finland, Rumania, and the Ukraine. The Russian bourgeois were looking to her to intervene in Russia and to restore them to their former position. Here was a situation which the British Government could exploit to its own benefit. The Bolsheviks would welcome British support.

On February 9th I had an interview of a more intriguing nature. Various commissions of the Central Powers peace delegation were actually working in St. Petersburg. Through a reliable channel I received a demand for an interview from one of the Bulgarian delegates. As I had nothing to risk in seeing him, I acceded to the request. In my diary he is entered merely as S. His name, I think, was Semidoff. In a long and interesting conversation he told me that Bulgaria was ripe for peace and revolution and that with encouragement (which, I assume, meant money) from England there would be little difficulty in starting a movement to dethrone King Ferdinand and expel the pro-German ministers. Obviously, the man may have been an agent-provocateur sent to me by the Bolsheviks. In this case, however, the odds are that he was genuine. I reported the incident to London and heard no more about it.

While awaiting Trotsky's return from Brest, we took advantage of this respite to establish our mission in a large and well-furnished flat on the Palace Quay almost directly opposite the Peter and Paul Fortress and within a few hundred yards of the Embassy. There was, too, an excellent cellar, which we took over at a reasonable price. We could, in fact, have had a palace for next to nothing. The unfortunate aristocracy, deprived of everything, was only too glad to find a foreign official who could, even temporarily, safeguard its property.

As a house-warming I gave a luncheon party to which I invited the Embassy staff and other prominent British officials in St. Petersburg. My chief guest was Robins. He arrived late, having just come from Lenin. He brought with him the news that Trotsky had refused to sign a shameful peace but that, as Russia could not fight, she would go on demobilising.

During luncheon Robins spoke little, but afterwards, when we assembled in the smoking-room, his tongue was loosed. Standing by the mantelpiece, his black hair smoothed back with characteristic gesture, he made a moving appeal for Allied support of the Bolsheviks. He began quietly, analysing the various Allied arguments against recognition and demolishing the ridiculous Allied theory that the Bolsheviks were working for a German victory. He drew a touching picture of a helpless people facing with courage and without arms the greatest military machine in history. We had nothing to hope from the demoralised Russian bourgeoisie, who were actually relying on German aid for the restoration of their rights and property. Then he began his eulogy of Trotsky. The Red Leader was "a four kind son of a bitch, but the greatest Jew since Christ. If the German General Staff bought Trotsky, they bought a lemon." As he worked up to his peroration, he became almost indignant over the folly of the Allies in "playing the German game in Russia." Then he stopped dramatically and took a piece of paper from the flap pocket of his uniform. I can see him now. Consciously or not, he had provided himself with an almost perfect setting. Before him a semi-circle of stolid Englishmen. Behind him the roaring log-fire, its tongues of flame reflected in weird shadows on the yellow-papered walls. Outside, through the window, the glorious view of the slender spire of Peter and Paul with the great fire-ball of the setting sun casting rays of blood on the snow-clad waters of the Neva. Once again he pushed his hair back with his hand and shook his head like a lion. "Have any of you read this?" he asked. "I found it this morning in one of your 'noospapers'." Then in a low voice, quivering with emotion, he read Major McCrae's poem:

> "We are the Dead. Short days ago
> We lived, felt dawn, saw sunset glow,
> Loved and were loved, and now we lie
>   In Flanders Fields.
> Take up our quarrel with the foe:
> To you from failing hands we throw
> The Torch; be yours to hold it high.
> If ye break faith with us who die
> We shall not sleep, though Poppies grow
>   In Flanders Fields."

When he had finished, there was an almost deathly silence. For what seemed an eternity Robins himself turned away and looked out of the window. Then, squaring his shoulders, he came back to us. "Boys!" he said. "I guess we're all here for one purpose—to see that the German General Staff don't win this war."

Three quick strides, and he was by my side. He wrung my hand. "Good-bye, Lockhart," he said. Four more strides, and he was gone.

As a dramatic performance Robins's effort was immense. To-day, it sounds like emotional hysteria. Doubtless, too, he had rehearsed all his effects before his shaving glass in the morning. But at the moment his words made a deep impression on everyone who heard him. There was not a laugh or a smile. Even "Benji" Bruce, with all his Ulster prejudices against revolution, was temporarily convinced that recognition or, at least, support of the Bolsheviks against German aggression was the right policy. General Poole, who afterwards commanded the ill-fated expedition to Archangel, was then of the same opinion.

Three days afterwards I had my first interview with Trotsky in the Russian Foreign Office. It lasted for two hours, during which we discussed all the modalities of Anglo-Russian co-operation. As one of the accusations levelled against me afterwards was that I had been infatuated from the first by Trotsky and was completely under his influence, I give my first impressions of him exactly as I entered them in my diary at the time:

"February 15th, 1918. Had a two hours' conversation with L.D.T. (Lev Davidovitch Trotsky). He struck me as perfectly honest and sincere in his bitterness against the Germans. He has a wonderfully quick mind and a rich, deep voice. With his broad chest, his huge forehead, surmounted by great masses of black, waving hair, his strong, fierce eyes, and his heavy protruding lips, he is the very incarnation of the revolutionary of the bourgeois caricatures. He is neat about his dress. He wore a clean soft collar and his nails were carefully manicured. I agree with Robins. If the Bosche bought Trotsky, he bought a lemon. His dignity has suffered an affront. He is full of belligerent fury against the Germans for the humiliation to which they have exposed him at Brest. He strikes me as a man who would willingly die fighting for Russia provided there was a big enough audience to see him do it."

Trotsky *was* angry with the Germans. At that moment he was not quite certain what the German reaction would be to his famous declaration of "no peace and no war," but he had a shrewd idea that it would be unpleasant.

Unfortunately, he was also full of bitterness against the English. We had not handled Trotsky wisely. At the time of the first revolution he was in exile in America. He was then neither a Menshevik nor a Bolshevik. He was what Lenin called a Trotskist—that is to say, an individualist and an opportunist. A revolutionary with the temperament of an artist and with undoubted physical courage, he had never been and never could be a good party man. His conduct prior to the first revolution had incurred the severest condemnation by Lenin. "Trotsky, as always," wrote Lenin in 1915, "is, in principle, opposed to the Socialist Chauvinists, but in practice he is always in agreement with them."

In the spring of 1917 Kerensky requested the British Government to facilitate Trotsky's return to Russia. Common sense seemed to indicate one of two courses: to refuse, on the grounds that Trotsky was a danger to the Allied cause; or to allow him to return unmolested. As usual in our attitude towards Russia, we adopted disastrous half-measures. Trotsky was treated as a criminal. At Halifax, New Brunswick, he was separated from his wife and children and interned in a prison camp at Amherst with German prisoners for four weeks. His finger-prints were taken. Then, having roused his bitter hate we allowed him to return to Russia. I am giving Trotsky's own account of the incident. I learnt afterwards that it was substantially correct. The outraged Trotsky came back to Russia, threw in his lot with the Bolsheviks, and relieved his injured feelings by writing a fiercely anti-British pamphlet entitled "A Prisoner of the English." Some trace of his resentment showed itself during our interview. I succeeded, however, in soothing him. The German danger was uppermost in his mind, and his last words, as I left him, were: "Now is the big opportunity for the Allied Governments."

I returned from my interview to our flat only to find an urgent message from Robins requesting me to come to see him at once. I found him in a state of great agitation. He had been in conflict with Saalkind, a nephew of Trotsky and then Assistant Commissar for Foreign Affairs. Saalkind had been rude, and the American, who had a promise from Lenin that, whatever happened, a train would always be ready for him at an hour's notice, was determined to exact an apology or to leave the country. When I arrived, he had just finished telephoning to Lenin. He had delivered his ultimatum, and Lenin had promised to give a reply within ten minutes. I waited, while Robins fumed. Then the telephone rang and Robins picked up the receiver. Lenin had capitulated. Saalkind was to be dismissed his post. But he was an old member of the Party. Would Robins have any objection if Lenin sent him as a Bolshevik emissary to Berne? Robins smiled grimly. "Thank you, Mr. Lenin," he said. "As I can't send the son of a bitch to hell, 'burn' is the next best thing you can do with him."

This was the beginning of what was to be a hectic month. The Germans lost little time in replying to Trotsky's refusal to sign their peace terms and, to the consternation of the Bolsheviks, began to advance on St. Petersburg. At first the Bolsheviks made some show of resistance. Orders were given in this sense to the fleet and to the army. Trotsky himself, whom I was now seeing daily, informed me that, even if Russia could not resist, she would wage a partisan war to the best of her ability. Very soon, however, it became clear that, in the military sense of the word, there could be no resistance. The Bolsheviks had come into power on a peace slogan. A war slogan might easily bring about their ruin. The bourgeoisie was openly delighted at the prospect of the German advance, which had emboldened the anti-Bolshevik Press to attack the Bolsheviks with a frenzied fury. The determining factor was the attitude of the troops. On the rumour that the war was to be renewed desertions from the front assumed the proportions of panic flight, and, after an all-night sitting of the Commissars, a telegram was sent to the Germans capitulating entirely and asking for peace on any terms.

In the Bolshevik-Left Social-Revolutionary coalition, of which the Lenin Government was composed, there was a holy-war Party. It included Bolsheviks like Petroff, Bucharin and Radek and, numerically, it was nearly as strong as the peace party. Lenin, however, was for peace. Without peace he could not consolidate his position. It was now that he formulated his policy of "lavirovat" of which the best translation is the French *"reculer pour mieux sauter."* Trotsky, as usual, steered a middle course. He wanted to fight. He considered that war was inevitable. If the Allies would send a promise of support, he informed me that he would sway the decision of the Government in favour of war. I sent several telegrams to London requesting an official message that would enable me to strengthen Trotsky's hands. No message was sent.

On February 23rd the German terms were received. They were considerably stiffer in their territorial demands than the Treaty of Versailles, and once again the ranks of the Bolsheviks were torn with dissension. The next day, after a fierce and passionate debate, the Central Executive Committee decided by 112 votes to 86 to accept the German terms. Lenin's cold, calculated logic dominated the meeting. There were, however, 25 abstentions. Among them was the vote of Trotsky, who during the discussion remained skulking in his room.

On the afternoon of the debate I telephoned to Trotsky. He had given me his private telephone, and he answered the call himself. "May I speak to Citizen Trotsky?" I asked. There was a growl of "No" from the other end. But I had recognised his voice. "Lev Davidovitch," I said quickly. "This is Lockhart. I want to see you immediately." There was a moment's silence. Then another growl:

"It's no use. But come at once if you like. I'm at Smolny."

Smolny—in Tsarist days a seminary for young girls of good

family—was the Bolshevik headquarters. It had a picturesque situation next door to a monastery—a pleasant blue and white building on the outskirts of the city. The Institute itself was grey, with an entrance like a Greek temple. It reminded me of the old Royal Military College building at Sandhurst.

As I made my way past the armed guards who with machine-guns and fixed bayonets were posted before the gates, my pass, signed by Trotsky himself, was subjected to the closest scrutiny. Finally, I was taken to the commandant, a tall sailor, whom I was to meet again in less pleasant circumstances, and in a few minutes I was being piloted upstairs through a maze of corridors and class-rooms to Trotsky's sanctum on the second floor. I made a mental note of the various notices still posted on the walls: Vth Class Dormitory, Linen Room, Drawing Class. Formerly these corridors had resounded to the gentle tramp of girls' slippers. Everything, one could be sure, had been immaculate; the only unseemliness a foolish giggle. Now all was dirt and confusion. Sailors, red guards, students and working-men lounged against the walls. None of them looked as if he had washed for a fortnight. Cigarette ends and crumpled news-sheets strewed the floors.

Trotsky's own room was an exception. Lofty and well-lit, it contained a red carpet. There was a fine birch-wood writing desk. There was even a wastepaper basket. The habitual neatness of its occupant was everywhere manifest.

The occupant himself, however, was in the worst of tempers. "Have you any message from London?" he asked, still scowling. I told him that I had not yet had a reply to my telegrams, but that, if the Bolsheviks would make a genuine effort to prevent half Russia from falling into German hands, I was confident that British support would not be withheld. "You have no message," he said. "Well, I have. While you are here trying to throw dust in my eyes, your countrymen and the French have been intriguing against us with the Ukrainians, who have already sold themselves to the Germans. Your Government is working for Japanese intervention in Siberia. Your other missions here are plotting against us with all the bourgeois

Одно изъ самыхъ слабыхъ мѣстъ въ рѣчи Бальфура есть заявленіе о томъ, что японцы идутъ на помощь русскимъ. К а к и м ъ и м е н н о р у с с к и м ъ?. Въ нынѣшней Россіи есть одна сила, по своей природѣ предназ для борьбы наченная не на жизнь, а на смерть противъ нападеній со стороны международ-аго имперіализма - это власть Совѣтовъ. Первымъ же шагомъ тѣхъ русскихъ, которымъ собираются "помогать" японцы, при возникновеніи слухавъ о приближеніи послѣднихъ было требованіе упраздненія Совѣтской власти. Въ случаѣ продвиженія японцевъ внутрь Сибири тѣ же "русскіе", которымъ японцы собираются "помогать", будутъ требовать упраздненія Совѣтовъ во всей Сибири. Чѣмъ же Совѣтская власть можетъ быть замѣнена? Единственное, что можетъ ее замѣнить, есть буржуазное правительство. Но буржуазія въ Россіи достаточно уже ясно показала, что можетъ держаться у власти лишь при помощи извнѣ. Если буржуазное правительство, опирающееся на помощь извнѣ, удержится у власти въ Сибири, и Восточная Россія будетъ потеряна для Совѣтской власти, то и въ Западной Россіи послѣдняя будетъ до такой степени ослаблена, что врядъ ли долго удержится, и ея наслѣдникомъ явится буржуазное правительство, которое и здѣсь также будетъ нуждаться въ помощи извнѣ. Держава, которая окажетъ эту помощь, будетъ, конечно, не Англія. Легко понять, какія перспективы сулитъ такая возможность.

Подтверждаю, что
это факсимиле моей
бесѣды съ Рансомомъ и
разговоръ нечатался.
Москва 23/Х 1918. Ленинъ.

[Translation overleaf]

One of the weakest spots in Balfour's speech is the statement that the Japanese are going to help the Russians. Which Russians? In Russia to-day there is one power, which by its nature is destined to wage a life and death struggle against the attacks of international Imperialism—that is the Power of the Soviets. The first step, however, of those Russians, whom the Japanese intend to "help," as soon as they heard rumours of the advance of the latter, was to demand the abolition of the Soviet Power. Should the Japanese move into Siberia, these same "Russians" whom the Japanese are going to "help," will demand the abolition of the Soviets throughout the whole of Siberia. What can take the place of the Soviet Power? The only power that can take its place is a bourgeois government. But the bourgeoisie in Russia has proved clearly enough that it can only remain in power with foreign help. If a bourgeois government, supported by outside help, should establish itself in power in Siberia and Eastern Russia become lost to the Soviet, then in Western Russia the Soviet Power would become weakened to such an extent, that it could hardly hold out for long; it would be followed by a bourgeois government, which would also need foreign help. The Power to give this help would, of course, not be England. It is easy to understand what avenues are opened up by this possibility.

I confirm that I really said this in a conversation with Ransome, and I give permission for it to be printed.

LENIN.

Moscow 23/vi/1928.

scum. Look at this," he shouted. He seized a bundle of papers on his desk and thrust them into my hands. They were the alleged originals of forged documents which had already been shown to me. They were typed on paper with the stamp of the German General Staff. They were signed by various German staff officers including, I think, Colonel Bauer. They were addressed to Trotsky and they contained various instructions, which he as a German agent was to carry out. One instruction was an order to facilitate the passage by rail of two German submarines from Berlin to Vladivostok.

I had seen these documents before. They had been hawked round the Allied missions in St. Petersburg for some time. One set of "originals" had been bought by an American agent. Months afterwards it was discovered that these letters, purporting to come from such different centres as Spa, Berlin, and Stockholm, had been written on the same typewriter.

I smiled, but Trotsky was not to be placated. "So this is what your agents waste their time and money on," he hissed. "Your intrigues here have only helped the Germans. I hope you are proud of your work. Your Foreign Office does not deserve to win a war. Your policy towards Russia right from the beginning has been indecisive and vacillating. Your Lloyd George is like a man playing roulette and scattering chips on every number. And now I have to put up with this. Do you know that, while your fools of spies are trying to prove that I am a German agent, my friends down there——" he waved his arm airily towards the room below where the Central Executive Committee was sitting—"are calling me an Ententophile." There was some justification for his attack. The British Government was entitled to regard Bolshevism as a scourge and an evil. It might make war on it or ignore it severely. But it was sheer folly to continue to regard it as a movement fostered solely for the furtherance of German ends. When I had told Trotsky that I had received no reply to my telegrams, I had been strictly truthful. I had, however, received messages from our Foreign Office. They still expressed Lord Robert Cecil's doubts and suspicions regarding Trotsky. If I had succeeded in convincing

Whitehall that Trotsky was not a German staff officer in disguise, he was still a German agent. It was an unsatisfactory interview. The most I could extract from Trotsky was that, if peace were signed, it would be of short duration. The Bolsheviks had no intention of observing the German terms. He promised, however, to keep me fully informed. The same night Pokrovsky, Chicherin, and Karachan left for Brest-Litovsk to sign the peace. With the dislocation of the railway traffic and the Bolshevik genius for protraction the actual signing was to be delayed for another week.

In the meantime the uncertainty regarding the peace negotiations and the advance of the Germans towards St. Petersburg had thrown the Allied Embassies into the wildest confusion. For hours on end there were long conferences regarding the policy to be pursued. Were the Embassies and missions to remain or were they to be evacuated? If they waited too long, they ran the risk of falling into the hands of the Germans. The decision to evacuate was forced by the action of the Germans, who refused to stop their advance until the Bolsheviks had actually signed the dictated peace treaty.

The decision having been taken, there remained the delicate task of obtaining Bolshevik visas for the large number of British officials and agents, many of whom were not entered on the diplomatic list. The Bolsheviks, who regarded the departure of the Allied Embassies in much the same manner as a gambler regrets the loss of an ace, were likely to make difficulties.

The securing of the visas was left to me, and, armed with a sheaf of passports, I drove down to the Foreign Office to try my luck. In the absence of Trotsky and Chicherin, I was received by Petroff, whose imprisonment in England had not increased his affection for British officials. After informing me that there could be no objection to the departure of bona fide diplomatists, he referred me to Lutsky, an unpleasant Jewish lawyer, who was in charge of the passport department.

He was seated at his desk in a large room, the only other occupant of which was a girl typist, who sat at a small table in the corner. Lutsky's rudeness made me boil with rage. He was a rat, and I should have liked to shake him. I kept my temper while he went through my huge pile of passports. "My orders are that only genuine diplomatists may receive visas," he said. "All these people are not on the Embassy staff." I explained patiently that my list was genuine and that the bearer of every passport was attached in some form or other to the Embassy. He scrutinised each photograph closely. To my relief he passed General Poole and various other officers who had been photographed in uniform. The pile was nearly finished, and I thought I was about to achieve a complete success. The rat, however, was enjoying his short reign. He was determined to let me feel his newly acquired power. He picked out a passport. "I know this man," he said. "He is a spy. You are trying to deceive me in the same way as the French and Italians have done." He stormed at me for a few minutes. "For this dupery I shall refuse all visas." I stood up, still keeping my temper under control. "In that case," I replied, "please allow me to telephone to Trotsky. Here is his private telephone number and here is my pass to him signed in his own handwriting." Lutsky hummed and hawed and changed his tune. "Very well then," he said, putting the rejected passport on one side, "I shall stamp the others, but this one I shall not stamp."

At this moment the Marchese Della Torretta, the Italian Chargé d'Affaires and later Italian Ambassador in London and Foreign Minister under Mussolini, was announced. Lutsky sprang to his feet. In preparing for a new scene, he became almost friendly to me. Once again he went rapidly through my passports. He rejected several which belonged to members of the British colony and added them to the passport which he had already turned down. He called his typist. "Sit down at my desk and stamp these passports," he said, pointing to the large pile. "The others are to be retained until further instructions."

Then, puffing out his little chest, he advanced to the middle of the room to receive the Italian Marchese standing. The scene that followed was the most extraordinary that I have ever witnessed, perhaps the most extraordinary that has ever taken place between two representatives of foreign Governments. As soon as the Marchese entered the room, Lutsky overwhelmed him with a torrent of abuse. There had been some row about an Italian deputy called Count Frasso, who had been arrested by the Bolsheviks and who had been included in the Italian official passport list. There seemed no end to the epithets which Lutsky showered on the unfortunate Italian. "Bandits, sneaks, sons of bitches," were among the mildest. Both men were of small stature. At first Torretta, gentle, correct and scrupulously polite, tried to remonstrate. His protests produced a further storm of violence. Torretta then became hysterical and almost tearful. His face went a ghastly white. With his silver-grey hair and his short black coat he reminded me of the Rabbit in *Alice in Wonderland*. His hands clutched nervously at his trouser legs. Then he, too, began to scream. It seemed only a matter of seconds before the two men must come to blows.

The scene fascinated me, but I had work of my own to do. Among my rejected passports was the passport of Terence Keyes, a brother of Admiral Keyes and a Colonel in our Intelligence Service. I knew that he had been engaged in various anti-Bolshevik schemes. If his passport were to be held up, things might be awkward. In the meantime the girl was stamping my passports with one eye on her work and the other on the drama which was taking place before us. She was pretty. I talked to her gently, and she smiled. I continued to talk, and, as we talked, I began to fiddle with the passports. As I was whispering to her, I slipped Keyes's passport into the large pile. And, God bless her blue eyes, she stamped it!

Just as her work was finished, I heard Lutsky flinging his last word at Torretta: "Not a single Italian is to leave," and, crestfallen and crumpled, the Marchese crept out of the room. Thoroughly satisfied with himself, Lutsky came over to his desk. I had the viséd passports, Keyes's among them, under my arm. The half-dozen rejected ones were still lying on his table. "May I go now?" I said politely.

"Certainly," he replied.

I walked away and then turned back.

"I think I had better take the rejected passports as well," I said. "Their owners may get into trouble without them."

He shrugged his shoulders. In his mind he was still fighting his battle with Torretta. "Take them," he said, and, picking them up slowly, I made a dignified exit.

That night the British and French officials (there were, of course, no Italians) left by special train for Bieloostroff and the Finnish frontier. Petroff, who was Acting Commissar for Foreign Affairs, went down on the engine for a final revision of the passports. There was trouble with the French, but all our party, including Terence Keyes, passed the frontier without a hitch.

If my mission in Russia failed in every other respect, it was at least successful in this, that it saved some forty or fifty British officials from the indignities and humiliations that were heaped upon their French and Italian colleagues.

There was a pleasant curtain to this passport drama. On the day after the departure of the Embassies Lutsky was arrested for granting visas to French subjects who were not entitled to them. He was accused of having accepted French money. That night I dined well on an affair that was well ended. I had used no bribes—only my innate Celtic persuasiveness and a pair of Russian eyes.

CHAPTER FOUR

THE ALLIED EMBASSIES left on February 28th. The next day I went to Smolny and had my first interview with Lenin.

I felt a little forlorn. My own position was now vaguer than ever. But I had decided to remain at my post for two reasons. The Bolsheviks had not yet signed the peace terms. They probably would do so, but even then the peace was likely to be of short duration. Here was a position which I might usefully exploit. Secondly, so long as the Bolsheviks held the reins of government in Russia, I felt that it would be foolish to cut off all contact with them and to leave the field open to the Germans. I was convinced that their internal strength was far greater than most foreign observers realised, and that there was no other power in Russia which was capable of replacing them.

This, indeed, was the fundamental difference between Whitehall and myself. The consensus of official opinion in London seemed to be that Bolshevism would be swept away within a few weeks. My instinct told me that, weak as the Bolsheviks were, the demoralised forces of the anti-Bolsheviks in Russia were still weaker. In the intensity of the civil strife which was now developing, the Great War had ceased to have any significance to all classes of Russians. In so far as Germany was our main enemy (and at this state few Englishmen regarded Bolshevism as a serious menace to Western civilisation), we had nothing to gain by stimulating civil war. If we took sides against the Bolsheviks, we should be backing the weaker horse and would have to employ large forces to ensure even a temporary success.

In informing Lindley of my desire to remain, I made use of these arguments. He made no objection. I therefore sent back to England Phelan and Birse, who in the situation which had now arisen could be of little service to me, and asked for Rex Hoare, whose views were in sympathy with my own and whose steadying influence would have been of great value to me. He was willing to stay on, but Lindley, perhaps rightly, decided that, as my mission was nominally an unofficial one, he was not justified in allowing me to retain the services of a professional diplomatist. He was quite willing that I should take on any official who was willing to remain and who was outside the permanent staff of the Embassy. There were several volunteers, and from them I selected Denis Garstin, a brother of the well-known novelist and a young cavalry captain, who spoke Russian with tolerable accuracy. Other English officials who remained were Captain Cromie, the naval attaché, who was determined not to let the Baltic Fleet fall into the hands of the Germans, Woodhouse, the Consul, Major McAlpine and Captain Schwabe of General Poole's mission, and various officers and officials of our intelligence services. They were entirely independent of me and supplied their own reports to London.

With Lindley's departure I was, therefore, left to my own resources. Moreover, the route through Finland was now closed, and for the next six months I was to be shut off from all communication with England except by telegraph. Robins, too, had joined the American Embassy in its flight to Vologda and had informed me by telephone that in all probability the Ambassador and his staff would leave the next day for America via Siberia. If I could receive any encouragement from Lenin he would remain and do his best to persuade the American Ambassador to follow his example.

It was, therefore, with a sinking feeling in my heart that I went to Smolny that morning to see the Bolshevik leader. He received me in a small room on the same floor as Trotsky's. It was untidy and bare of all trappings except a writing desk and a few plain chairs. It was not only my first interview with Lenin. It was the first time that I had set eyes on him. There was nothing in his personal appearance to suggest even faintly a resemblance to the super-man. Short of stature, rather plump, with short, thick neck, broad shoulders, round, red face, high intellectual forehead, nose slightly turned up, brownish moustache, and short, stubbly beard, he looked at the first glance more like a provincial grocer than a leader of men. Yet in those steely eyes there was something that arrested my attention, something in that quizzing, half-contemptuous, half-smiling look which spoke of boundless self-confidence and conscious superiority.

Later I was to acquire a considerable respect for his intellectual capacity, but at that moment I was more impressed by his tremendous will-power, his relentless determination, and his lack of emotion. He furnished a complete antithesis to Trotsky, who, strangely silent, was also present at our interview. Trotsky was all temperament—an individualist and an artist, on whose vanity even I could play with some success. Lenin was impersonal and almost inhuman. His vanity was proof against all flattery. The only appeal that one could make to him was to his sense of humour, which, if sardonic, was highly developed. During the next few months I was to be pestered with various requests from London to verify rumours of serious dissensions between Lenin and Trotsky— dissensions from which our Government hoped much. I could have given the answer after that first interview. Trotsky was a great organiser and a man of immense physical courage. But, morally, he was as incapable of standing against Lenin as a flea would be against an elephant. In the Council of Commissars there was not a man who did not consider himself the equal of Trotsky. There was not a Commissar who did not regard Lenin as a demi-god, whose decisions were to be accepted without question. Squabbles among the Commissars were frequent, but they never touched Lenin.

I remember Chicherin giving me an account of a Soviet Cabinet meeting. Trotsky would bring forward a proposal. It would be violently opposed by another Commissar. Endless discussion would follow, and all the time Lenin would be writing notes on his knee, his attention concentrated on some work of his own. At last someone would say: "Let Vladimir Ilyitch (Lenin's Christian name and patronymic) decide." Lenin would look up from his work, give his decision in one sentence, and all would be peace.

In his creed of world-revolution Lenin was as unscrupulous and as uncompromising as a Jesuit, and in his code of political ethics the end to be attained justified the employment of any weapon. On occasions, however, he could be amazingly frank, and my interview was one of them. He gave—correctly as events proved—all the information for which I asked. It was quite untrue that the peace negotiations had broken down. The terms were such as one might expect from a militarist régime. They were scandalous, but they would have to be accepted. They would be signed preliminarily the next day and would be ratified by the overwhelming majority of the Party.

How long would the peace hold? He could not say. The Government was to be transferred to Moscow to enable him to consolidate his power. If the Germans forced their hands and tried to instal a bourgeois government, the Bolsheviks would fight even if they had to withdraw to the Volga and the Urals. But they would fight on their own conditions. They were not to be made a cat's-paw for the Allies.

If the Allies understood this, there was an excellent opportunity for co-operation. To the Bolsheviks Anglo-American capitalism was almost as hateful as German militarism, but for the moment German militarism was the immediate menace. For that reason he was glad that I had decided to remain in Russia. He would give me all facilities, guarantee, as far as lay in his power, my personal safety, and grant me a free exit from Russia whenever I wanted to leave. But—he was sceptical about any possibility of co-operating with the Allies. "Our ways," he said, "are not your ways. We can afford to compromise temporarily with capital. It is even necessary, for, if capital were to unite, we should be crushed at this stage of our development. Fortunately for us, it is in the nature of capital that it cannot unite. So long, therefore, as the German danger exists, I am prepared to risk a co-operation with the Allies, which should be temporarily advantageous to both of us. In the event of German aggression, I am even willing to accept military support. At the same time I am quite convinced that your Government will never see things in this light. It is a reactionary Government. It will co-operate with the Russian reactionaries."

I expressed my fears that, now that peace was a certainty, the Germans would be able to throw all their forces against the Western front. They might then crush the Allies, and where would the Bolsheviks be then? Even more serious was the danger that Germany would be able to relieve her starving population with grain forcibly exported from Russia. Lenin smiled. "Like all your countrymen you are thinking in concrete military terms. You ignore the psychological factor. This war will be settled in the rear and not in the trenches. But even from your point of view your argument is false. Germany has long ago withdrawn her best troops from the Eastern front. As a result of this robber peace she will have to maintain larger and not fewer forces on the East. As to her being able to obtain supplies in large quantities from Russia, you may set your fears at rest. Passive resistance—and the expression comes from your own country—is a more potent weapon than an army that cannot fight."

I went home in a thoughtful mood to find a batch of telegrams from the Foreign Office. They were full of complaints about the peace. How could I insist that the Bolsheviks were not pro-German, when they proposed giving half Russia away to Germany without firing a shot. There was, too, a strongly-worded protest against Litvinoff's activities in London. Would I warn the Bolshevik Government immediately that such conduct could not be tolerated. As I sat paraphrasing the sense of the protest into Russian, the telephone rang. It was Trotsky. He had received news that the Japanese were preparing to land troops in Siberia. What did I propose to do about it and how could I explain my own mission in the face of this open act of hostility? I queried the authenticity of his information and sat down again at my desk. My servant brought in yet another telegram. It was from Robins, advising me to come to Vologda. I got on to him by telephone, told him that I was going to see things through to the bitter end in St. Petersburg, and requested him to inform his Ambassador about the Japanese imbroglio. Japanese intervention in Siberia would destroy all possibility of an understanding with the

Bolsheviks. Common sense seemed to indicate that as a measure for reconstructing an Eastern front against Germany it was ludicrous. The final blow of a shattering day was a telegram from my wife—cryptically worded, but conveying unmistakably the information that my efforts were meeting with no sympathy in London. I was to be careful or my career would be ruined.

London had neither approved nor disapproved my decision to remain on after Lindley's departure. From the fact that the Foreign Office continued to bombard me with telegrams I concluded that it had acquiesced in the new situation. I indulged in a minor orgy of self-pity, which stiffened my obstinacy. Assuredly, my lot was a hard one. Then I went to bed and read the life of Richard Burton. In the circumstances it was perhaps the most dangerous tonic I could have taken. Burton had fought against Whitehall all his life, and the results had been disastrous.

Life in St. Petersburg during this period was a curious affair. The Bolsheviks had not yet succeeded in establishing the iron discipline which to-day characterises their régime. They had, in fact, made little attempt to do so. There was no terror, nor was the population particularly afraid of its new masters. The anti-Bolshevik newspapers continued to appear and to attack the Bolshevik policy with violent abuse. In particular Gorky, then editor of the *Novaia Zizn*, excelled himself in denouncing the men to whom to-day he has given his whole-hearted allegiance. The bourgeoisie, still confident that the Germans would soon send the Bolshevik rabble about its business, was more cheerful than one might have expected in such disturbing circumstances. The population was starving, but the rich still had money. Restaurants and cabarets were open, and the cabarets at any rate were crowded. On Sundays, too, there were trotting races before our house, and it was strange to contrast these beautiful, well-groomed horses with the starved and skeleton nags of the unfortunate "droschke" drivers. The only real danger to human life during these early days of the Bolshevik revolution was furnished, not by the Bolsheviks, but by the

Anarchists—bands of robbers, ex-army officers, and adventurers, who had seized some of the finest houses in the city and who, armed with rifles, hand-grenades, and machine-guns, exercised a gangsters' rule over the capital. They lurked at street corners for their victims and were utterly unscrupulous in their methods of dealing with them. They were, too, no respectors of persons. One evening, on his way back from Smolny to the centre of the city, Uritsky, who was subsequently head of the St. Petersburg Cheka, was pulled from his sleigh by bandits, stripped of all his clothes, and left to continue his journey in a state of nudity. He was fortunate to escape with his life. When we went out at night, we never went alone, no matter how short the distance. We walked, too, in the middle of the road, and we kept our finger tight on the gun in our overcoat pocket. Desultory firing went on all through the night. The Bolsheviks seemed quite incapable of dealing with this pest. For years they had been crying against the Tsarist suppression of free speech. They had not yet embarked on their own campaign of suppression.

I mention this comparative tolerance of the Bolsheviks, because the cruelties which followed later were the result of the intensification of the civil war. For the intensification of that bloody struggle Allied intervention, with the false hopes it raised, was largely responsible. I do not say that a policy of abstention from interference in the internal affairs of Russia would have altered the course of the Bolshevik revolution. I do suggest that our intervention intensified the terror and increased the bloodshed.

On Saturday, March 3rd, the preliminary peace was signed by the Russian delegates at Brest, and the next day a Congress of all the Soviets was summoned to meet at Moscow on March 12th, in order to give the formal ratification. At the same time the Bolsheviks announced the formation of a new Supreme War Council and issued an order for the arming of the whole people. Trotsky was appointed President of the new Council, and Chicherin took his place at the Bolshevik Foreign Office.

I saw Chicherin on his return from Brest. He was dejected

and therefore friendly. He informed me that the German terms had raised a feeling of resentment in Russia similar to that in France after 1870, and now was the most favourable moment for a demonstration of Allied sympathy. The peace was a dictated peace which Russia would break as soon as she was strong enough. This, indeed, was the attitude of every Commissar with whom I came into contact.

As St. Petersburg was now to be evacuated by the Government, I asked Chicherin what arrangements he could make to house my mission in Moscow. As usual, he was all promises and vagueness. I therefore went to Trotsky, who, when he was in the mood, could get things done—and done quickly. I found him in a state of exaltation. His sense of the dramatic had adapted itself to his new office. Almost in a night he had become a soldier. His whole conversation breathed war. Ratification or no ratification, there would be war. At the small committee meeting of the leading Bolsheviks, which had already decided on ratification, he had abstained from voting. He would not attend the formal ratification in Moscow. He was remaining in St. Petersburg for another week. He would be glad if I would remain with him. He would take me with him, when he left, and would be personally responsible for my comfort in Moscow. Preferring the virile action of Trotsky to the vacillations of Chicherin, I decided to stay on.

In spite of more trouble about Japanese intervention, the mention of which never failed to rouse the fire in Trotsky's eyes (incidentally, it made no appeal to the Russian bourgeoisie, who rightly concluded that it would not relieve their sufferings), my last week in St. Petersburg was not unpleasant. I saw Trotsky every day, but otherwise I had less work than usual. The weather, too, was at its best, and we passed our time happily enough in entertaining our Russian friends.

It was at this time that I first met Moura ——, who was an old friend of Hicks and Garstin and a frequent visitor to our flat. She was then twenty-six. A Russian of the Russians, she had a lofty disregard for all the pettiness of life and a courage which was proof against all cowardice. Her vitality, due perhaps to an iron constitution, was immense and invigorated everyone with whom she came into contact. Where she loved, there was her world, and her philosophy of life had made her mistress of all the consequences. She was an aristocrat. She could have been a Communist. She could never have been a bourgeoise. Later, her name was to become linked with mine in the final drama of my Russian career. During those first days of our meeting in St. Petersburg I was too busy, too pre-occupied with my own importance, to give her more than a passing thought. I found her a woman of great attraction, whose conversation brightened my daily life. The romance was to come afterwards.

Cromie, our Naval Attaché, was another of her friends, and on his birthday Moura gave a little luncheon party to which we all came. It was during Maslennitsa or Butter Week, and we ate innumerable "bliny" (pancakes and caviare) and drank vodka. I wrote a doggerel verse for each guest, and Cromie made one of his witty speeches. We toasted our hostess and laughed immoderately. For all of us it was almost the last care-free hour we were to spend in Russia.

Of the four English guests at that luncheon I am the sole survivor. Cromie died gloriously, defending the Embassy from Bolshevik intrusion. Poor Denis Garstin, who had worked with all his boyish enthusiasm for an understanding with the Bolsheviks, was taken from me by the War Office and sent to Archangel, where he fell a victim to a Bolshevik bullet. Will Hicks, or "Hickie," as everybody called him, died of consumption in Berlin in the spring of 1930.

It was a very peaceful St. Petersburg during this last week. Never had it looked more beautiful, and its deserted streets added to its charm.

The centre of gravity had now been transferred to Moscow. Lenin had left on March 10th. It was not until the afternoon of the 15th that Trotsky informed me we were to leave on the following morning. He had just been appointed Commissar for War. At the very moment when his appointment was announced, the Congress of Soviets, which was to ratify the peace, had opened, and Lenin was making his historic answer to his pro-war critics: "One fool can ask more questions in a minute than twelve wise men can answer in an hour."

The next morning, having stored most of our heavy luggage in the Embassy, we rose at seven and arrived at Smolny at eight, only to wait till ten before the Trotsky baggage train was ready. Most of that day we spent at the station, lolling about in the glorious sunshine and watching the 700 Letts, who furnished the Prætorian Guard of the new Red Napoleon, entrain. They looked a dour lot, but their discipline was excellent. The tediousness of our long wait was relieved by the drolleries of Bill Shatoff, a cheerful scoundrel with a sense of humour. He had spent his years of exile in New York and had a rich fund of East-side stories. Most of them were at the expense of Russia and the Russians for whom, in spite of his Communist beliefs, he had a slight contempt. His appearance was even funnier than his yarns. A miniature Carnera, he wore a suit of overalls over his ordinary clothes and sheepskin coat. The whole was surmounted by a large checked English cap. A pair of huge revolvers was strung from a belt at his hips. The general effect was a cross between a gunman and the rotund gentleman who furnishes the advertisement for Michelin tyres.

At last, at four o'clock, Trotsky arrived, resplendent in a khaki overcoat. We saluted, shook hands, and then he conducted us personally to our compartments. There were two of them, and, as, including our two Russian servants, we were only six strong, the accommodation was more than generous, more especially as the train was overcrowded. We travelled alone, but just before we reached Liuban we received a message from Trotsky. He would be glad if we would dine with him.

I shall remember that dinner to the end of my days. We dined at the head of a long table in the station restaurant. I sat on Trotsky's right and Hicks sat on his left. The fare was plain but good, a thick "shtshi" soup, veal cutlets with fried potatoes and sour gherkins, and a huge "torte." There was, too, beer and red wine. Trotsky, however, drank mineral water.

He was in one of his genial moods and made an excellent host. Huge crowds, dumb and open-mouthed, watched us while we ate. The whole neighbourhood seemed to have assembled to see the man who had given peace to Russia and now did not want it. At the end of dinner I congratulated him formally on his appointment as Minister for War. He replied that he had not yet accepted the post and that he would not accept it unless Russia were going to fight. At the time I believe he was sincere. Almost at the same moment the station-master came in and handed him a telegram. It was from Moscow. It contained the news that the Congress of Soviets had ratified the peace by an enormous majority.

We slept none the less soundly and arrived at Moscow the next morning without further incident.

At the station Trotsky gave another exhibition of good manners. He had secured rooms for us at the only hotel which was still functioning. He insisted on sending us off in his two cars, while he himself waited at the station.

CHAPTER FIVE

IN ONE SENSE I was glad to be back in Moscow. I knew nearly
every stone of its cobbled streets. It was almost my home. I had
spent more years of my life inside its walls than in any other
city in the world.

Yet it was a new Moscow that I found. Many of my old
Russian and English friends had left. Chelnokoff had fled to
the South. Lvoff was in hiding. Most of the fine houses of the
rich merchants were occupied by Anarchists, whose outrages
were even more daringly executed than in St. Petersburg.
The city, too, was abnormally gay with a gaiety that shocked
me. The bourgeoisie was awaiting the Germans with impatience and was already celebrating in advance the hour of its
relief. Cabarets flourished. There was even one in the Elite
Hotel, which was now our headquarters. Prices were high,
especially for champagne, but there seemed no lack of money
among the guests, who nightly thronged the tables until the
early hours.

I had, however, little time for moralising. Within twenty-
four hours of my arrival I was plunged into a whirlpool of
turbulent activity. I found Robins and his Red Cross Mission
at the Elite, where between us we had secured comfortable
suites with sitting-rooms and bathrooms. General Lavergne
and a large French military mission had also made Moscow
their headquarters. General Romei was there with a smaller
Italian mission. Major Riggs represented American military
interests. If there was not to be the wildest confusion of opinion,
it was essential that we should co-ordinate our efforts.

I called on all the Allied representatives, and at Romei's suggestion we had a daily conference in my rooms, at which Lavergne,
Romei, Riggs and myself were always present. Robins also
attended frequently. We succeeded in establishing a remarkably
smooth co-operation. Almost to the bitter end we were in complete agreement regarding policy. We were watching the situation from the inside, and we realised that without Bolshevik
consent military intervention would result only in a civil war,

which, without very large Allied forces, would be disastrous to our prestige. Intervention with Bolshevik consent was the policy which we sought to carry out, and within ten days of my arrival we passed a common resolution condemning Japanese intervention as futile. In self-defence I should make it plain that all our actions were influenced by the situation on the Western Front, where the great German March offensive was in full swing. We knew that the burning anxiety of the Allied High Command was to detach as many German soldiers from the West as possible. But taking every factor into consideration, we could not believe that this object could be attained by support of Alexeieff or Korniloff, who were at that time the forerunners of Denikin and Wrangel. These generals, like Skoropadsky, who was installed by the Germans as head of a White Government in Kieff, were not immediately interested in the war in the West. They may have been sincere in their desire to reconstitute an Eastern front against Germany, but, before they could do so, they had to deal with the Bolsheviks. Without strong foreign aid they were not powerful enough for this task. Outside the officer class—and it, too, was demoralised —they had no support in the country. Although we realised that the Bolsheviks would fight only if they were forced into war by German aggression, we were convinced that this situation might easily develop and that by a promise of support we might help to shape events in the form we desired. We could understand the resentment of the Allied Governments against the Bolsheviks. We could not follow their reasoning.

In this miniature Allied council Romei and I were independent. Romei reported direct to the Italian General Staff. He was not under the Italian Embassy. Since the departure of our own Embassy, I was alone. Lavergne, although the head of a military mission, was also military attaché. He was directly under the control of his Ambassador. Riggs was in an even more subordinate position. And the Allied Ambassadors were at Vologda, a little provincial town, hundreds of miles away from the centre of events. It was as if three foreign Ambassadors were trying to advise their governments on an English cabinet crisis from a village in the Hebrides. They were, too, strangely ill-fitted for their task. Francis, the American Ambassador, was a charming old gentleman of nearly eighty—a banker from St. Louis, who had left America for the first time to be plunged into the vortex of the revolution. Noulens, the French Ambassador, was also a new arrival. He was a professional politician, whose attitude was determined by the prevailing policy of his own Party in the French Chamber. Lavergne, too, had a Socialist on his staff—Captain Jean Sadoul, the well-known French barrister and former Socialist deputy. Sadoul, who was on friendly terms with Trotsky, was a legacy of Albert Thomas. He served Lavergne well and faithfully, but to Noulens he was like a red rag to a bull. Politician mistrusted politician. There was continual friction. Noulens held up Sadoul's correspondence with Thomas, and in the end his obstinacy and his oppression drove the unfortunate Sadoul into throwing in his lot with the Bolsheviks. Torretta, the Italian Chargé d'Affaires, knew Russia well and spoke the language. His Russia, however, was the Russia of the old régime. Even had he wished to do so, he was morally incapable of standing up against the virile and aggressive Noulens. Moreover, he had had that desperate interview with Lutsky. There was not much to be hoped for from Torretta.

Vologda, even more than London and Paris, lived on the wildest anti-Bolshevik rumours. Rarely a day passed without Lavergne's being ordered by his Ambassador to investigate some new evidence of Bolshevik pro-Germanism. Romei and I roared with laughter when Lavergne asked us if we had heard anything of a German Control Commission in St. Petersburg. At the head of it was Count Frederiks, the former Court Minister of the Tsar. It was working behind the scenes, but it had complete control over the Bolshevik Foreign Office, and not a single foreigner could leave Russia without its permission. "Another telegram from Vologda!" we said. But Lavergne did not laugh. These little excitements of M. Noulens had to be taken seriously, and, while Lavergne made inquiries on his own, down would go Sadoul to Trotsky to register an official protest against the establishment of such a mission. Trotsky would look blank. Sometimes he would be angry. At other times he would laugh and offer to write out a bromide prescription to calm the nerves of their Excellencies of Vologda. His father had been a chemist, and his acquaintance with a drug store had enriched his vocabulary. Lavergne had to take the tedious journey to Vologda fairly frequently. Romei and I went only once. Romei's comment was that "If we had put all the Allied representatives there in a cauldron and stirred them up, not one drop of common sense would have come out of the whole boiling."

The month of March, 1918, was the period during which the Bolsheviks were most amenable to an understanding with the Allies. They were afraid of further German aggression. They had little confidence in their own future. They would have welcomed the assistance of Allied officers in training the new Red Army which Trotsky was now forming.

A coincidence of misfortune had provided us with a remarkable opportunity of supplying the Bolshevik War Minister with the Allied officers whom he required. A large French military mission, headed by General Berthelot, had just arrived in Moscow from Rumania. Holding the view that it was better that the Red Army should be trained by Allied officers than by Germans, we proposed to Trotsky that he should make use of General Berthelot's services. The Red leader, who had already shown his good-will by appointing a committee of Allied officers to advise him, accepted the proposal with alacrity. At the first meeting of this new committee, which was composed of General Romei, General Lavergne, Major Riggs and Captain Garstin, Trotsky made a formal request for help. General Lavergne accepted the invitation, and it was agreed that General Berthelot's mission should remain. We seemed to have secured a tactical advantage.

Two days later the whole scheme was wrecked. M. Noulens had intervened. General Lavergne was hauled over the coals for exceeding his powers, and General Berthelot and his staff of officers were ordered to return immediately to France. The barometer of Trotsky's temperament suffered a severe depression, and the *Izvestia* came out with a leading article declaring that "only America had known how to treat the Bolsheviks decently and it was the Allies themselves who, by disregarding the wishes of the Russian people, were preventing the creation of a pro-Ally policy."

If General Lavergne had his troubles, my own were just as great. With the help of our secret service agents the British Government had discovered a new pro-German scare. According to the reports it had received, Siberia was teeming with German regiments composed of war prisoners, who had been armed by the Bolsheviks. They were in control of a vast area. Here was a further proof that the Bolsheviks were handing over all Russia to the enemy. I received a querulous telegram pointing out the difference between my reports and the actions of the Bolsheviks.

I referred the matter to my Allied colleagues in Moscow. Common sense told me that the story was a mare's nest. Siberia, however, was far away. We could not quote the evidence of our own eyes. Robins and I, therefore, went down to the Commissariat for War to interview Trotsky. His reply was unequivocal. It was no use his issuing a denial. We should not believe him. We must go—and see for ourselves. There and then he offered full facilities to anyone we liked to send to carry out an investigation on the spot.

Ill as I could spare him, I decided to send Hicks, my most reliable assistant. He left that night together with Captain Webster, an officer of the American Red Cross Mission. Trotsky carried out his promise. He gave to both officers a personal letter instructing the local Soviets to give them the fullest assistance. They were to be allowed to go anywhere and to see everything.

Hicks was not to return for six weeks. During that time he travelled all over Siberia, inspecting the prison camps and carrying out his investigations with great thoroughness. His telegrams to me contained some startling information, especially regarding Semenoff, the Cossack general, who behind the

Chinese frontier was waging a brigand warfare against the Bolsheviks. But of armed German or Austrian war-prisoners in Siberia he had seen no trace.

I paraphrased his reports and ciphered them to the War Office. The immediate reaction of London was a telegram from the War Office ordering Hicks to return to England at once. I was in a quandary. I had a shrewd idea why Hicks had been recalled. Moreover, I could not spare him. I had already more work than I could cope with, and no one on my staff was an expert cipherer. At the end of a long day's work I had to sit up late and take a hand in the ciphering myself. I sent a telegram to the Foreign Office pointing out my difficulties. At the same time I added that Hicks had been sent to Siberia on my responsibility and that, if he were to be recalled, there was no other course than for me to ask for my own recall. I received a private telegram from George Clerk, whose kindness and patience with my shortcomings I remember with gratitude, informing me that Hicks could remain.

The incident closed, but it did not increase my popularity in London. Within four days I received two alarming telegrams from my wife. The second ran as follows: "Have fullest information. Do nothing rash. Am anxious about your future career. I understand your personal feelings but hope to see you soon. Would be better for you. Please acknowledge immediately, also wire about no sympathy here."

The meaning was unmistakable. I knew from whom my wife had received her information. I was to throw in my hand and come home. I kept a stiff upper lip and my troubles to myself.

Quite apart from the major question of policy, life at this moment was full of minor excitements. There were perpetual pin-pricks between the British and Russian Governments—pin-pricks which served to confuse the real issue. We had small missions all over Russia, and each mission had a different policy. At the same time we were making every kind of protest against the Bolshevik confiscation of Allied property. The Bolsheviks retaliated by attacks on the war aims of the Allies and attempts to influence British Labour in their favour. Litvinoff, in particular, was making himself a nuisance in London. In this game of protest and counter-protest I was a sadly battered shuttlecock between the battledores of the two Governments.

Nevertheless, there were rays of light in this murky situation. The German successes on the Western front had alarmed the Bolsheviks. They were prepared to go so far as to agree to Allied intervention in the event of renewed aggression by the Germans. The atmosphere in Moscow at this stage may best be illustrated by the fact that in its account of the March fighting on the Western front the Bolshevik Press suppressed all German bulletins. The bourgeois Press published them in full.

The Germans, too, seemed to be playing into our hands in Russia. Their attitude towards the Bolsheviks was truculent and overbearing. They made numerous protests against our presence at Murmansk, which we still occupied, and for form's sake the Bolshevik Foreign Office sent me several notes, which in accordance with its practice of so-called open diplomacy were published in the official Press. I took the notes to Chicherin. "What am I to do with them?" I asked. He replied that it would help if we would take the local soviet into greater consideration. "Otherwise," he said cynically, "you can put them in your waste-paper basket."

Trotsky, although almost in despair over the attitude of the Allies, was no less friendly. "Just when we are on the verge of going to war," he said, "the Allied governments do everything they can to help the Germans." In the history of the Jews, which at that time was—not without reason—my bed-side literature, I found the prayer of Bar Cochba, the Jewish "Son of the Star," in his struggle against the Romans in A.D. 132. "We pray Thee not to assist our enemies: us Thou needst not help." The words were almost the same as those which Trotsky addressed to me daily.

It was at this time that Trotsky gave me one remarkable proof of his physical courage. I was talking to him in the

Commissariat for War in the square behind the Cathedral of the Saviour. Suddenly, a startled assistant burst into the room in a state of panic. There was a large crowd of armed sailors outside. They had not been paid or their pay was insufficient. They wanted to see Trotsky. If he did not come, they would storm the place.

Trotsky rose at once, his eyes blazing, and went down into the square. I watched the scene from the window. He made no attempt to satisfy the sailors. Instead, he lashed them with a withering blast of invective. They were dogs totally unworthy of the Fleet, which had played such a glorious part in the revolution. He would look into their complaints. If they were justified, they would be rectified. If not, he would brand them as traitors to the revolution. In the meantime they were to go back to their barracks or he would disarm them and take away their privileges. The sailors slunk away like beaten curs, and Trotsky returned to me to resume his conversation where he had left off. Was Trotsky another Bar Cochba? At any rate he was very bellicose.

Lenin, whom Robins saw frequently, was more guarded, but he, too, was prepared to go a long way to secure the friendly co-operation of the Allies.

Nor were the other Commissars behind-hand in their evidence of friendliness. I had established smooth-working relations with Karachan, who, together with Chicherin and Radek, formed a kind of triumvirate at the Bolshevik Foreign Office. An Armenian, with dark, waving hair and a well-trimmed beard, he was the adonis of the Bolshevik Party. His manners were perfect. He was an excellent judge of a cigar. I never saw him in a bad temper, and during the whole period of our contact, and even when I was being denounced as a spy and an assassin by his colleagues, I never heard an unpleasant word from his lips. This is not to imply that he was a saint. He had all the guile and craft of his race. Diplomacy was his proper sphere.

Radek, however, was our chief delight among the Commissars. A Jew, whose real name is Sobelsohn, he was in some respects a grotesque figure. A little man with a huge head, protruding ears, clean-shaven face (in those days he did not wear that awful fringe which now passes for a beard), with spectacles, and a large mouth with yellow, tobacco-stained teeth, from which a huge pipe or cigar was never absent, he was always dressed in a quaint drab-coloured Norfolk suit with knickers and leggings. He was a great friend of Ransome, the correspondent of the *Manchester Guardian*, and through Ransome we came to know him very well. Almost every day he would turn up in my rooms, an English cap stuck jauntily on his head, his pipe puffing fiercely, a bundle of books under his arm, and a huge revolver strapped to his side. He looked like a cross between a professor and a bandit.

Of his intellectual brilliance, however, there was no doubt. He was the virtuoso of Bolshevik journalism, and his conversation was as sparkling as his leading articles. Ambassadors were his game and Foreign Ministers his butts. As Assistant Commissar for Foreign Affairs he received the Ambassadors and Ministers in the afternoon, and the next morning, under the thinly-disguised pseudonym of Viator, he attacked them in the *Izvestia*. He was a Puck full of malice and with a delicious sense of humour. He was the Bolshevik Lord Beaverbrook.

When the German Embassy arrived, he sorely tried the patience of the Kaiser's representatives. For, in those days, at any rate, this little man was violently anti-German. He had been at Brest-Litovsk, where he had taken an impish delight in puffing the smoke of his vile cheroot into General Hofmann's face. He had voted on every occasion against peace. Hot-headed and impulsive, he chafed under the restraint which from time to time had to be placed on his conduct by his more cautious colleagues. And, when he came to us and was rewarded with a half-pound tin of navy tobacco, he would air his grievances with scintillating abandon. His satirical shafts were aimed at all and sundry. He spared nobody—not even Lenin, and certainly not the Russians. When the peace was ratified, he exclaimed, almost in tears: "My God, if we had had any other race but Russians behind us in this struggle, we should have upset the world." He had a poor opinion of both Chicherin and Karachan. Chicherin was an old woman. Karachan he described as the "osel klassicheskoi krasoty"—the donkey of classical beauty. He was an amusing and entertaining comedian and, kept in proper check, the most dangerous propagandist that the Bolshevik movement has so far produced.

During our first two months in Moscow Robins and I enjoyed a privileged position. We had no difficulty in seeing the various Commissars. We were even allowed to be present at certain meetings of the Central Executive Committee. On one occasion we went to hear the debate on the new army. In those early days the Bolshevik Parliament held its meetings in the main restaurant of the Metropole Hotel, which had been re-named the "First House of Soviets." The deputies were seated in chairs set out in rows as for a concert. The various speakers spoke from the little pulpit from which formerly Konchik, the leader of the orchestra, had stirred countless bourgeois souls with the sobbing of his violin. On this particular occasion the chief speaker was of course Trotsky. As a demagogic orator Trotsky is wonderfully effective until he loses his temper. He has a fine command of language, and the words stream from his mouth in a torrent, which never seems to abate. At its highest pitch his voice sounds almost like a hiss.

That night he was at his best. He was the man of action reporting the first progress of his great achievement—the creation of the Red Army. There was just sufficient opposition (in March and April there were still several Mensheviks in the Central Executive Committee) to rouse him to a great effort but not to make him lose his control, and he demolished his opponents with vigour and obvious relish. The enthusiasm he aroused was remarkable. His speech was like a declaration of war. He himself was an incarnation of belligerent hate.

Before the debate began, Robins and I were given tea and biscuits and were introduced to various Commissars whom we had not yet met: the mild-mannered and silky-tongued

Lunacharsky; Bucharin, diminutive in size but a man of great personal courage and the only Bolshevik who was not afraid to criticise Lenin or to cross swords with him in a dialectical duel; Pokrovsky, the eminent Bolshevik historian; Krylenko, an epileptic degenerate, the future Public Prosecutor, and the most repulsive type I came across in all my connections with the Bolsheviks. These four men, together with Lenin and Chicherin, represented the purely Russian element in a hotch-potch of Jews, Georgians, Poles and other nationalities.

During the debate we sat at a side table with Radek and Gumberg, Robins' Jew-American assistant. Lenin came into the hall several times. He sat down and chatted with us for a few minutes. He was, as usual, in a good humour—indeed, I think of all the public figures I have met he possessed the most equable temperament—but he took no part in the debate. The only attention he paid to Trotsky's speech was to lower his voice slightly in his own conversation.

There were two other Commissars whom I met that night for the first time. One was Derjinsky, the head of the Cheka and a man of correct manners and quiet speech but without a ray of humour in his character. The most remarkable thing about him was his eyes. Deeply sunk, they blazed with a steady fire of fanaticism. They never twitched. His eyelids seemed paralysed. He had spent most of his life in Siberia and bore the traces of his exile on his face. I also shook hands with a strongly-built man with a sallow face, black moustache, heavy eyebrows, and black hair worn *en brosse*. I paid little attention to him. He himself said nothing. He did not seem of sufficient importance to include in my gallery of Bolshevik portraits. If he had been announced then to the assembled Party as the successor of Lenin, the delegates would have roared with laughter. The man was the Georgian Djugashvilli, known to-day to the whole world as Stalin, the man of steel.

Of these new acquaintances the one who made the deepest impression on me was Lunacharsky. A man of brilliant intellect and wide culture, he has been more successful than anyone in converting bourgeois intellectuals to Bolshevism or to tolerance of the Bolshevik régime. It was he who brought back Gorky to the Bolshevik fold, to which, perhaps without knowing it, he had always belonged. It was he, too, who insisted on the preservation of the bourgeois arts, who provided protection for the treasures of the Russian museums, and who is primarily responsible for the fact that to-day Moscow has still its opera, its ballet, and its famous Art Theatre. It was also Lunacharsky, who, as an original adherent to the Orthodox Faith, started the "Bolshevising" movement inside the Russian Church. A brilliant speaker, he advanced many original arguments in support of his revised religion. It was during that first year of Bolshevism that he made his famous speech in which he compared Lenin's persecution of the capitalists with Christ's expulsion of the money-lenders from the Temple, finishing with the startling peroration that "if Christ were alive to-day, he would be a Bolshevik."

Robins and I had one more thrilling experience during this period of March and April, 1918. One of Trotsky's first tasks as Commissar for War had been to rid Moscow of the anarchist bands who were terrorising the city. At three in the early morning of April 12th he carried out a simultaneous raid on the twenty-six anarchist nests. The venture was a complete success. After a desperate resistance the Anarchists were evicted from the houses they had occupied, and all their machine-guns, their rifles, their ammunition, and their loot were captured. Over a hundred were killed in the fighting. Five hundred were arrested. Later in the day on Derjinsky's invitation, Robins and I made a tour of the different fighting areas. We were given a car and an armed escort. Our cicerone was Peters, Derjinsky's Lettish assistant and my future gaoler-in-chief.

The Anarchists had appropriated the finest houses in Moscow. On the Povarskaia, where the rich merchants lived, we entered house after house. The filth was indescribable. Broken bottles littered the floors, the magnificent ceilings were perforated with bullet-holes. Wine stains and human excrement blotched the Aubusson carpets. Priceless pictures had been slashed to strips. The dead still lay where they had fallen. They included officers in guards' uniform, students—young boys of twenty—and men who belonged obviously to the criminal class and whom the revolution had released from prison. In the luxurious drawing-room of the House Gracheva the Anarchists had been surprised in the middle of an orgy. The long table which had supported the feast had been overturned, and broken plates, glasses, champagne bottles, made unsavoury islands in a pool of blood and spilt wine. On the floor lay a young woman, face downwards. Peters turned her over. Her hair was dishevelled. She had been shot through the neck, and the blood had congealed in a sinister purple clump. She could not have been more than twenty. Peters shrugged his shoulders. "Prostitutka," he said. "Perhaps it is for the best."

It was an unforgettable scene. The Bolsheviks had taken their first step towards the establishment of discipline.

CHAPTER SIX

IF WE LIVED in a state of chronic crisis, life was not without its relaxations. Thanks to the American Red Cross, we were well supplied with stores and tobacco. Hicks, too, was an excellent organiser, and in the days when the going was still good he provided us with a cellar which nearly lasted out our stay. We dined in our rooms, entertaining our colleagues and making as brave a show as we could in return for the more sumptuous hospitality which their larger numbers and their superior accommodation enabled them to offer. After dinner there was generally a game of poker with the Americans. Robins did not play. He read his Bible or talked to me. But his staff did. My fellows were no match for them, and, when I took a hand in the game, I, too, had to pay for my education. There was an Irish-American called O'Callaghan, whose equal as a poker-player I have yet to discover. He was a confirmed pessimist. Every time he played he would take out his watch and say: "The luck changes at twelve o'clock, when it gets worse." His own luck or skill never changed. He took our money with unfailing regularity.

On Sundays we went to the ballet. Except that the Imperial box was crowded with "comrades," the performance was the same as in Tsarist days, and excellent it was. For a few hours we could forget our troubles, and, watching the same scenery and the same dancers, I found it hard to remember that we were in the middle of the greatest revolution the world has ever known. Then the curtain would go down. The orchestra would strike up "The International," and we returned to the grim realism of the time in which we lived. In the space of a few months "The International" was the third national anthem I had heard played by the same orchestra.

When the spring came, we made excursions into the country, picnicked in the woods and played rounders in the fields. It was our only form of exercise. Our favourite resort was Archangelskoe, the beautiful country home of Prince Yusupoff. It was strange to see the place deserted. The peasants had taken over the land, but, as far as we could see, they had not touched the house, and everything seemed intact. After Moscow the solitude was vastly soothing. There was no traffic on the roads, and, once we were clear of the outskirts of the city, we rarely saw a living soul. The absence of traffic, in fact, was a danger which nearly brought me to disaster. Coming back one night after dusk, we ran into a toll-bar. The turn-pike keeper had gone to sleep. Fortunately, we were not going very fast, and beyond a smashed wind-screen our car suffered no damage. My hands, however, were badly cut by the broken glass, and I bear the scars of the adventure to this day.

We even went to a cabaret—a cellar called the "Podpolye" in the Okhotny Riad. It was a stupid escapade, for the place was illegal, and if we had been caught we should have looked foolish. The hall was crowded with bourgeois of the richer class. There was an excellent stage, tables on the floor, and a row of boxes at the end. Prices were high, but there was champagne on every table. We took a box and sat down to listen to a first-class entertainment such as only Russians can provide. It was here that I heard for the first time Vertinsky, a decadent young genius, whose songs, written and sung by himself, expressed the disillusionment of the Russian intelligentsia. One song, in particular, made a deep impression on me: "Ya nye znaiu zachem" ("I do not know why"). It was an anti-war song, and Vertinsky, his face powdered a deathly white, sang it with immense effect. I can remember only the first few lines:

> "I do not know why
> or for what purpose.
> Who sent them to death
> With relentless, untrembling hand.
> Only it was all so useless,
> So pitiless . . . . ."

The song was encored again and again. It reflected the mood of an anti-Bolshevik audience which had lost its soul and its morale. It was the song of a class which had already abandoned all hope—a class which would go almost to any length to avoid death by fighting. Yet only that morning I had received a telegram from the Foreign Office giving the view of a British military expert that all that was required in Russia was a small and resolute nucleus of British officers to lead the "loyal Russians" on to victory.

As I sat reflecting on the hard fate of the man on the spot, there was a sudden rush at the door and a stern roar of "hands up!" Twenty men in masks had entered the room and were covering the audience with Browning pistols and revolvers. There was a deathly stillness. Quickly and without fuss, four of the bandits went through the pockets of the audience, collecting money, jewellery and everything of value. Most of them wore officers' uniform—whether with right or not I had no means of determining. When they reached our box, the leader noticed the English uniforms of Hill and Garstin. I had already handed over my watch and note-case. The man saluted. "You are English officers," he said. With my arms still stretched towards heaven, I answered "Yes." He returned me my money and my watch. "We do not rob Englishmen," he said. "I apologise for the state of my country which forces me to adopt this manner of earning our living."

We were in luck. Fortunately, we were never in a position to repeat the experiment. When Trotsky exterminated the Anarchists, he closed the cabarets as well.

As far as Moscow was concerned, we Allies were a not unhappy family. Lavergne and Romei were splendid companions, and, during the eight trying months we were together, we never had a quarrel or a cross word. Romei, in particular, was a great stand-by. He was the most stolid Italian I have ever met. He faced every crisis with complete objectiveness and could always be relied upon to give a common-sense solution to every problem. He had no illusions about the collapse of Russia as a fighting machine and opposed himself resolutely to any scheme of adventure.

With the other British missions in Russia my relations were not so good. I maintained as close a contact as possible with Cromie, the naval attaché, and was able to assist him in his

work by bringing him into touch with Trotsky. He was a
gallant and extremely efficient naval officer, but was without
experience of political work. Occasionally, too, I saw McAlpine,
a former Treasury official and a man of first-class intellect. His
headquarters were in St. Petersburg. He, too, was able to take
an objective view of the situation and remained to the end a
convinced opponent of intervention. There were, however,
other British officials, who I knew disapproved of my policy
and, without knowing what I was doing, intrigued against me.
The truth is that our various missions and remnants of missions
were at sixes and sevens. There was no one in a position of
authority, and, although the Foreign Office addressed me in
their telegrams as "British Agent, Moscow," and the Bolsheviks insisted on labelling me "British Diplomatic Representative," I was completely in the dark regarding the work of a
whole group of British officers and officials for whose presence
in Russia and for whose protection my position with the
Bolsheviks was the only guarantee.

There was no British policy, unless seven different policies
at once can be called a policy. And, for the furtherance of this
vagueness, the Foreign Office insisted on keeping my own
position as vague as possible. If in the House of Commons
some irate interventionist wished to know why in the name
of decency the British Government maintained an official
representative with a government of cut-throats, who boasted
of their determination to destroy civilisation, Mr. Balfour or
his Under-Secretary would then reply quite truthfully that we
had no official representative accredited to the Bolshevik
Government. On the other hand, when some revolutionary-
minded Liberal charged the British Government with the
folly of not maintaining an accredited representative in
Moscow in order to protect British interests and to assist the
Bolsheviks in their struggle with German militarism, Mr.
Balfour would reply, with the same strict regard for the truth,
that in Moscow we had a representative—an official with great
experience of Russia—who was charged precisely with these
duties.

Obviously, the British Government was faced with a problem of immense difficulty. It was not in a position to send large forces to Russia. If it supported the small officer armies in the South, it ran the risk of driving the Bolsheviks into an unholy league with the Germans. If it supported the Bolsheviks, there was, at the beginning at any rate, a serious danger that the Germans would advance on Moscow and St. Petersburg and set up their own pro-German bourgeois Government. (Personally, I should have preferred this course, as it would have drawn more German troops into Russia. Without German military support no bourgeois Government could have maintained power for a month. The Bolsheviks would always have mastered the forces of the anti-Bolshevik Russians.) Moreover, it was physically impossible for our Government to keep pace with the situation, which changed radically every forty-eight hours. That British Ministers were unable to see any sign of order in the prevailing chaos was natural enough. Where they were to blame was in listening to too many counsellors, and in not realising the fundamental truth that in Russia the educated class represented only an infinitesimal minority, without organisation or political experience and without any contact with the masses. It was the crowning folly of Tsarism that outside its own bureaucracy it had sternly repressed every political outlet. When Tsarism collapsed, the bureaucracy collapsed with it, and there was nothing left but the masses. In Moscow, with one's fingers on the pulse of the events, everyone except the most obstinate traditionalist could realise that here was a cataclysm which had shattered all previous conceptions of Russia. London, however, continued to regard it as a passing storm, after which the glass would return to "set fair." The most dangerous of all historical aphorisms is the catch-phrase: "*plus ça change, plus c'est la même chose.*" During the spring and summer of 1918 it was constantly on the lips of the British pro-interventionists. History has its ebbs and flows, but unlike the tide the ebb comes slowly and, rarely, if ever, in one generation.

Another heavy weight on my shoulders during this period

was my contact with my old political friends of pre-revolutionary days. Those who had remained in Moscow came to see me. They came, some in anger, some in sorrow, and some in friendship. They could be divided into three classes: those who were in favour of general peace; those who were in touch with the White Generals in the South and who believed in the so-called Allied orientation; and those who realised sadly that the Bolsheviks had come to stay. I do not include the out-and-out pro-Germans in this classification. They did not come to see me.

These interviews were a source of genuine grief to me. These men had been my friends and colleagues in the task of promoting Anglo-Russian friendship. To refuse them help seemed almost like treachery. With the advocates of a general peace (the idea was that we should make peace with Germany and allow the Germans to deal with Bolshevism) my task was comparatively simple. I could only shake my head sorrowfully and say that in the light of the situation on the Western front this object seemed unattainable. Nevertheless, they persevered, and, when the German Embassy arrived in Moscow, one prominent Russian informed me that he had consulted the German Ambassador and was in a position to arrange a private interview for me with him at the Russian's house. I referred the matter to the Foreign Office and was instructed to have nothing to do with the proposal.

Much more trying was my position with the advocates of Allied intervention. Situated as I was, I was not in a position to offer them any promise of help or of support. Nor did I do so, although for the sake of information I maintained a more or less regular contact with them. I was visited, too, by various emissaries from General Alexeieff, General Korniloff, and, later, General Denikin, but, as I was surrounded by agents-provocateurs and could not be certain of their bona fides, I was severely non-committal in my answers.

The third class whom I may call the realists were few in number. They included men like Avinoff, the former Assistant Minister of the Interior, and young Muravieff, ex-secretary of

Izvolsky and a brother of the first Lady Cheetham. Avinoff, a man of great intelligence and objectivity, was the most understanding of all my friends. He was a man whom no one could help liking. His manners were as charming as his culture. His wife, born a Countess Trubetskaia, belonged to one of the oldest families in Russia. The revolution had destroyed everything he held dear in life. But, prescient beyond most of his compatriots, he saw clearly. And in the course of a brilliant *exposé* of the revolutionary movement he told me sadly that the Bolsheviks were the only government that had shown the slightest sign of strength since the revolution, that in spite of its dictatorial tyranny its roots were in the masses, and that the counter-revolution had no chance of success for years to come.

We had, too, other visitors in the form of stranded English missions returning from Rumania and the South. There was Le Page, a self-possessed and bearded naval officer, who had the arduous task of maintaining relations with the Russian Fleet in the Black Sea. There was de Candolle, a railway expert, who had been engaged on a mission in Rumania. On his return home through Moscow, he left me his assistant, Tamplin, whom I added to the strength of my own mission. A little later, I picked up Lingner, who had been employed on a propaganda mission in Tiflis and who, in order to reach Moscow, had completed a real Odyssey of dangerous adventure. Both Tamplin, who spoke Russian perfectly, and Lingner, who had a good business head, were of great help to me. Nor must I forget to mention Arthur Ransome, the correspondent of the *Manchester Guardian*, who, if not a member of our mission, was something more than a visitor. He lived in our hotel and we saw him almost daily. Ransome was a Don Quixote with a walrus moustache, a sentimentalist, who could always be relied upon to champion the under-dog, and a visionary, whose imagination had been fired by the revolution. He was on excellent terms with the Bolsheviks and frequently brought us information of the greatest value. An incorrigible romanticist, who could spin a fairy-tale out of nothing, he was an amusing and good-natured companion. As an ardent fisherman who had written some charming sketches on angling, he made a warm appeal to my sympathy, and I championed him resolutely against the secret service idiots who later tried to denounce him as a Bolshevik agent.

Our most exciting visitors, however, were the Germans, whom we saw frequently but never greeted. As a direct result of the peace of Brest-Litovsk the Germans had appointed Count Mirbach Ambassador in Moscow. He was due to arrive on April 24th. The first of a long series of duels began on April 22nd, when the Bolsheviks roused me to fury by requisitioning forty rooms in my hotel for the new Ambassador and his staff. Most of the rooms were on the same floor as my own.

White with passion, I went to Chicherin and protested vigorously against this insult. Chicherin was apologetic, but impotent. I stormed and I blustered. Chicherin looked up wearily, his ferret-eyes blinking with amazement at this fierce outburst from so good-natured a person as myself. He wrung his hands, pleaded for time, promised that the intrusion would be only for a few days, and excused himself on the ground that there was no other accommodation available.

In despair I went to Trotsky, who, at any rate, could be relied upon to give a decision. He was not to be found. He had, however, an extremely able and tactful secretary, Evgenia Petrovna Shelyepina, who is now an English subject and the wife of Arthur Ransome. I told her that I must speak to Trotsky immediately and that the matter was one of the utmost urgency. Within five minutes I was speaking to him on the telephone. In the most vigorous Russian I could command I told him that I would not tolerate this insult, and, that, unless the requisition order were rescinded at once, I should move myself, my mission, and my baggage to the station and camp there, until he gave me a train. I demanded an immediate answer.

Trotsky, who was in the middle of a Commissars' meeting at the Kremlin, took my outburst splendidly. He agreed that our position would be intolerable. He promised to take immediate action. He was as good as his word. Half an hour later he telephoned to me to say that the matter had been settled.

He had given categorical orders that other quarters—he did not know where—were to be found for the Germans. For several days they were lodged uncomfortably in a second-rate hotel. Then they moved to a magnificent private house in the Denejni Pereulok. This minor triumph I owed entirely to Shelyepina. I rewarded her later, when she wanted to leave Russia, by giving her a British passport—an illegal act, for which I hope I shall not be held responsible to-day.

On April 26th Count Mirbach presented his credentials at the Kremlin. He was received, not by Lenin, but by Sverdloff, the President of the Central Executive Committee. The proceedings were formal and acidly polite. In his speech Sverdloff said: "We greet in your person the nation with whom we concluded the Treaty of Brest-Litovsk."

The staff of the German Embassy was composed almost entirely of Russian experts. Mirbach himself had been Counsellor of the German Embassy in St. Petersburg before the war. Riezler, his chief assistant, had had a long and varied experience of Russian politics. Hausschild, the first secretary, was an old friend of mine. He had come to Moscow as Vice-Consul at the same time as myself. He was a man of sterling character. Until the outbreak of war he had always been pro-English.

Although they possessed so wide a knowledge of Russian affairs, I do not believe that the Germans were more successful in their dealings with the Bolsheviks than we were. Certainly, they made as many mistakes, and at no time was their position secure or happy. We went everywhere unarmed and unattended. The Germans never moved out of their quarters without a guard.

Their presence in Moscow, however, was a considerable embarrassment to us, and the Bolsheviks must have found a childish amusement in playing us off against each other. They did it very effectively. They herded us together in the same waiting-room at the Foreign Office. If they wished to annoy Mirbach they received me first. If the British Government had offended them in any way, they were suave to Mirbach and kept me waiting. If the Germans were too insistent in their demands, the Bolsheviks would threaten them with Allied intervention. When the Allies tried to force intervention on the Bolsheviks, they would draw an alarming picture of the dangers of a German advance on Moscow. As neither the Germans nor the Allies could make up their minds on a clear-cut policy towards Russia, Bolshevik diplomacy had all the advantages.

My meetings with the Germans at the Bolshevik Foreign Office caused me acute discomfort. Sometimes we were left together for nearly an hour, during which we turned our backs on each other and gazed out of the window or read the *Izvestia*. My most painful encounter was the first time I came face to face with Hausschild. He was alone in the waiting-room when I entered, and he came forward to greet me with a frank smile. I turned away as if I did not know him. It was an act which I have regretted ever since. Later, when I was arrested and in danger of my life, he put me to shame by associating himself with the diplomatic representatives of the neutral Powers in the demand for my release. Through the Swedish Chargé d'Affaires, he sent a friendly message to me when I was in prison. To-day, he is dead, and I have never been able to repay my debt of gratitude or to apologise for my action.

There was one other visitor, who, like Arthur Ransome, became a permanency. This was Moura. Since saying good-bye to her in St. Petersburg at the beginning of March, I had missed her more than I cared to admit. We had written to each other regularly, and her letters had become a necessary part of my daily life. In April she came to stay with us in Moscow. She arrived at ten o'clock in the morning, and I was engaged with interviews until ten minutes to one. I went downstairs to the living-room, where we had our meals. She was standing by a table, and the spring sun was shining on her hair. As I walked forward to meet her, I scarcely dared to trust my voice. Into my life something had entered which was stronger than any other tie, stronger than life itself. From then onwards she was never to leave us, until we were parted by the armed force of the Bolsheviks.

CHAPTER SEVEN

WITH THE ARRIVAL of the German Embassy in Moscow the prospects of a renewal of the war between Germany and Russia began to diminish. The great opportunity for an understanding between the Bolsheviks and the Allies had been in February and March, when the Soviet Government was still uncertain what the Germans would do. By the beginning of May, Lenin's peace policy had made headway even among those Bolsheviks, who were most opposed to the treaty of Brest-Litovsk. Strangely enough, the Foreign Office, who in February and March had given me no encouragement, now began to show signs of approval. Thus I was urged to do my utmost to secure Bolshevik consent to an Allied military intervention in Russia.

The moment was not so favourable, but it had not entirely passed. There were still certain factors in our favour, of which the most important was the attitude of the German troops in the territory they had occupied. They had set up a bourgeois Russian Government in the Ukraine, whose first action was to restore the land to its former owners. This naturally provoked a peasant revolt which was suppressed with great cruelty. The Bolsheviks and Left-Social Revolutionaries, who came from the South, were furious and were doing everything they could to stimulate a partisan war against the Germans. The latter could take and hold the towns by their military strength. They never succeeded in controlling the countryside. Moreover, the military support, which the Germans had afforded to the White Finns in the Finnish Civil War, was another factor to our advantage. Germany seemed to be taking the side of reaction. It was therefore natural that the forces of the Left should turn to us for aid.

Trotsky, too, was still talking of war as though it were inevitable. When I asked him if he would accept Allied intervention, he replied that he had already asked the Allies to make a proposition. He wanted safeguards about non-interference in Russia's internal affairs. I then said that, if the Allies would come to an agreement on this point, could we have a half-hour's conference to draw up a working arrangement. His reply was characteristic: "When the Allies agree among themselves, it is not half an hour but a whole day that I shall give you."

It is true that Lenin's views were less satisfactory. He, too, thought that war was inevitable and was in favour of an arrangement with the Allies. But he was determined to fix his own date of inevitability. I saw him for the last time on May 7th. He informed me frankly that to him it appeared clear that sooner or later Russia would become a battle-field for the two opposing Imperialist groups and that he was determined, for the sake of Russia herself, to prevent this for as long a period as was possible.

Nevertheless, right up to the end of June, there was a reasonable prospect of arriving at a *modus vivendi*. Unfortunately, although both the British and American Governments made some attempt to play with the idea of Allied intervention with Bolshevik consent, no definite policy was ever formulated. And in Vologda there was M. Noulens, the French Ambassador, intent only on one aim: to have no dealings with the cut-throats, who had insulted him. On April 29th we had a meeting of the Allied representatives in my rooms. General Lavergne informed us that M. Noulens was in favour of intervention without Bolshevik consent and without asking for it. The General, who had been at Vologda, admitted that his Ambassador had been unable to advance a single military argument in favour of his proposal. Romei, Riggs and I again affirmed our adherence to a policy of co-operation with the Bolsheviks.

There were, too, minor frictions between the Bolsheviks and ourselves—frictions which played an important part in wrecking the working agreement we sought to achieve. Japanese intervention was one stumbling block. At one moment we would be reporting favourable progress with Trotsky. The next day we would be back to where we were before. The Japanese had landed troops at Vladivostok. Scowls from Trotsky. All privileges to the British stopped. Telegrams to London. And after days of delay the answer would come that the incident was to be regarded as purely local.

Prospects of an agreement were not enhanced by a well-intentioned speech of Mr. Balfour, who declared that the Japanese were coming to help the Russians. In a conversation with Ransome Lenin at once raised the question of "which Russians," and in a shrewd analysis of the problem set out his reasons why Japanese intervention would benefit neither England nor Bolshevik Russia. He typed out his analysis and in his own handwriting added his attestation that it correctly represented his views. I reproduce the document in facsimile with an English translation on another page (1) as a specimen of Lenin's handwriting and (2) as an illustration of the workings of his mind.

Another source of trouble was the Czech army which, formed of Czech prisoners, had been fighting for Russia up to the period of the Bolshevik revolution. The Czechs, who were a well-disciplined and fully-armed force, were under the control of French officers. My services, however, were requisitioned to secure their evacuation, presumably because of the privileged position I enjoyed with the Bolshevik Government. The evacuation was no simple matter. Not unnaturally, the Germans protested violently against the presence, on what was now neutral Russian territory, of a large force, which was to be used against them. Nevertheless, I succeeded in securing Trotsky's good-will, and but for the folly of the French I am convinced that the Czechs would have been safely evacuated without incident. My task was not made easier by the last-minute requests of the British Government to use my influence to persuade Trotsky to divert the Czechs to Archangel. This, too, at a time when General Poole was already in North Russia, advocating a policy of intervention, which was subsequently adopted and which never amounted to anything more than an armed intervention against Bolshevism.

Ultimately, the Czechs were the cause of our final breach with the Bolsheviks. How I wish to-day that President Mazaryk had remained in Russia during this trying period. I am convinced that he would never have sanctioned the Siberian revolt. The Allies would have listened to him, and we should have been

СОВѢТЪ НАРОДНЫХЪ
Комиссаровъ.

Петроградъ.

27 - февраля 1918 г.

№ 564

Прошу всѣ Организаціи, Совѣты и Комиссаров

вокзалов оказывать всяческое содѣйствіе членам

Англійской Миссіи гов⟨п⟩ Р.Б. ЛОКАРТУ, В.Л.ГИК-

СУ и Д. ГАРСТИНУ.

Комиссар по иностранным Дѣлам *[signature]*

за Секретарь *[signature]*

P.S. [handwritten note]

[stamp]

[Translation overleaf]

SOVIET OF THE PEOPLE'S COMMISSARS.

————

Petrograd

27th February, 1918.

No. 567.

————

I request all Organisations, Soviets and Commissars of Railway Stations to give every assistance to the members of the English Mission, Messrs. R. B. Lockhart, V. L. Hicks and D. Garstin.

Commissar for Foreign Affairs,

L. TROTSKY.

Secretary,

SERGEIEFF.

P.S.—Personal stores of provisions not to be confiscated.

L. TROTSKY.

spared the crowning folly of an adventure which sent thousands of Russians to their deaths and cost the British taxpayer millions of pounds in money.

The sands were running out. We were drifting rapidly towards the inevitable tragedy. In Moscow, too, I was not alone in receiving no support from home. Robins had lost ground in Vologda. He had a formidable opponent in Summers, the American Consul-General in Moscow, who, married to a Russian of good family, was heart and soul for the old régime. When Summers died suddenly towards the end of April, there were slanderers, who declared that he had been poisoned by the Bolsheviks and who looked askance at Robins. The French, too, had put a spoke in Robins' wheel by playing on the American Ambassador's vanity. In his presence a member of the French Embassy had asked who was the American Ambassador—Francis or Robins—because they always said the opposite of each other. As a result of these intrigues Robins' position became intolerable, and early in May he left Russia in order to make a personal appeal to President Wilson. The night before he left he dined with us. He had been reading Rhodes' life and after dinner he gave us a wonderful exposition of Rhodes' character. Like Lord Beaverbrook, he possessed in a remarkable degree the talent of extracting exactly what he wanted from everything he read, and dramatising it afterwards in his conversation. He was a great personality and a man of sterling character and iron determination. His departure was a great loss to me. In the almost lone hand I was playing his moral courage had been an immense support.

Lavergne, too, willy-nilly, had been forced to adopt the Noulens policy. Even Romei, who as a soldier preferred action to inaction, was beginning to reach the stage when intervention even without Bolshevik consent seemed better than no intervention at all. At this stage the position was that President Wilson was still opposed to intervention without Bolshevik consent. The French were working vigorously for military support of the anti-Bolshevik forces. The British Foreign Office —I write Foreign Office intentionally, because the British War

Office seemed to have a totally different policy—was pressing us hard for an immediate acceptance by the Bolsheviks of Allied military support. Presumably, although I do not think the conditions were ever laid down, they were prepared, in return for this consent, to guarantee to the Bolsheviks complete non-interference in Russia's internal affairs.

In this gloomy vacuum a ray of hope was suddenly propelled. Trotsky had been more than usually amenable. The Germans had been very aggressive in the South, and he had reacted in the usual belligerent manner. He had been conciliatory about Murmansk and about our stores at Archangel. He had even asked for a British naval mission to re-organise the Russian Fleets and had offered to put an Englishman in charge of the Russian railways. I had telegraphed this news to London and for several days I received no answer. I was not astonished. The telegraph service was erratic, and delays and a break in the sequence of numbers were frequent. Then one evening I received a telegram, which was as long as a despatch. I sat up until late into the night deciphering it. It was from Mr. Balfour. I learnt later that he had drafted personally nearly all the telegrams I received in Russia. I have no copy of this telegram. I cannot remember all its details, but its beginning and its end are firmly fixed in my memory. It began: "There are three duties of a diplomatist: one is to make himself *persona grata* to the government of the country to which he is accredited. In this you have succeeded admirably. The second is to interpret to his own government the policy of the government of the country to which he is accredited. In this you have also been successful. The third is to interpret to the Government of the country to which he is accredited, the policy of his own government. In this it seems to me that you have not been so successful." Then followed a list of British grievances against Bolsheviks. When the list was completed, there was a sudden change. "Since writing this," the telegram went on, "I have received your telegram informing me of Trotsky's request for British naval and technical experts. This is good news. If you can, indeed, persuade Trotsky to resist German penetration, you will have earned the gratitude of your own country and of all humanity."

The telegram, although affording me fresh hope, was a little unkind. Admittedly, I had been unsuccessful in interpreting the policy of His Majesty's Government to the Bolsheviks. But for three months London had given me no indication of its policy or policies. In my reply I referred to my previous telegrams and requested humbly to be supplied with a more precise statement. It was not forthcoming. No naval mission was sent. No Englishman was appointed to the control of the Russian railways. But General Poole and a staff of officers were sent to Archangel and Murmansk.

Altogether May was a hectic and nerve-racking month. It began with an impressive parade of the Red Army on the Red Square. Trotsky took the salute in the presence of the foreign diplomatic representatives. Mirbach watched the review from his motor car. At first he smiled superciliously. Then he looked serious. He was the representative of the old German Imperialism. There was an unmistakable living force in the ill-clad, unorganised men who marched past him. I was impressed. The bourgeoisie, however, could not read the signs. They were obsessed with a strange story of a miracle, which had taken place that day. On the Nikolskaia the Bolsheviks had draped an ikon with red bunting. As soon as they put it up, the cloth was miraculously torn.

On May 6th the American Ambassador paid a visit of several days to Moscow. I had several interviews with him and liked him. He was a kind, old gentleman, who was susceptible to flattery and swallowed any amount of it. His knowledge of anything beyond banking and poker was severely limited. He had a travelling spittoon—a contraption with a pedal—which he took with him everywhere. When he wished to emphasise a point, bang would go the pedal, followed by a well-aimed expectoration. During his Moscow visit he was responsible for a story which deserves to rank with Dumas' account of the loving couple plighting their troth under the shade of the "Kliukva" (cranberry)! One afternoon Norman Armour, the efficient secretary of the American Embassy, came into the Ambassador's room.

"Governor," he said, "would you like to go to the opera to-night?"

"Nope," was the reply, "I think I'll play poker."

"Do come, Governor," said Armour. "You really ought not to miss it. It's Evgenie Onegin."

"Evgenny what?" said the Ambassador.

"Oh! you know," replied Armour. "Pushkin and Chaikovsky."

There was a crash from the pedal of the spittoon.

"What!" said the Ambassador ecstatically. "Is Pushkin singing to-night?"

On May 7th I had an excitement of a more disturbing nature. At six o'clock in the evening Karachan telephoned to me requesting me to come to see him. He had an extraordinary story to tell. That afternoon a British officer had walked boldly up to the Kremlin gate and had demanded to see Lenin. Asked for his credentials, he had declared that he had been sent out specially by Mr. Lloyd George to obtain firsthand news of the aims and ideals of the Bolsheviks. The British Government was not satisfied with the reports it had been receiving from me. He had been entrusted with the task of making good the defects. He had not seen Lenin but he had been interviewed by Bonch-Brouevitch, a Russian of good family and the closest personal friend of the Bolshevik leader. Karachan wished to know if the man was an impostor. The name of the officer, he said, was "Relli." I was nonplussed, and, holding it impossible that the man could have any official standing, I nearly blurted out that he must be a Russian masquerading as an Englishman or else a madman. Bitter experience, however, had taught me to be prepared for almost any surprise, and, without betraying my amazement, I told Karachan that I would inquire into the matter and let him know the result. That same evening I sent for Boyce, the head of the Intelligence Service, and told him the story. He informed me that the man was a new agent, who had just come out from England. I blew up in a storm of indignation, and the next day the officer came to me to offer his explanation. He swore that the story Karachan had told me was quite untrue. He admitted, however, that he had been to the Kremlin and had seen Bonch-Brouevitch. The sheer audacity of the man took my breath away. I knew instinctively that on this occasion Karachan had adhered strictly to the truth. Now I was faced with the unpleasant and even dangerous task of saving a British agent, who, unless I denied him, might compromise me and for whose safety, although he was in no way subordinate to me, I felt myself in some measure responsible. Although he was years older than me, I dressed him down like a schoolmaster and threatened to have him sent home. He took his wigging humbly but calmly and was so ingenious in his excuses that in the end he made me laugh. Fortunately, I was able to arrange matters with Karachan so that his suspicions were not unduly aroused.

The man who had thrust himself so dramatically into my life was Sidney Reilly, the mystery man of the British secret service and known to-day to the outside world as the master spy of Britain. My experiences of the war and of the Russian revolution have left me with a very poor opinion of secret service work. Doubtless, it has its uses and its functions, but political work is not its strong point. The buying of information puts a premium on manufactured news. But even manufactured news is less dangerous than the honest reports of men, who, however brave and however gifted as linguists, are frequently incapable of forming a reliable political judgment. The methods of Sidney Reilly, however, were on a grand scale, which compelled my admiration. We shall hear more of him before my story is ended.

About this time, too, I received a mysterious visit from a tall, clean-shaven Russian. He addressed me as "Roman Romanovitch." I looked at him blankly. As far as I knew, I had never seen him before.

"You do not recognise me?" he said.

"Frankly, no," I replied.

He covered his chin and mouth with his hand. It was Fabrikantoff, a Social-revolutionary and an intimate friend of Kerensky. The last time I had seen him, he had worn a beard! He was in dire trouble. Kerensky was in Moscow and wanted to leave Russia. The only way he could go was by Murmansk or Archangel. Fabrikantoff had been to see Wardrop, the British Consul-General, in order to obtain the necessary visa. Wardrop had refused to give it without first referring the matter to London. Several days might elapse before the answer came. There was an immediate opportunity of smuggling Kerensky out with a platoon of Serbian soldiers, who were returning home via Murmansk. Every hour he remained in Moscow exposed him to the danger of betrayal to the Bolsheviks. If the British refused to give him a visa, they might be responsible for his death. What did I propose to do about it?

I made up my mind very quickly. I dared not telephone to Wardrop lest our conversation might be tapped. If he had no authority to give a visa without reference to London, he was not likely to change his mind. I had no time to go to see him. I could not expose Fabrikantoff to the disappointment and even danger of sending him away and asking him to return. I had no authority to give visas. I was an Ishmaelite, to be owned and disowned as the British Government thought fit. I had no certainty that my visa would be accepted by the British authorities at Murmansk. We were living, however, in strange times, and I was prepared to go a long way to avoid endangering the unfortunate Kerensky's life. I therefore took the Serbian passport, which Kerensky had procured, wrote out a visa, and sealed my signature with the rubber stamp, which made apology for our official seal. That same evening Kerensky, disguised as a Serbian soldier, left for Murmansk. Not for three days, when I knew he must be safe, did I telegraph to London, reporting my action and my reasons for taking it. I was afraid that the Bolsheviks had a key to our ciphers.

My fears were not entirely groundless. Karachan himself had confessed to me that the Bolsheviks had made every attempt to procure the German ciphers. They had staged a raid on the

German courier. He even suggested to me that, if our cipher experts could decipher them, he could furnish me with copies of the German telegrams. I suspect that my own popularity with the Bolsheviks was due to the fact that they knew from my telegrams that I was opposed to any form of intervention without Bolshevik consent.

Between May 15th and 23rd Cromie came down twice from St. Petersburg to confer with me. He was anxious about the Black Sea Fleet, which, owing to the German advance along the Black Sea coast, was now in imminent danger of capture. Together we went to see Trotsky. During Cromie's visit I had several interviews with the Red Minister for War, and, although he was now full of suspicions against the Allies, he was reassuring about the Fleet and not unfriendly. After several days of negotiation he informed me that he had given orders for the destruction of the Black Sea Fleet. A little later it was, in fact, blown up. This was the last interview I ever had with Trotsky. From now onwards his door was to be shut against me.

The next day (May 24th) was young Tamplin's twenty-first birthday, and we gave him a dinner at Streilna, the restaurant outside the city, where Maria Nikolaievna and her Tsiganes held their court. By what means I do not know, the place had escaped the vigilance of the Bolshevik authorities, and we were able to relax to our heart's content. We were all a little excited. We felt instinctively that our stay in Russia was coming to an end, and the minor orgy, which I suppose every gipsy party must be called, was a welcome relief to the high tension of the previous weeks. We drank innumerable "charochki," while Maria Nikolaievna sang to us as she had never sung before. She, too, realised that the days of her reign were numbered. One by one, she went through all our old favourites: "Two Guitars," "Once Again," "To the last Copeck," "Black Eyes."

> "Po obichaiyu chisto-ruskomu;
> Po obichaiyu po-moskovskomu.
> Zit nye mozem my bez shampawskavo
> E bez penya, bez tziganskavo."

(In the true Russian fashion,
In the manner that is Moscow's.
We cannot live without champagne
Without our songs and our Tziganes.)

The haunting minor chords of the guitars, the deep bass notes of Maria Nikolaievna's glorious voice, the warm stillness of the summer night, the rich fragrance of the lime-trees. How it all comes back to me like every experience which we cannot repeat.

There was one song which I have never heard from any other lips than Maria Nikolaievna's. In those days it was in tune with my own turbulent soul, and that night I made her repeat it again and again, until at last she laughed and kissed me on both cheeks. It was called "I Cannot Forget," and it began:

"They say my heart is like the wind,
That to one maid I can't be true;
But why do I forget the rest,
And still remember only you."

In English idiotic, but sung by Maria Nikolaievna in Russian a throbbing plaint of longing and desire.

We drank deep into the night. Hicks, Tamplin, Garstin, Hill and Lingner went out into the garden at different intervals to cool their heads, until I was left alone. When they returned, they found me sitting at the middle of the table—still erect and very serious and greeting them with a sigh: "Roman Romanovitch patchti pyan"—Roman Romanovitch is almost drunk. It was *almost* true.

Their return broke the spell. I pulled myself together, and, when the dawn broke, I sent the others home and drove out with Moura to the Sparrow Hills to watch the sun rise over the Kremlin. It came up like an angry ball of fire heralding destruction. No joy was to come with the morning.

The next day I received news from St. Petersburg that General Poole was expected in Archangel that evening. Colonel Thornhill, the former assistant military attaché, had already arrived in Murmansk and had paid a recent visit to St. Petersburg. Although I had heard nothing of these movements from London—indeed, the Foreign Office were still pressing me (1) to secure the consent of the Bolsheviks to Allied military assistance, and (2) to expedite the departure of the Czech Army from Russia—it was obvious that the interventionists were gaining ground.

I had further proof of their activities when on the same evening General Lavergne came to our daily meeting. He brought with him an invitation for me to go to Vologda to see the Allied ambassadors. Mr. Francis and M. Noulens wished to see if we could not co-ordinate our views and find a common formula.

Although I was scarcely in a position to refuse, I accepted with some reluctance. My visit to Vologda was to have an all-important influence on my career. Yet, although I realise to-day that it would have been better for me if I had remained in Moscow, this journey into the wilderness was a valuable experience.

Vologda itself was a sleepy provincial town with almost as many churches as inhabitants. As a connecting link with Moscow it was as useless as the North Pole. Its only advantage as a retreat for the Allied representatives was its proximity to Moscow.

On my arrival I called on M. Noulens, who received me with every mark of friendliness. After a short preliminary discussion I went off to dine with the American Ambassador, who was comfortably lodged in an old club-house and who was to be my host during my stay. The serious business was to be left until the next day.

My evening with the Americans had the merit of being amusing as well as instructive. Mr. Francis was a charming host. At his house I met the Japanese Chargé d'Affaires, the Brazilian Minister, and the serious and still perturbed Torretta. We sat up late into the night, but Russia figured hardly at all in our conversation. From Francis I gathered that President Wilson was strongly opposed to Japanese intervention. Otherwise, he

did not seem to have any decided views about Russia. Knowledge of Russian politics he had none. The only political entry
in my diary for that evening is the laconic note: "Old Francis
doesn't know a Left Social Revolutionary from a potato." To
do him justice, he made no pretence of professing to understand the situation. He was as simple and as fearless as a child.
It never entered his head that he himself was in any personal
danger. At dinner he asked me a few questions about life in
Moscow. I answered him with commendable brevity, and the
rest of the meal was devoted to chaffing the Brazilian Minister.
This gentleman was the one joy of Vologda. I hope he is still
alive and that he is still serving his country. He had reduced
the art of diplomacy to a simple formula: do nothing, and
promotion and honours are certain. He did his best to live
up to his own formula. He slept all day and played cards all
night. When the American Ambassador twitted him with
doing no work, he turned the tables by wagering that his
telegram bill was higher than the American's. His statement
was correct. True it is that since February, 1917, he had sent
only one telegram to his Government. But it had cost over a
thousand pounds. He had translated and telegraphed to Rio
the whole of Kerensky's first speech on the revolution! Having
proved his case, he then proceeded to justify his philosophy.
When he had entered the service as a young attaché, he had
been full of zeal. He had gone to London as second secretary.
He had worked strenuously on a report on the Brazilian coffee
trade with England. He had made certain recommendations.
His reward had been a reduction in rank and a transfer to the
Balkans. When later he was transferred to Berlin, he resumed
his zeal and furnished his Government with an admirable
report on technical education in Germany. Once again he
suffered a reduction in rank. Then wisdom came to him. Zeal
had obviously no place in diplomacy, and he made up his mind
to do nothing in future to remind his Government of his
existence. From that moment his diplomatic career had been
one long triumph and his promotion had been as regular as
clockwork. The formula is not so absurd as the layman may

imagine. It has stood more than one British diplomatist in good stead.

As soon as dinner was over, Francis began to fidget like a child who wishes to return to its toys. His rattle, however, was a deck of cards, and without loss of time they were produced. The old gentleman was no child at poker. We played late, and, as usually happens when I play with Americans, he took my money.

The next day I lunched with the French Ambassador. There was nothing childish about M. Noulens. If he played poker, he played without cards. Politics—and politics viewed from the narrow, logical angle of a Frenchman—was his only game. General Lavergne had given him a copy of the report we had drafted on the military needs of the situation. It was based on the supposition that the Bolsheviks would give their consent to our intervention. Together we discussed the report. M. Noulens was flatteringly congratulatory. He agreed with the report. He had only one amendment to make. If the Bolsheviks would not give their consent, we must intervene without their consent. He advanced many arguments in support of this new formula. He referred to the critical situation on the Western front. He quoted telegrams from the French General Staff. The war would be lost or won on the Western front. And the French General Staff insisted on the necessity of some diversion in Russia which would prevent the Germans from transferring more troops from the East. It was essential that the various Allied representatives in Russia should present a united front. Dissensions in Allied policy had been the chief cause of delay in achieving victory. He would go far to obtain unity. He would accept our formula. He hoped I would agree to his amendment. I looked at Lavergne. I knew he had already capitulated. Romei had not come to Vologda, but he, too, had been subjected to pressure from Italian headquarters. As a soldier he was not likely to stand out against his own General Staff. I was alone. Robins had left. Sadoul, the French Robins, had been side-tracked. M. Noulens had taken away his right of telegraphing direct to Albert Thomas. Feverishly I tried to summarise my own position in my mind. Perhaps I could still pull off a big coup with Trotsky. Perhaps M. Noulens was cleverer than I realised. I was in a corner. If I refused to agree, M. Noulens would go ahead with his own policy. He would carry the Italians, the Japanese, and even Francis with him. If I consented, at least I should escape the stigma of having stood out against the united opinion of all the other Allied representatives. I capitulated.

In the blazing sunshine we walked across to the Ambassadors' meeting. Francis was in the chair, but Noulens dominated the proceedings. He was, in fact, the only Allied representative in Vologda who knew his own mind. He was at one with us regarding the number of troops that would be required for a successful intervention. Even with regard to the Czech Army, which was then stretched like a serpent from the Volga to Siberia, he was strangely conciliatory. We discussed this question from all its angles and decided that the Czechs should be evacuated as soon as possible. After the meeting I said good-bye to M. Noulens. He was all smiles and affability. When, twenty-four hours later, I arrived in Moscow, I was met by Hicks with the news that there had been a serious clash in Siberia between the Bolsheviks and the Czechs. How the clash had arisen is unclear to me to this day. The report from the French officers, who were accompanying the Czechs, stated that the Bolsheviks, yielding to German demands, had tried to disarm the Czechs. The Czechs resisted and were now continuing their journey by the force of their own arms. The Bolsheviks maintained that at the instigation of the French the Czechs had made an unprovoked attack on the local Bolshevik authorities and had taken the law into their own hands. From which side the provocation came will probably remain a matter of dispute for all time. Nevertheless, what the result of this affair was to be was quite clear. The first plank in the platform of the interventionists had been laid.

I found Moscow in a state of siege. The Czech diplomatic council had been arrested. Numerous counter-revolutionaries had been rounded up and put in prison. The newspapers had been suppressed. There was an urgent request from Chicherin, begging me to use my influence to settle the Czech incident amicably. There was also a telegram from Cromie urging me to come to St. Petersburg to see one of General Poole's officers who was arriving the next day.

I spent the next afternoon in interviewing Chicherin and Karachan. In the absence of details of what was happening in Siberia we were unable to make much headway about the Czech incident. That the Bolsheviks were anxious to settle the affair amicably was evident, but, as I had not time to receive instructions from London, I could only promise to do my best. My interview, however, left me with one clear impression. The suspicions of the Bolsheviks were now fully aroused. They were, as I had always believed, accurately informed about the activities of the French. They knew that General Poole had arrived in North Russia. Already they had a shrewd idea that the Czechs were to be the vanguard of an anti-Bolshevik intervention. I gave them the only answer I could: that the British Government's offer of military aid against Germany was still open. Chicherin laughed bitterly. The Allies were siding with the counter-revolutionaries. There was no choice for the Bolsheviks. They would oppose Allied intervention against Russia's wish in the same way as they would oppose German intervention.

The same evening, having decided that I could just afford the time, I left for St. Petersburg. There I saw Cromie and McGrath, the English officer who had come out with General Poole. In one sense McGrath was reassuring. Some weeks before Trotsky, in a moment of depression, had suggested that I was merely a tool, used by the British Government to keep the Bolsheviks quiet while it was preparing an anti-Bolshevik coup. At the time I had been furiously indignant. Now I was perturbed. McGrath, however, set my mind at rest. The intervention plan, he said, was not very far advanced, and England had no policy at all as far as Russia was concerned. Nothing would be decided until Poole reported home.

If there was a negative comfort in this statement McGrath

gave me several shocks. Poole himself was in favour of intervention. Thornhill, who was at Murmansk, was a rabid interventionist. Moreover, Lindley, who had been our Chargé d'Affaires when I arrived in St. Petersburg, was coming out again. This could mean only one thing. London had no confidence in me. I returned to Moscow in a state of dejection, aggravated by the humiliation that all St. Petersburg should know of Lindley's pending arrival before my own Government had thought fit to inform me of the fact.

On my return to Moscow I found instructions from London regarding the Czech affair, and the same afternoon, together with my French and Italian colleagues, I went to the Russian Foreign Office. The proceedings were severely formal. Chicherin's room was long and bare of any furniture except the desk in the middle. We sat on wooden chairs facing him and Karachan. One by one, we read out our protests. Mine was the strongest. I told the two Commissars that for months I had done my best to bring about an understanding with the Allies, but that they had always put me off with evasions. Now, after promising a free exit to the Czechs, who had fought for the Slav cause and who were going to France to continue the fight against a foe, who was still the Bolshevik enemy as well as ours, they had yielded to German threats and had wantonly attacked those, who had always been their friends. I was instructed by my Government to inform them that any attempt to disarm the Czechs, or to interfere with them in any way, would be regarded as an act inspired by Germany and hostile to the Allies.

The Bolsheviks listened to our protests in silence. They were scrupulously polite. Although they had a case, they made no attempt to argue it. Chicherin, looking more like a drowned rat than ever, stared at us with mournful eyes. Karachan seemed stupidly bewildered. There was a painful silence. Everyone was a little nervous and none more than myself, whose conscience was not quite clear. Then Chicherin coughed. "Gentlemen," he said, "I have taken note of what you said." We shook hands awkwardly and then filed out of the room.

Our protest had made a profound impression. Months afterwards, when I was in prison, Karachan told me that both he and Chicherin had been completely surprised by the vehemence of my language. Their first suspicions of me had dated from that day. The suspicions were well-founded. Almost before I had realised it I had now indentified myself with a movement which, whatever its original object, was to be directed, not against Germany, but against the de facto government of Russia.

I must explain the motives which had driven me into this illogical situation. For four and a half months I had opposed Japanese intervention and, indeed, every kind of intervention which had not received the sanction of the Bolsheviks. I had little faith in the strength of the anti-Bolshevik Russian forces and none at all in the feasibility of reconstituting an Eastern front against Germany. Moreover, I had been in close touch with the Czech Council. The Czech Army, whose revolt had brought matters to a head, was composed of war-prisoners. They were Slavs, who, although technically Austrian subjects, had deserted in their thousands to the Russians at the beginning of the war. They bore no love to the Tsarist régime, which had always refused to recognise their separate nationality. They were democrats by instinct, and their sympathies were with the Russian Liberals and the Social-Revolutionaries. They were not likely to co-operate smoothly with the Tsarist officers, who supplied the main strength to the armies of the anti-Bolshevik Generals.

Why then had I given my adherence to a policy which seemed to hold out little promise of success and which was to expose me to widespread accusations of inconsistency? Although I desire to be strictly truthful, the answer is not easy. Fortunate indeed are the traditionalists, who accept the existing order of society in their cradle, and who solve every political problem by the simple formula of "these men are my friends and those my enemies." I could not see the situation in this light. I had been sent back to Russia mainly in order that I might keep the British Government informed about the real state of affairs.

That task I had tried to fulfil to the best of my ability. I had no special sympathy for the Bolsheviks, nor did the numerous accusations of pro-Bolshevism augment unduly the obstinacy with which I strove to maintain an objective and unbiased view of the situation. At the same time, I could not help realising instinctively that, behind its peace programme and its fanatical economic programme, there was an idealistic background to Bolshevism which lifted it far above the designation of a mob movement led by German agents. For months I had lived cheek by jowl with men who worked eighteen hours a day and who were obviously inspired by the same spirit of self-sacrifice and abnegation of worldly pleasure which animated the Puritans and the early Jesuits. If to realise that I was living in a movement, which was likely to assume even greater proportions in history than the French revolution, was to be pro-Bolshevik, then I am entitled to the label of pro-Bolshevism. I knew from my wife's telegrams—later they were to be confirmed from other sources—that my views were unpalatable to the British Government. I ought to have resigned and come home. To-day, I should have been enjoying the reputation of a prophet who had predicted the various phases of the Russian revolution with remarkable accuracy.

I did not do so. It would be easy for me to say that my first duty was to my country, that, when my country had decided on another policy, I had no right to oppose it, and that to resign in the middle of the war would have been equivalent to deserting my post in the face of the enemy. I do not plead these excuses. They were not my motives. Three months later, when I was in prison, Karl Radek wrote a letter to Arthur Ransome, in which he described me as a "carrièriste," who, when he had seen that his own policy had no chance of being accepted, sought feverishly to regain the favour of his employers. This, too, although nearer the mark, is an unfair accusation. The motives for my conduct were two. Subconsciously, although I did not put the question to myself at the time, I was unwilling to leave Russia because of Moura. The other motive—and it was the all-compelling one, of which

I was fully conscious—was that I lacked the moral courage to resign and to take a stand which would have exposed me to the odium of the vast majority of my countrymen.

There was perhaps one other more creditable motive. In my conceit I imagined that, if the Allies were bent on a military intervention in Russia, my special knowledge of the Russian situation would be of some value in aiding them to avoid the major pitfalls. I knew the Bolsheviks more intimately than any Englishman knew them at that time. I had had my finger on the pulse of events in Russia since January. The clam-jamfrey of military experts, who from outside were screaming for intervention and who regarded the Bolsheviks as a rabble to be swept away with a whiff of grape shot, was deprived by its geographical situation of that knowledge. Having gone over to intervention, I did my best to ensure that it would have at least some chance of success. To the last I opposed the theory that the "loyal" Russians were capable of overthrowing the Bolsheviks even if supported by Allied munitions and money and led by Allied officers. To the last I insisted on the need for large Allied forces, without which the whole scheme was bound to fail. I even devised a special formula: that the support which we would receive from the "loyal" Russians would be in direct proportion to the number of troops we sent ourselves. For all the good I did I might have saved my breath for my own porridge. My volte-face had discredited me with everybody. The interventionists looked on me as an obstinate young mule, who had at last come over to their way of thinking. I was an obstacle which had been successfully removed. My views could now be safely disregarded. The Bolsheviks shared Radek's opinion of me. I had fallen between two stools. To this day I have suffered from my tumble. To the Bolsheviks I am the incarnation of counter-revolution. To the interventionists I am still the pro-Bolshevik, who wrecked their plans!

CHAPTER EIGHT

THE INTERVENTION ITSELF did not take place until August 4th. The two months from June to August were a purgatory, during which our position gradually deteriorated. And, as a result of the increased danger which now threatened them, the Bolsheviks tightened up their discipline.

On June 10th "Benji" Bruce arrived in Moscow. He had come to fetch his bride, the beautiful and charming Karsavina. He brought me a large bundle of mail and my first real news from England. There was a letter from George Clerk, then Head of the War Department in the Foreign Office. It was full of nice things. Indeed, he and Colonel Kisch, who was then at the War Office, are almost the only senior officials who have been generous enough to sympathise with my attitude and to admit that my estimate of the situation had not been far wrong. Bruce, however, left me with no illusious regarding my unpopularity in England during the period of my so-called pro-Bolshevism. He informed me that in March I had nearly been recalled. He stayed only twelve hours in Moscow, but, in spite of the news he brought me, his visit was like a breath of wind coming over the desert. After being shut off from the world for five months I was thrilled by his account of the situation in England and on the Western front. Karsavina and he had a nightmare of adventure before reaching Murmansk. They had to travel without a Bolshevik permit. My powers to help them had ceased.

June was a dreary month. Perhaps because my conscience was uneasy, I lived in an atmosphere of suspicion. Trotsky would have no more dealings with us, and, although I continued to see Chicherin, Karachan, and Radek almost daily, we avoided the real issue in our conversations. With the alteration in the political attitude of the Bolsheviks came a change in our material position. We found it increasingly difficult to obtain supplies of fresh meat and vegetables. Without the tinned rations supplied to us by the American Red Cross mission we should have fared badly.

Through Hicks I increased my contact with the anti-Bolshevik forces. As far as we were concerned, they were represented in Moscow by an organisation called the "Centre" which was subdivided into two wings of Left and Right, and by the League of the Regeneration of Russia founded by Savinkoff. There were constant bickerings between the two organisations. The Centre was in close touch with the White Army in the South. The White generals regarded Savinkoff with suspicion. Indeed, about this period I received a letter from General Alexeieff in which he stated that he would sooner co-operate with Lenin and Trotsky than with Savinkoff or Kerensky. Both organisations were agreed on one point only. They wanted Allied aid and Allied money. I saw one or two of the leaders, notably Peter Struve, a brilliant intellectual, who at one time had been a Socialist and had helped Lenin to frame his first Communist manifesto, and Michael Feodoroff, a former Assistant Minister. Both were men of fine character. Both were unswervingly loyal to the Allies. I was, however, very guarded in my conversations with them. As far as I knew officially, the British Government had not yet decided on intervention. Until the decision was brought to my notice I gave no support to the Whites either in cash or in promises.

In this my attitude differed from that of the French, who, as I knew from their own admission, were supplying funds to Savinkoff. Their promises, too, were extravagant. The Whites were led to believe that Allied military support would be forthcoming in decisive strength. The figure generally mentioned was two Allied divisions for Archangel and several Japanese divisions for Siberia. Encouraged by these hopes, the anti-Bolshevik forces began to increase their activities. On June 21st Volodarsky, the Bolshevik Commissar for Press Affairs in St. Petersburg, was assassinated on his return from a meeting at the Obuchoff Works. The Bolshevik reply was swift. In his speech to the St. Petersburg Soviet Uritsky, the head of the local Cheka, made a violent attack on England in which he accused the English of organising the dead

Commissar's murder. The next day Schastny, the Commander-in-Chief of the Baltic Fleet, who had been a prisoner in the Kremlin, was condemned to death and shot. At the trial Trotsky distinguished himself by the violence of his language. The Terror was beginning.

I went to see Chicherin to protest against Uritsky's accusation. He put me off with semi-apologetic explanations. It was deplorable, but what else could we expect if we insisted on infringing Russia's neutrality. Russia wanted only to be left alone and to enjoy the fruits of her dearly-bought peace. He was amusing about Trotsky, who, with his back to the wall, was always wanting to fight somebody and was now advocating strong measures against the Allies. "It is strange," said Chicherin, "how the military idea has gone to Trotsky's head. In March Lenin had to use his influence to prevent Trotsky from declaring war on Germany. Now it is Lenin's cool brain which is holding Trotsky back from declaring war on the Allies."

Although the intervention appeared to be hanging fire, our stay in Moscow seemed near its end. None of us was very happy. Denis Garstin had already left us. He had been ordered to join General Poole at Archangel. He, too, had to leave clandestinely owing to the difficulty in securing a Bolshevik pass for him. He went with a sad heart. He would have liked to remain with us to the end. Poor boy! He was one of the first victims of the intervention. Still, we were not without optimism. Believing that the Allies would land in force, we were convinced that the Bolsheviks would be unable to offer a serious resistance. Even Ransome, whose opposition to intervention without Bolshevik consent had remained constant, told us that "the show was over" and began to make preparations to leave. Before we ourselves were to be allowed to depart we were to have our fill of excitement.

One extraordinary adventure during this period was the murder of Count Mirbach, the German Ambassador. This assassination, accompanied as it was by an internal revolt against the Government, was the most dramatic political murder of modern times. As I myself was an uncomfortable eye-witness of the attempted *coup d'état*, I give my own account of the affair in full detail.

To understand the situation, the reader must remember that after the Bolshevik revolution in November, 1917, the extreme wing of the Russian Social-Revolutionary Party joined hands with the Bolsheviks and co-operated with them in the formation of the new Government. They received a few posts in the various Commissariats, retained their places in the Soviets, and were strongly represented in the All-Russian Central Executive Committee, which, when the Congress of Soviets is not sitting, is the supreme legislative and executive power of the Russian Socialist Federative Soviet Republic. For the first eight months of its existence the Soviet Government was, in fact, a coalition.

As a party the Left Social-Revolutionaries were quite as extreme as the Bolsheviks in their hatred of capitalism and Imperialism. They were therefore as violent as the Bolsheviks in their denunciation of the Allies. In internal politics, while they differed from the Bolsheviks on agrarian questions, they upheld the Soviet system and supported the Bolsheviks in the prosecution of the civil war. Two members of the party, Colonel Muravieff, an ex-police officer, and Lieutenant Sablin, the son of the proprietor of the Korsh Theatre in Moscow, were during the first period of the Bolshevik régime the most successful military commanders of the new Government.

Unlike the Bolsheviks, however, the Left Social-Revolutionaries were not prepared to go to any lengths in their desire for peace. They had been opposed to the Brest-Litovsk Peace and, although they retained their representatives in the Government, had never accepted it. They drew most of their support from the Ukraine, which had been occupied by the Germans, and the Germans were hard taskmasters who had installed a dummy reactionary Russian Government and restored the land to the Russian landowners.

The Left Social-Revolutionaries had not accepted this situation, and ever since the peace they had carried on a violent

partisan war in the Ukraine against both the Russian land-
lords and the German troops of occupation. By both sides this
miniature warfare was conducted with appalling cruelty.
Goaded almost to despair by the sufferings of their compatriots in the Ukraine, the Left Social-Revolutionaries protested vigorously against the servile attitude of the Bolsheviks
before the Germans and denounced the Bolshevik Commissars
as Mirbach's lackeys. As even the official Press had to admit,
almost daily, some fresh German breach of the Brest Treaty,
considerable point was given to the caustic comments on the
cringing tone of Chicherin's mild protests and the barely civil
replies of the German Ambassador.

The real difference between the two Russian Government
Parties was that the Left Social-Revolutionaries regarded
Germany as the chief menace to the revolution. The Bolsheviks,
or rather Lenin, for he alone saw clearly in this confused
atmosphere, were determined to do nothing which might
endanger the fragile fabric of their peace. They were now more
afraid of Allied intervention than of further aggression by the
Germans. The two parties were of course at heart both anti-
German and anti-Entente. The situation, however, was not
without its comic side. While the Bolsheviks were publicly
denouncing the activities of the Left Social-Revolutionaries
in the Ukraine, they were supplying them secretly with the
funds for their partisan warfare against the Germans.

There was one other grievance which further divided the two
Parties. Among the peasants the chief supporters of the Left
Social-Revolutionaries were the Kulaks. Partly in order to
strengthen their own position in the country and partly to
obtain more grain, the Bolsheviks had organised so-called
Poverty Committees, composed of poorer peasants, who were
encouraged to attack the richer Kulaks and to seize their
grain.

Here obviously were dissensions, which were bound to come
to a head. Secretly, the Left Social-Revolutionaries began to
prepare fantastic plans for the overthrow of the Bolshevik
Government and for a renewal of the war with Germany. By

July 4th, the opening day of the Fifth All-Russian Congress, the political situation was ripe for the inevitable explosion.

For this Congress the Left Social-Revolutionaries had made special preparations. In spite of Bolshevik manipulation at the elections, they succeeded in returning about one-third of the eight hundred delegates present, and for the first time since November, 1917, the Bolsheviks were confronted, in their own carefully hedged-in Parliament, with a real official opposition.

The Congress took place in the Moscow Opera House. In the parterre, where once sat the "balletomanes" and the richly bejewelled ladies of the Moscow plutocracy, now are ranged the official delegates: on the right, facing the stage, the Bolshevik majority, composed mainly of soldiers in khaki; on the left the Left Social-Revolutionary opposition, whose brawny arms and loose shirts proclaim their village origin.

On the high stage, from which Chaliapin first gave his immortal rendering of Boris, now sit the members of the Central Executive Committee—a motley gathering of about one hundred and fifty intellectuals with a strong predominance of Jews.

At a long table across the front of the stage is the Presidium, with Sverdloff, the President, in the centre. A Jew so dark that he might almost be suspected of "colour," his black beard and his fierce black eyes make him look like some modern incarnation of the Spanish inquisitors. On his left are Afanasieff, the Secretary of the Central Executive Committee, an insignificant young Jew with nervous twitching eyes, and Nakhamkis, the editor of the *Izvestia*, and better known to the public under his pseudonym of Stekloff. At this table, too, sits Zinovieff, the President of the St. Petersburg Commune. Clean shaven and with an enormous forehead, he looks as intelligent as he is reputed to be. On the right of Sverdloff sit the Left Social-Revolutionary leaders: Kamkoff, Karelin, both young Jews, clean shaven, well dressed, and clearly of the intellectual class; Cherepanoff; and at the extreme end Maria Spiridonova, the thirty-two-year-old leader of the Party. Very simply dressed, her dark hair brushed smoothly back over her head, and with pince-nez with which she toys continuously, she looks for all the world like Olga, the schoolmistress, in Chehoff's "Three Sisters." In 1906, while still a girl, she had made herself famous by her assassination of Lujinovsky, the notorious Councillor of the Government Administration of Tamboff. She had been selected by her Party to carry out this terroristic act, and in the middle of winter she waited for Lujinovsky on the platform of the station at Borisogliebsk and fired on him with a revolver as he stepped out of the train. Her shots were successful, but an attempt to end her own life failed, and she was dragged from the platform and later raped by the Cossack soldiery. She had been condemned to death, but, yielding to a strong plea for mercy on account of her age, the Tsar had changed her sentence to one of penal servitude for life. The earnest, almost fanatical, expression in her eyes shows that her sufferings have affected her mind. She is more hysterical than practical, but her evident popularity with her own followers shows that she is still one of the few sentimental figures of the revolution.

Behind the Presidium table in serried rows are ranged the other members of the Central Executive Committee. Here are to be found the real Bolshevik leaders and the chief Commissars. They are present in full force from Trotsky to Krylenko, the scowling, twitching, Public Prosecutor. Only Derjinsky and Peters are absent. These grim exponents of Bolshevik justice have no time for Congresses. Lenin, too, is late, as usual. He will slip in later, quietly, unobtrusively, but at the opportune moment.

In the boxes and galleries all around are the friends and supporters of the various delegates. Admission is by ticket only, and every entrance, every corridor, is guarded by groups of Lettish soldiers, armed to the teeth with rifle, pistol, and hand-grenade. In the great Imperial box are the representatives of the official Press. I take my place in the large parterre box on the right hand of the stage, together with Lavergne, Romei, and the other members of the Allied Missions. Just above us are the representatives of the German, Turkish and Bulgarian Embassies. Fortunately for our enjoyment of the spectacle, we are not face to face.

From the first the atmosphere is charged with electricity. The opening day is devoted to speeches by minor delegates. The speeches are on strictly party lines. The three great crimes are the Brest-Litovsk peace, the Poverty Committees and the death sentence. The Left Social-Revolutionaries denounce all three. They support their denunciation of the Peace Treaty with bloodcurdling accounts of the German atrocities in the Ukraine. The Bolsheviks are on the defensive.

The real battle comes on the second day, when the heavy artillery on both sides is engaged. It is opened by Sverdloff, who wisely anticipates the Left Social-Revolutionary attack. He admits the horrors of the German occupation, but pleads that Russia is too weak to fight. He is less successful in his defence of the Poverty Committees. He scores a point over the Left Social-Revolutionary attitude towards the death sentence. The Left Social-Revolutionaries, he says, protested against the death sentence on Admiral Schastny. At the same time they have co-operated closely with the Bolsheviks in the Extraordinary Commissions. One of their members is Vice-President of the Moscow Cheka, which has carried out numerous death sentences without any trial. Are they, then, to understand that the Left Social-Revolutionaries are against the death sentence in cases of trials but in favour of it when there is no trial. He resumes his seat amidst laughter and Bolshevik applause.

Spiridonova then rises, and from her first words one realises that this is no ordinary Congress, that to-day the Bolsheviks and the Left Social-Revolutionaries have come to the parting of the ways. She is obviously nervous. Her delivery, too, is monotonous, but, as she warms to her subject, she acquires a hysterical passion which is not unimpressive. Her attack is concentrated on the Poverty Committees. With pride she refers to the fact that her whole life has been dedicated to the welfare of the peasants. Keeping time to the rhythm of her sentences with an up-and-down movement of the right arm, she bitterly attacks Lenin. "I accuse you," she says, addressing Lenin, "of betraying the peasants, of making use of them for your own ends, and of not serving their interests." She appeals to her followers: "In Lenin's philosophy," she shrieks, "you are only dung—only manure." Then, working up to an hysterical peroration, she turns on the Bolsheviks: "Our other differences are only temporary, but on the peasant question we are prepared to give battle. When the peasants, the Bolshevik peasants, the Left Social-Revolutionary peasants, and the non-party peasants, are alike humiliated, oppressed and crushed—crushed as peasants—in my hand you will still find the same pistol, the same bomb, which once forced me to defend——" The end of the sentence is drowned in a wild torrent of applause. A Bolshevik delegate in the parterre hurls an indecent assault at the speaker. Pandemonium ensues. Brawny peasants stand up in their seats and shake their fists at the Bolsheviks. Trotsky pushes himself forward and tries to speak. He is howled down, and his face blenches with impotent rage. In vain Sverdloff rings his bell and threatens to clear the theatre. Nothing seems more certain than that he will have to carry out his threat. Then Lenin walks slowly to the front of the stage. On the way he pats Sverdloff on the shoulder and tells him to put his bell away. Holding the lapels of his coat, he faces the audience—smiling, supremely self-confident. He is met with jeers and cat-calls. He laughs good-humouredly. Then he holds up his hand, and with a last rumble the tumult dies. With cold logic he replies point by point to the criticisms of the Left Social-Revolutionaries. He refers with gentle sarcasm to their illogical and frequently equivocal attitude. His remarks produce another storm of interruption. Again Sverdloff becomes excited and grasps his bell. Again Lenin raises his hand. His self-confidence is almost irritating. Then, swaying slightly forward as he accentuates his points, but with strangely little gesticulation, he proceeds as calmly as though he were addressing a Sunday-School meeting. To the taunts of servility towards the Germans he replies that the Left Social-Revolutionaries, in wishing to renew the war, are carrying out the policy of the Allied Imperialists. Coldly and without a trace of sentiment he defends the Brest Treaty, points out how bitter a humiliation it has been, but underlines the grim doctrine of necessity. He almost exaggerates the difficulties of the present situation, praises the courage of those who are fighting the battle of Socialism, counsels further patience, and promises a reward for that patience in a glowing picture of the future, when war-weariness must inevitably produce a revolution in all countries. Gradually the sheer personality of the man and the overwhelming superiority of his dialectics conquer his audience, who listen spell-bound until the speech ends in a wild outburst of cheering, which, although many of the Left Social-Revolutionaries must know of the preparations for the morrow, is not confined to the Bolsheviks.

The effect on the Left Social-Revolutionaries, however, is only temporary. Lenin is followed by Kamkoff, a brilliant orator who lashes himself into a passion of fury. His is a fighting speech, and I marvel at his foolhardiness. He spares no one. His peroration is magnificent in its dramatic emotion. He turns towards the box in which the Germans are sitting. "The dictatorship of the proletariat," he thunders, "has developed into a dictatorship of Mirbach. In spite of all our warnings the policy of Lenin remains the same, and we are become, not an independent Power, but the lackeys of the German Imperialists, who have the audacity to show their faces even in this theatre."

In an instant the Left Social-Revolutionaries are on their feet shouting and shaking their fists at the German box. The theatre rings with roars of: "Down with Mirbach! Away with the German butchers! Away with the hangman's noose from Brest!" Hurriedly Sverdloff rings his bell and declares the session closed, and in a fever of excitement the delegates stream from the hall.

One incident gives me cause for reflection. During Kamkoff's speech a French intelligence officer in our box applauds fiercely. His attitude is typical of that of many of my Allied colleagues. They cannot realise that to both Bolsheviks and Left Social-

Revolutionaries foreign intervention, whether by Germany or by the Allies, means counter-revolutionary intervention. When our own intervention took place it received no support from the Left Social-Revolutionaries.

The debate which had ended so dramatically on the evening of July 5th was not destined to be resumed on the Saturday afternoon of the 6th. The Congress, indeed, reassembled, but the Bolshevik leaders were absent. The stage revolution of yesterday had been transferred to the streets and to the barricades.

I went to the Opera House at four o'clock. It was a hot and sultry afternoon, and the atmosphere of the theatre was like a Turkish bath. The parterre was filled with delegates, but many of the seats on the platform were vacant. There was no Trotsky, no Radek. By five o'clock most of the other Bolshevik members of the Central Executive Committee had disappeared. The box allotted to the representatives of the Central Powers was empty. There was, however, a considerable number of Left Social-Revolutionaries including Spiridonova. She looked calm and composed. There was nothing in her manner to betray the fact that her Party had already decided to put its whole existence to the supreme test of war.

Yet this was what had happened, although it was some time before we realised the truth. At six o'clock Sidney Reilly came into our box with the news that the theatre was surrounded by troops and that all exits were barred. He had only the vaguest idea of what had occurred. He knew, however, that there had been fighting in the streets. Something had gone wrong. Our apprehension was not diminished by a loud explosion in the corridor above us. A careless sentry had dropped a hand grenade. Fearful that the Bolsheviks might search them before they were allowed to leave the theatre, Reilly and a French agent began to examine their pockets for compromising documents. Some they tore up into tiny pieces and shoved them down the lining of the sofa cushions. Others, doubtless more dangerous, they swallowed. The situation was too tense for us to appreciate its comic side, and, deciding that in this case inaction was the best policy, we sat down to await the dénouement with as brave a show of patience as we could assume.

Finally, at seven o'clock, we were relieved by Radek, who gave us the whole story. The Left Social-Revolutionaries had assassinated Mirbach, hoping thereby to provoke Germany into restarting the war. Headed by Sablin and Alexandrovitch, the Vice-President of the Cheka, they had planned to arrest the Bolshevik Leaders during the Congress in the Theatre. Instead, they themselves had been caught in the trap which they had set for their opponents.

The story of their *coup d'état* may be told in a few words. At a quarter to three on the Saturday afternoon a motor car with two men drove up to the German Embassy in the Denejni Pereulok. The Embassy itself was guarded by a detachment of Bolshevik troops. The occupants of the car, however, had no difficulty in obtaining an entrance, for they were provided with special passes signed by Alexandrovitch in his capacity as Vice-President of the Cheka. A man named Blumkin, who for months had lived in the room next to me in my hotel, was the chief actor in the ensuing tragedy. Himself an official of the Cheka, he was received immediately by Riezler, the Councillor of the German Embassy. He informed Riezler that he must see Mirbach personally. The Cheka had discovered an Allied plot for the assassination of the German Ambassador. In view of Blumkin's credentials and the seriousness of his information, Dr. Riezler himself took him into Count Mirbach's presence. When the Count asked him how the assassins proposed to act, Blumkin took a Browning from his pocket, replied, "Like this," and emptied his pistol into the body of the unfortunate Ambassador. Then, leaping out of an open window, he hurled a hand grenade behind him in order to make doubly sure, and escaped.

In the meantime the Left Social-Revolutionaries had assembled such troops as they could persuade to support them in the Pokrovsky Barracks. They included one unit of two thousand men who had been bought over by Popoff, an agent of the Cheka, some disaffected soldiers from other regiments, and a few hundred sailors from the Black Sea Fleet. For an hour they enjoyed a slight success. They arrested Derjinsky. They captured the telegraph office. Then, however, their imagination failed them, and, beyond sending out telegrams all over the country to announce the success of their *coup d'état*, they did nothing. Towards evening they made a half-hearted attempt to approach the Opera House, but, finding it already surrounded by a strong detachment of Bolshevik forces, they retired to their headquarters. So feeble was their military effort that the vast majority of the Moscow population never realised until the next day that an attempted revolution was in progress.

In the meantime Trotsky had not been idle. He had called in two Lettish regiments from the suburbs. He had assembled his armoured cars. Within a few hours the Left Social-Revolutionary troops, opposed by overwhelming strength, laid down their arms. Some of the leaders escaped. Alexandrovitch, however, was caught at the Kursk railway station and promptly shot. The Social-Revolutionary delegates in the Opera House were arrested without even a protest. The revolution, which was conceived in a theatre, ended in the same place.

The only effect of this opera bouffe of the Left Social-Revolutionaries was to strengthen the hands of the Bolsheviks and the peace party. The repercussion in the country was insignificant. A few days later Muravieff, the commander-in-chief of the Bolshevik forces on the Volga, attempted to move his troops against Moscow. By this time, however, the failure of the *coup d'état* in Moscow was known, and he was arrested by his own men. He ended his life dramatically by shooting himself in the presence of the Simbirsk Soviet. Spiridonova and Cherepanoff were imprisoned in the Kremlin, where, later, I was to be their companion in misfortune. Blumkin, the assassin, escaped. Most of the rank and file, in order to save themselves from reprisals, went back on their leaders, condemned their action, and were re-admitted into the Bolshevik fold.

This miserable affair, which should have been an object-lesson to the Allies in the sense that it proved beyond all doubt that Russia would do almost anything to avoid fighting either the Germans or the Allies, had certain reactions both on our own position and that of the Germans. The German Government was furious, but, convinced now of the certainty of Allied intervention, it did not declare war on the Bolsheviks. It demanded the right to send a battalion of German soldiers to guard its Moscow Embassy, but, when the Bolsheviks refused this request, it confined its action to a diplomatic protest. The reaction in our own case was more comic. Two days after Mirbach's murder Radek came to see me and informed me that the Bolshevik Government wished to place a guard at my disposal. There was a broad grin on his face. He knew what my reply would be. I told him to put his guard where the Khyber Pass veteran had put the workhouse Christmas pudding. It was almost the last laugh we had together.

Our situation was, in fact, none too pleasant. During the Congress Lindley had arrived at Vologda, and his first telegram to me was vaguely alarming. It gave me, however, no indication either of policy or of the date of our intervention. The attempted counter-revolution was already uncomfortably near. Savinkoff, egged on by French assurances of Allied help, had seized Yaroslavl, and Yaroslavl was between Moscow and Archangel, our only port of exit. Incidentally, Trotsky accuses me in his Autobiography of having fomented and financed the Yaroslavl affair. This is wholly untrue. Never at any time did I furnish Savinkoff with financial aid. Still less did I encourage him in any action he took. Trotsky, too, had issued an order that all French and British officers were to be refused travelling passes on account of their counter-revolutionary activities. Although technically this ukase did not apply to my mission, I knew that in practice there would be no difference. Moreover, there was great delay in the telegraph service to England, and I was never sure when this source of communication would be cut off from us altogether.

On the evening of July 17th I received from Karachan the official intimation of the murder of the Tsar and his family at Ekaterinburg. I believe that I was the first person to convey the news to the outside world. The only first-hand evidence of this crime that I can give concerns the official attitude of the Bolshevik Government. My own impression is that, alarmed by the approach of the Czech troops, who had now turned in their tracks and were at open war with the Bolsheviks, the local Soviet had taken the law into its own hands, and that the approval of the Central Government was subsequent. Certainly, there was no question of disapproval or disavowal. In its leading articles the Bolshevik Press did everything it could to justify the murder and reviled the Tsar as a tyrant and a butcher. It announced that it would begin immediate publication of his diaries. Later, a few instalments were published. All that they revealed was that the Emperor was a devoted husband and a loving father. When it was seen that their effect was to win sympathy for the Tsar, the instalments were stopped. Karachan, it is true, professed to be shocked and pleaded extenuating circumstances. He advanced the theory that the menace of Allied intervention was the direct cause of the Emperor's death. I am bound to admit that the population of Moscow received the news with amazing indifference. Their apathy towards everything except their own fate was complete, yet symptomatic of the extraordinary times in which we were living.

While this stark tragedy was taking place at Ekaterinburg, a drama, rich in its comic situations, was being enacted at Vologda. The Bolsheviks had sent Radek to this Allied Elysium in a last attempt to persuade the Allied Ambassadors to come to Moscow. Perhaps they were animated by a genuine desire to come to an amicable settlement. It is more probable that, realising that intervention was now inevitable, they desired to hold the Ambassadors in Moscow as hostages. For this delicate task they had chosen the Bolshevik Puck, and, if his effort failed, he richly satisfied his own sense of humour. He appeared before the Ambassadors with his revolver. He argued, cajoled, and even threatened. He interviewed them jointly and singly, but the Ambassadors stood firm. Then, in the evening, he went to the local telegraph office and gave an account of the failure of his mission by direct wire to Chicherin.

His joy-ride in Arcady had an amusing sequel. I received a word-for-word report of the Radek-Chicherin direct wire conversation from one of our secret agents. The document was so obviously genuine that the American Consul-General in Moscow sent a translation of it to his Ambassador. Without reading it, Francis put it in his pocket and took it to the Ambassadors' daily conference. "Gentlemen," he said, "I have received an interesting document from Moscow. It is Radek's account of his negotiations with ourselves. I shall read it to you." Fumbling with his pince-nez, he began: "Ambassador Francis is a stuffed shirt-front." It was only too true, but, coming from the Ambassador's lips, it was a little startling. Richer jests followed, and the climax came with the closing sentence: "Lindley is the only man who has any sense. He practically admits that he considers Noulens' behaviour childish in the extreme." Sir Francis Lindley has faced many difficult situations with unfailing courage and equanimity. I doubt, however, if he has ever felt quite so awkward as at that moment.

There was to be one more comedy before the final tragedy. On July 22nd an official British Economic Mission, composed of Sir William Clark, now British High Commissioner in Canada, Mr. Leslie Urquhart, Mr. Armistead, and Mr. Peters of the Commercial Diplomatic Service, arrived in Moscow. They had come to discuss the possibilities of trade relations with the Bolsheviks. Their arrival staggered me. As far as I knew—and I had no certain knowledge—our intervention was only a matter of days. The Czech army was now advancing towards the West. It had taken Simbirsk and was then besieging Kazan. The Czechs were our Allies. In so far as we were supporting them we were supporting war against the Bolsheviks. Savinkoff, too, was holding Yaroslavl, and Savinkoff was being financed by the French. Moreover, at that very moment British troops must have been on their way to Archangel. Yet here was a British Economic Mission in Moscow breathing

peace and commercial treaties to the Bolsheviks. Was there
ever a more Gilbertian situation? Could I be surprised when,
later, the Bolsheviks accused me of Machiavellian duplicity
and supplemented their denunciation of my crimes with well-
documented references to Albion's perfidy. Alas! here was
no guile or treachery. It was merely another example of one
department in Whitehall not knowing what the other was
doing. I took Sir William Clark to see Chicherin and Bronsky,
the Trade Commissioner. I cannot say that I enjoyed the
interview. Nor did I learn much from the English visitors.
Sir William Clark knew nothing of the Allies' plans regarding
Russia. Urquhart, who had mining interests in Siberia, was a
convinced interventionist. I was glad when, after two days of
abortive negotiations, they left for St. Petersburg. Had they
stayed twelve hours longer, they might have been detained
indefinitely.

The next day, with startling suddenness came the news that
the Allied Embassies had left Vologda and had fled to Archangel. Although they issued a futile statement to the effect
that their departure was not to be regarded as a rupture, the
Bolsheviks rightly interpreted it as the prelude to intervention.
Their flight, carried out without a word of warning to the
Allied Missions in Moscow, left me in an unenviable position.
All too clearly I saw that the rôle of hostages, which had
originally been destined for the Ambassadors, would now be
reserved for us. Together with my French, American, and
Italian colleagues I went to see Chicherin in order to feel our
way. He was studiously polite and obviously anxious to avoid
any act which would put the blame for any rupture of relations
on the Bolsheviks. He pressed us to remain in Moscow and
assured us that, whatever happened, we should be allowed to
leave whenever we wanted to go. We gave a non-committal
answer. We were still without any official intimation from
our Governments. We took it for granted that the Allies had
decided to land troops. We assumed that they would land
in force at Archangel, Murmansk, and Vladivostok. We knew
nothing for certain.

It was, however, clear that our own position in Moscow was no longer tenable, and I returned to my rooms to take the preliminary steps for our departure. The next few days were the most miserable of my whole stay in Russia. Moura had left Moscow some ten days before in order to visit her home in Esthonia. Owing to the fighting on the Czech and Yaroslavl fronts travelling on the railways was now strictly controlled. I could not communicate with her. It seemed any odds on my having to leave Russia without seeing her again. For four days and nights I never slept. For hours on end I sat in my room playing patience and badgering the unfortunate Hicks with idiotic questions. There was nothing we could do, and in my despair my self-control left me and I abandoned myself to the gloomiest depression. Then on the afternoon of July 28th my telephone rang. I picked up the receiver. Moura herself was speaking. She had arrived in St. Petersburg after six days of terrible adventure, during which she had crossed the no-man's land between Esthonia and Russia on foot. She was leaving that night for Moscow.

The reaction was wonderful. Nothing now mattered. If only I could see Moura again, I felt that I could face any crisis, any unpleasantness the future might have in store for me.

CHAPTER NINE

THE SEQUENCE OF events was now to be swift. On the day after Moura's return, General Eichhorn, the German Commander-in-Chief in Russia, was assassinated at Kieff. A young Moscow student called Donskoi, who was a member of the Social-Revolutionary Party, had carried out this act of terror. He had hired a cab and, passing the General, had hurled a bomb at him with fatal effect. I was sitting with Chicherin and Karachan when the news was conveyed to them by telephone. They made no concealment of their joy—especially Chicherin, who turned to me and said: "You see what happens when foreigners intervene against the wishes of the people." Their glee shocked me. My reason should have told me that in Bolshevik eyes the General was an oppressor, whose murderer was to be regarded as a liberator in just the same manner as bourgeois children are taught to admire Jaël or Brutus. To the Bolsheviks German generals and English generals were in the same category as soon as they set foot on Russian soil. They were the agents of counter-revolution and, therefore, outside the law. Both Allies and Germans, however, made the mistake of regarding Russia solely in the light of their own conflict. At the German court-martial of Donskoi two days later the first two questions asked of the prisoner were: "Do you know Lockhart? Do you know the head of the English mission in Moscow?"

On August 1st we received notice to leave our hotel. It had been requisitioned for the General Council of Russian Trades Unions. The Bolsheviks were showing their horns. No longer were we worthy of special consideration. Fortunately, I succeeded in obtaining occupation of my old flat in the Khliebny Pereulok, and we were able to avoid an awkward predicament.

On August 4th Moscow went wild with excitement. The Allies had landed at Archangel. For several days the city was a prey to rumour. The Allies had landed in strong force. Some stories put the figure at 100,000. No estimate was lower than two divisions. The Japanese were to send seven divisions through Siberia to help the Czechs. Even the Bolsheviks lost their heads and, in despair, began to pack their archives. In the middle of this crisis I saw Karachan. He spoke of the Bolsheviks as lost. They would, however, never surrender. They would go underground and continue the struggle to the last.

The confusion was indescribable. On the day after the landing I went to see Wardrop, our Consul-General, who had established his office in the Yusupoff Palace close to the Red Gates. While I was talking to him, the Consulate-General was surrounded by an armed band. It was composed of agents of the Cheka. They sealed up everything, and everyone in the building was put under arrest except Hicks and myself. The special pass I had received from Trotsky still held good. This raid had an amusing aspect. While the Cheka agents were cross-examining our Consular officials downstairs, our intelligence officers were busily engaged in burning their ciphers and other compromising documents upstairs. Clouds of smoke belched from the chimneys and penetrated even downstairs, but, although it was summer, the Cheka gentlemen noticed nothing untoward in this holocaust. As we were to learn later, the Cheka was terrifying but far from clever.

At the same time a similar raid was carried out on the French Mission and Consulate-General. Although the Italians and Americans were left alone, this outrage (it is true that in Bolshevik eyes our landing at Archangel was also an outrage against international law) could not be ignored, and the next day we all went to Chicherin to give formal notice of the rupture of relations and to demand our passports. Chicherin did not actually refuse. He seemed overwhelmed by the situation, and made his usual plea for time. The unfortunate Chicherin was, indeed, sorely harassed. Only that morning he had received a similar visit from Helfferich, who had succeeded Count Mirbach as German Ambassador. Helfferich, too, seemed to treat the Allied intervention as a serious menace to the Bolsheviks. He had no intention of sharing Count Mirbach's fate or of being caught in Moscow when the Allied troops marched in. The same night he took the train for Berlin, leaving only a small staff to carry on in Moscow.

Deserted now by both the Allies and the Germans, the Bolsheviks seemed to be in a hopeless position. The Czech army had captured Kazan, and, although the Bolsheviks had retaken Yaroslavl from Savinkoff's Russians, they seemed incapable of offering any serious opposition to the large Allied force which was supposed to be advancing from Archangel. For forty-eight hours I deluded myself with the thought that the intervention might prove a brilliant success. I was not quite sure what we should be able to do when we reached Moscow. I could not believe that a bourgeois Russian Government could be maintained in Moscow without our aid. Still less did I believe that we could persuade any considerable number of Russians to renew the war with Germany. In the circumstances the intervention was bound to assume an anti-Bolshevik rather than anti-German character. It was, therefore, likely that our occupation of Moscow would last indefinitely. But, with the adequate forces, which I assumed we had at our disposal, I had no doubt of our being able to reach the Russian capital.

Disillusionment was to follow swiftly. On August 10th the Bolshevik newspapers splashed their front page with headlines announcing a great Russian naval victory over the Allies at Archangel. I regarded this report as a joke or, at best, as a feeble attempt on the part of the Bolsheviks to stimulate the courage of their own followers. But that afternoon, when I saw Karachan, I had misgivings. His face was wreathed in smiles. The dejection of the previous days had gone, and his relief was too obvious to be put down to play-acting. "The situation is not serious," he said. "The Allies have landed only a few hundred men."

I smiled sceptically. Later, I was to discover that his statement was only too true. The naval victory was a myth. The Bolsheviks had sunk an Allied barge in the Dvina. But the account of the strength of the Allied forces was literally correct. We had committed the unbelievable folly of landing at Archangel with fewer than twelve hundred men.

It was a blunder comparable with the worst mistakes of the Crimean War. In the chaotic state of Russia it was obvious that, if intervention was to be a success, it must start well. It had begun as badly as it could, and no individual gallantry could ever repair that initial mistake. The plan of the pro-interventionist Russians was to hold the line of the Volga with the Czechs and to join up with the Allies in the North and with Generals Alexeieff and Denikin in the South. The latter had been advised to proceed via Tsaritzin to Samara, while it was hoped that the Allies would be able to advance almost unopposed to Vologda and Viatka. The weakness of our landing force in the North resulted in the loss of the Volga line and in the temporary collapse of the anti-Bolshevik movement in European Russia.

All my worst fears were speedily justified.

In the absence of a strong lead from the Allies the various counter-revolutionary groups began to quarrel and bicker among themselves. The accuracy of my dictum that the support we would receive from the Russians would be in direct proportion to the number of troops we sent ourselves was speedily proved. The broad masses of the Russian people remained completely apathetic.

The consequences of this ill-conceived venture were to be disastrous both to our prestige and to the fortunes of those Russians who supported us. It raised hopes which could not be fulfilled. It intensified the civil war and sent thousands of Russians to their death. Indirectly, it was responsible for the Terror. Its direct effect was to provide the Bolsheviks with a cheap victory, to give them a new confidence, and to galvanise them into a strong and ruthless organism. To have intervened at all was a mistake. To have intervened with hopelessly inadequate forces was an example of spineless half-measures which, in the circumstances, amounted to a crime. Apologists for this policy maintain that it served a useful purpose in preventing Russia from falling into the hands of Germany and in detaching German troops from the Western Front. By June, 1918, there was no danger of Russia being overrun by Germany. The effect of the intervention on the German situation in the West was insignificant. The fact remains that, whatever may have been the intentions of the Allied Governments, our intervention was regarded by those Russians, who supported it, as an attempt to overthrow Bolshevism. It failed, and, with the failure, our prestige among every class of the Russian population suffered.

Karachan's optimism was a bitter disillusionment, but now that the intervention had begun I had to do my best to aid it. My efforts during August were concentrated (1) on securing our own departure, and (2) on furnishing financial assistance to the Russians who were supporting us.

As far as our own departure was concerned, we had reached a deadlock. Chicherin had assumed an attitude which was typical of Bolshevik diplomatic finesse. Of course we could have our passports. We could leave as soon as we liked. But where did we intend to go? The Germans were in control in Finland. The Turks were in Constantinople. He did not suppose we should like to make the long "trek" to the Afghan or Persian frontiers. Yet these seemed the only exits.

I cut short this long rigmarole. "What about Archangel?" I asked. He washed his hands apologetically. "The English counter-revolutionaries are at Archangel," he said. "We cannot let you go there." We seemed to be checkmated. It was only too likely that we should be held in Moscow as hostages. There was only one hope: that the Finnish-German bourgeois Government would guarantee us a safe conduct through Finland. We put ourselves in the hands of the diplomatic representatives of the neutral Powers, who at once began negotiations with the Finnish and German Governments.

I took advantage of this period of waiting to supply financial aid to the pro-ally organisations, who were badly in need of funds. For weeks the French had furnished this aid single-handed, and my refusal to co-operate in this work had been a sore point with Alexeieff's and Denikin's political representatives. Now that we had reached an open rupture with the Bolsheviks, I contributed my share. Although the banks were closed and all dealings in foreign exchange illegal, money was easily available. There were numerous Russians with hidden stores of roubles. They were only too glad to hand them over in exchange for a promissory note on London. To avoid all suspicion, we collected the roubles through an English firm in Moscow. They dealt with the Russians, fixed the rate of exchange, and gave the promissory note. In each transaction we furnished the English firm with an official guarantee that it was good for the amount in London. The roubles were brought to the American Consulate-General and were handed over to Hicks, who conveyed them safely to their destined quarters.

Apart from this excitement the days passed drearily. There was almost no other work that we could do. With the exception of a small pocket code for emergency messages we had destroyed all our ciphers and all our documents. We had a daily meeting of the Allied representatives at the American Consulate-General, which was now our safest refuge. For, strangely enough, although the United States had associated itself with this landing at Archangel, the Bolsheviks showed no animosity against the Americans. Their name was always excluded from the official protests against the alleged atrocities by the French and British troops in North Russia. They were never mentioned in the violently anti-French and anti-British articles in the Moscow Press.

We made plans for our departure—the negotiations with the Finnish and German Governments were proceeding slowly but not unsatisfactorily. At immense expense the French kept a train waiting with steam up so that we might leave without a moment's delay. From the British in St. Petersburg we were completely cut off. Through the Dutch Legation I sent Cromie a message informing him that I could do nothing to help him and that he had better conduct his own negotiations for the departure of himself and the other British officials. I had several discussions with Reilly, who had decided to remain on in Moscow after our departure.

It was an extraordinary situation. There had been no declaration of war, yet fighting was proceeding on a front stretching from the Dvina to the Caucasus. We were unable to leave Moscow, yet our liberty of action inside the city was almost unrestricted. On the other hand, we knew little of what was going on outside. All that seemed clear was that the Bolsheviks were holding their own.

We struggled successfully against dejection. We dined with the French, and they with us, and played bridge. We renewed our unsuccessful encounters with the Americans at poker. Here I must pay my tribute to Poole, the American Consul-General, and to Wardwell, the head of the American Red Cross Mission. They would have had little difficulty in arranging their own departure. Yet they stood solidly by us to the end.

In the afternoons we had strenuous football matches at the British Consulate-General. There was one historic encounter between the British and the French, for which even General Lavergne, complete in shirt, military riding breeches, braces, and military boots, turned out. He performed prodigies of valour, his silver hair sparkling gaily in the August sun. Sadoul, the French Socialist deputy, who was afterwards to join the Bolsheviks, kept goal. As there was no referee, the charging was terrific. The French had several heavy-weights, and, shod as we were with tennis shoes, we suffered several casualties. The result, however, was the same as at Waterloo—this time without the aid of the Germans, and, the victory clinched, we carried the General off the field to toast his health in Russian beer. It was the last game of football I ever played.

A few days after this international contest—on August 15th, to be exact—I received a visit which was to cause international diversions of a more serious nature. I was lunching in my flat, when the bell rang and my man announced two Lettish gentlemen. One was a short, sallow-faced youth called Smidchen. The other, Berzin, a tall, powerfully-built man with clear-cut features and hard, steely eyes, called himself a colonel. He was, in fact, in command of one of the Lettish regiments which formed the Prætorian Guard of the Soviet Government. Smidchen brought a letter from Cromie. Always on my guard against agents-provocateurs, I scrutinised the letter carefully. It was unmistakably from Cromie. The handwriting was his. The text referred to a previous communication which I had addressed to him through the Swedish Consul-General. The expression that he was making his own arrangements to leave Russia and hoped "to bang the 'dore' before he went out" was typical of this very gallant officer. Above all, the spelling was his. No forger could have faked this, for like Prince Charles Edward, Frederick the Great, and Mr. Harold Nicolson, poor Cromie could not spell. The letter closed with a recommendation of Smidchen as a man who might be able to render us some service.

I asked the two men what they wanted. Berzin did most of the talking. He explained that while the Letts had supported the Bolshevik revolution, they could not fight the Bolsheviks' battles indefinitely. Their one ambition was to return to their own country. As long as Germany was powerful this was impossible. On the other hand, if the Allies, as now seemed likely, were to win the war, it was clear that the Allies and not Germany would have the final word regarding the future of Latvia. They were therefore determined not to put themselves wrong with the Allies. They had no intention of fighting against General Poole's forces at Archangel. If they were sent to that front, they would surrender. Could I arrange matters with General Poole so that they would not be shot down by the Allied troops?

It was an interesting and plausible proposal. It would have to be considered seriously, but, before holding out any encouragement, I wanted to consult my colleagues. I told the two conspirators that, while I understood their reluctance to fight against the Allies, I was not in a position to help them. I was not in touch with General Poole. Moreover, I was expecting to leave Russia at any moment. Their best plan would be to send their own messenger to General Poole. In this connection I might be able to assist them. I arranged for them to call on me at the same time the next day.

That afternoon I thrashed out the whole matter with General Lavergne and M. Grenard, the French Consul-General and subsequently French Minister to Jugoslavia. We decided that, while we must be very careful not to compromise our own position in any way, it was probable that the Letts had no desire to fight against the Allies. There could be little harm in encouraging them to send a messenger to General Poole. We would assist them in this matter. As the negotiations for our own departure were now nearing a happy conclusion, we would put them in touch with Sidney Reilly, who was staying on. Reilly could keep an eye on their movements and help to stimulate their reluctance to oppose our troops. The next day I saw the two Letts, gave them a paper saying "please admit bearer, who has an important communication for General Poole, through the English lines," and put them into touch with Reilly.

Two days later Reilly reported that his negotiations were proceeding smoothly and that the Letts had no intention of being involved in the collapse of the Bolsheviks. He put forward a suggestion that after our departure he might be able, with Lettish help, to stage a counter-revolution in Moscow. This suggestion was categorically turned down by General Lavergne, Grenard, and myself, and Reilly was warned specifically to have nothing to do with so dangerous and doubtful a move. Reilly then went "underground"—that is, into hiding, and, until he escaped to England, I never saw him again.

For another fortnight our enforced idleness continued. Our departure, so the neutral diplomatists informed us, was now decided in principle. The actual date would be fixed at any moment. We packed our clothes, deciding rightly that we should have to travel light, and with heavy heart I resigned myself to the abandonment of all the belongings in my flat— my collection of Oriental books, my furniture, and my wedding presents. One night we went out to "Streilna" to say good-bye to Maria Nikolaievna, our gipsy queen. "Streilna" had been closed, but we found her in her "dacha" close by. She wept over us copiously, sang a few of our favourite songs to us in a low voice, which was scarcely louder than a whisper, and, kissing me on both cheeks, begged us to remain with her.

She saw tragedy ahead of us. She would disguise us, hide us and feed us, and arrange for our departure to the South. Her advice, as sound as it was well meant, could not be taken. She came to the gate to see us off, and we said good-bye beneath the giant firs of the Petrovsky Park with the harvest moon casting ghostly shadows around us. It was an eerie and emotional farewell. We never saw her again. Vaguely I heard that she died a few years ago in poverty.

The tragedy which she had foreseen came with a pistol shot. On Friday, August 30th, Uritsky, the head of the St. Petersburg Cheka, was murdered by a Russian Junker called Kannegiesser. The next evening a Social-Revolutionary, a young Jewish girl called Dora Kaplan, fired two shots point-blank at Lenin as he was leaving Michelson's factory, where he had been speaking at a meeting. One bullet penetrated the lung above the heart. The other entered the neck close to the main artery. The Bolshevik leader was not dead, but his chances of living were at a discount.

I received the news within half an hour of the actual shooting. It could hardly fail to have serious consequences, and, with a premonition of our impending fate, Hicks and I sat up late, discussing in low whispers the events of the day and wondering how they would affect our own unenviable situation.

We went to bed at one o'clock, and, worn out by months of strain, I slept soundly. At three-thirty a.m. I was awakened by a rough voice ordering me to get up at once. As I opened my eyes, I looked up into the steely barrel of a revolver. Some ten armed men were in my room. One man, who was in charge, I knew. He was Mankoff, the former commandant of Smolny. I asked him what this outrage meant. "No questions," he answered gruffly. "Get dressed at once. You are to go to Loubianka No. 11." (Loubianka No. 11 was the headquarters of the Moscow Cheka.) A similar group of Cheka agents was dealing with Hicks, and, while we dressed, the main body of the invaders began to ransack the flat for compromising documents. As soon as we were ready, Hicks and I were bundled into a car and, with a gunman on each side of us, were driven off to the Cheka headquarters. There we were put into a square small room, bare of all furniture except a rough table and a couple of plain wooden chairs.

After a long wait I was taken along a dark corridor. The two gunmen, who accompanied me, stopped before a door and knocked. A sepulchral voice said: "Come in," and I was brought into a long, dark room, lit only by a hand-lamp on the writing table. At the table, with a revolver lying beside the writing-pad, was a man, dressed in black trousers and a white Russian shirt. His black hair, long and waving as a poet's, was brushed back over a high forehead. There was a large wrist watch on his left hand. In the dim light his features looked more sallow than ever. His lips were tightly compressed, and, as I entered the room, his eyes fixed me with a steely stare. He looked grim and formidable. It was Peters. I had not seen him since the day he had accompanied Robins and myself on our tour of inspection of the Anarchists' strongholds.

"You can go," he said to the two gunmen, and then there was a long silence. At last he turned his eyes away and opened his writing folder. "I am sorry to see you in this position," he said. "It is a grave matter." He was scrupulously polite, but very serious. I asked for information, pointing out that I had come to Moscow on the invitation of the Soviet Government and that I had been promised full diplomatic privileges. I made a formal protest against my arrest and demanded to speak to Chicherin.

He ignored my protests. "Do you know the Kaplan woman?" I did not, but I decided that in the circumstances it was better to answer no questions. I repeated as calmly as I could that he had no right to question me.

"Where is Reilly?" was his next question. Again I made the same answer.

Then he produced a paper from his folder. It was the pass to General Poole which I had given to the Letts. "Is that your writing?" he asked.

Yet again I replied with studious politeness that I could answer no questions.

He made no attempt to bully me. He fixed me again with a long stare. "It will be better for you if you speak the truth," he said.

I made no reply. Then he rang a bell, and I was taken back to Hicks. Again we were left alone. We hardly spoke and, when we did, we talked trivialities. We realised that our conversation was likely to be overheard. I had only the vaguest idea of what had happened. It was obvious, however, that the Bolsheviks were trying to link us up with the attempt on Lenin's life. This manœuvre did not disconcert me. The attempt on Lenin might be an indirect consequence of Allied intervention, but we had had nothing to do with it. I was more uneasy about the mention of Reilly's name and the production of my pass to Poole. I guessed that there had been a hitch somewhere and that my two Lettish visitors were agents-provocateurs.

As, holding the lapels of my coat, I tried to review the situation in my mind, I suddenly felt in my breast pocket a note-book, which contained in cryptic form an account of the moneys I had spent. The Cheka agents had ransacked my flat —they were probably searching it at that moment, but they had not thought of searching the clothes we had put on when we were arrested. The note-book was unintelligible to anyone except myself. But it contained figures, and, if it fell into Bolshevik hands they would find some means of rendering it compromising. They would say that the figures represented movements of Bolshevik troops or moneys I had spent on fomenting counter-revolution. That note-book preyed on my mind. How was I to be rid of it? We might be searched at any moment. In the circumstances there seemed only one solution to the problem. I asked permission of our four sentries to go to the lavatory. It was granted, but the affair was not so simple. Two gunmen accompanied me to the door, but, when I started to close it, they shook their heads. "Leave it open," they said and took up their stand in front of me. It was an embarrassing moment. Should I take the risk or not? Fortunately, the decision was made for me by the insanitary conditions of the place. There was no paper. The walls were smeared with stains of human excrement. As calmly as I could, I took out my notebook, tore out the offending pages and used them in the manner in which the circumstances dictated. I pulled the plug. It worked, and I was saved.

I went back to Hicks and sat down to wait. At six in the morning a woman was brought into the room. She was dressed in black. Her hair was black, and her eyes, set in a fixed stare, had great black rings under them. Her face was colourless. Her features, strongly Jewish, were unattractive. She might have been any age between twenty and thirty-five. We guessed it was Kaplan. Doubtless, the Bolsheviks hoped that she would give us some sign of recognition. Her composure was unnatural. She went to the window and, leaning her chin upon her hand, looked out into the daylight. And there she remained, motionless, speechless, apparently resigned to her fate, until presently the sentries came and took her away. She was shot before she knew whether her attempt to alter history had failed or succeeded.

At nine o'clock in the morning Peters himself came in and informed us that we could go home. We were discharged. We heard afterwards that he had been uncertain how to act and had telephoned to Chicherin for instructions. Chicherin had protested against our arrest.

It was Sunday morning and it was raining. We found an old "droschke" and, tired and dejected, we made our way home. The flat was all upside down. The cook and our two men servants had disappeared. Moura, we learnt from the porter downstairs, had been taken off to the Cheka.

On the way home we had bought a paper. It was full of bulletins about Lenin's condition. He was still unconscious. There were, too, violent articles against the bourgeoisie and against the Allies. But there was no mention of our arrest, no effort to incriminate us in the assassination of Uritsky or the attempt on Lenin.

After a bath and a shave I went round to the Dutch Legation to see Oudendyke, the Dutch Minister, who was now in charge of our interests. He was a little man who had spent most of his life in China. His wife was English, and he spoke our language perfectly. I found him in a state of great agitation. There had been a terrible tragedy in St. Petersburg. On the same day as I had been arrested, a band of Cheka agents had burst into our Embassy there. The gallant Cromie had resisted the intrusion and, after killing a commissar, had been shot down at the top of the staircase. All British officials in St. Petersburg had been arrested.

With a sinking feeling in my heart I went to find Wardwell. I was anxious about Moura and my servants, and hoped that he would be able to secure their release. He promised to do his best, and his quiet assurance did much to restore my self-control. He had been unable to see Chicherin, but had been promised an interview for the next day. He, too, was unaware of what lay behind these arrests. He supposed that, as a result of the attempt on Lenin's life, the Bolsheviks had lost their heads. He was afraid that the threat of a Red Terror, which now filled the newspapers, would soon be put into execution.

As I walked back to my flat I was struck by the emptiness of the streets. Such people as went about their business did so with quick steps and furtive glances. The street corners were guarded by little groups of soldiers. A new fear was abroad. In forty-eight hours the whole atmosphere of the city had changed. The next day, unable to bear the suspense about Moura's fate any longer, I went down to the Foreign Office and demanded to see Karachan. I was received at once. Avoiding all political discussion, I went straight to the point. Whatever grievances the Bolsheviks might have against me, it was inhuman that they should seek to hit at me through the arrest of Moura. I appealed to his decency and begged him to release her. He promised to do what he could. It was my thirty-first birthday, and I spent it alone with Hicks, who prepared us a meal of coffee, black bread, and sardines.

On the Tuesday we read the full tale of our iniquities in the Bolshevik Press, which excelled itself in a fantastic account of a so-called Lockhart Plot. We were accused of having conspired to murder Lenin and Trotsky, to set up a military dictatorship in Moscow, and by blowing up all the railway bridges to reduce the populations of Moscow and St. Petersburg to starvation. The whole plot had been revealed by the loyalty of the Lettish garrison, whom the Allies had sought to suborn by lavish gifts of money. The whole story, which read like a fairy-tale, was rounded off with a fantastic account of my arrest. I had been surprised, it was stated, at a conspirators' meeting. I had been taken to the Cheka and, as soon as my identity was established, I had been immediately released. An equally fantastic story described the events in St. Petersburg. Cromie's murder was depicted as a measure of self-defence by the Bolshevik agents, who had been forced to return his fire. Huge headlines denounced the Allied representatives as "Anglo-French Bandits," and in their comments the leader-writers shrieked for the application of a wholesale terror and of the severest measures against the conspirators.

At first I was inclined to regard this outburst as a typical Bolshevik attempt (1) to excuse their murder of Cromie, which I felt sure they had never intended, and (2) to galvanise their own supporters and to strike terror into the heart of would-be counter-revolutionaries in Moscow itself. Reilly, whose name figured largely in the plot, had disappeared. Unless he had completely lost his head, the whole story was a tissue of invention.

I found that Poole, the American Consul-General, took a more serious view of the conspiracy. He was inclined to regard Reilly as an agent-provocateur, who had staged this plot for the benefit of the Bolsheviks. One account of the conspiracy mentioned a project whereby Lenin and Trotsky were not to be murdered, but were to be led through the streets of Moscow in their shirts. This fantastic proposal could have emanated only from Reilly's fertile imagination. I laughed at Poole's fears. Later, I was to know much more of Reilly than I did at that time, but my estimate of his character did not alter. He was then in his forty-sixth year. He was a Jew with, I imagine, no British blood in his veins. His parents came from Odessa.

His real name was Rosenblum. The name of Reilly he had taken from the second name of his first wife's father, an Irishman called Callahan. How he became a British subject I do not know to this day. Prior to the war he had spent most of his time in St. Petersburg, where he had earned considerable sums of money as a commission agent in various forms of business. He was a man of great energy and personal charm, very attractive to women and very ambitious. I had not a very high opinion of his intelligence. His knowledge covered many subjects, from politics to art, but it was superficial. On the other hand, his courage and indifference to danger were superb. Moreover, Captain Hill, his associate in his dangerous plan to remain on in Moscow after our departure, was a man whose loyalty was beyond suspicion. He was as brave and as bold as Reilly. He spoke Russian just as well. If there had been any double-crossing by Reilly, Hill would hardly have failed to detect it. Ridiculous as this story was, I found nevertheless that through Poole it had gained some credence in England. When two months later I reached London, I had to go bail with the Foreign Office for Reilly's bona fides when, after a series of hair-breadth escapes, this remarkable man succeeded in making his way to Bergen. I did so without the slightest hesitation.

But, although I never questioned Reilly's loyalty to the Allies, I was not sure—indeed, I am not sure to this day—how far he had gone in his negotiations with the Letts. He was a man cast in the Napoleonic mould. Napoleon was his hero in life and at one time he possessed one of the finest collections of Napoleana in the world. He saw himself being left alone in Russia and the prospect of playing a lone hand may have inspired him with a Napoleonic design. In conversation afterwards he always denied most of the Bolshevik allegations. His own theory was that Berzin and the other Letts, whom he saw, were at first sincere in their desire to avoid fighting against the Allies. When they realised that the Allied intervention was not serious, they went back on him and betrayed him to save their own skins. Be this as it may, the so-called Allied plot was to have serious consequences for all of us.

Reilly's subsequent career was curious. On his return to England, he speedily established himself with Mr. Churchill and the advocates of post-war intervention, and went to South Russia as a British agent with Denikin's forces. When that venture ended ir disaster, Reilly allied himself with Savinkoff, who was then besieging the statesmen of England and France with requests for support for his so-called "Green" movement. Reilly, who was a lavish spender, exhausted his financial resources on Savinkoff. He became hard up and, in a last desperate endeavour to re-establish his fortunes, set out for Russia in 1926 on some counter-revolutionary scheme alleged to be organised by ex-Guards officers. His subsequent fate is not known with certainty. The Bolsheviks announced that he had been shot while trying to cross the Finnish frontier. Such evidence as is available would seem to prove that he walked into a Bolshevik trap, that his Guards officers, whom he met abroad, were really Cheka agents, and that he was taken to a "dacha" outside Moscow and then shot.

After this long digression, which contains the whole truth, so far as I know it, about the so-called Lockhart Plot, I must return to my own situation in Moscow. The account of the Allied conspiracy had appeared in the Russian papers of September 3rd. In spite of the serious nature of the allegations I was left at liberty throughout that day. I discovered later that there was considerable difference of opinion in Bolshevik official circles regarding the procedure to be observed towards me. There were several Commissars who were not prepared to swallow the whole of the Cheka's story without some dilution. The next day I determined to approach Karachan again in order to make a last appeal for Moura, who was still in prison. He was not unfriendly. I told him that the story in the Soviet Press was a tissue of lies, and he laughed good-humouredly. "Now you know," he said, "what we have to put up with from your newspapers." He was, however, not very hopeful about Moura, and, deciding on desperate remedies, I made up my mind to approach Peters himself. I walked up from the Russian Foreign Office to the Loubianka and asked to see him. My request caused some excitement and much whispering among the guards in the entrance hall. It took me half an hour to gain admission and still longer to obtain access to Peters. When he received me, I tackled him at once about Moura. I told him that the conspiracy story was a fake and that he knew it. Even if there were a grain of truth in it, Moura knew nothing about it. I begged him to release her at once. He listened to me patiently and promised that my assurance of her innocence would receive every consideration. Then he looked me straight in the face. "You have saved me some trouble," he said. "My men have been looking for you for the last hour. I have a warrant for your arrest. Your French and English colleagues are already under lock and key." This last statement was not strictly accurate. Some of them had avoided capture by what was to prove the one comic expedient in our ignominious situation. But this I shall recount later. As far as I myself was concerned, this time I was to be a prisoner in all seriousness.

CHAPTER TEN

MY TERM OF imprisonment lasted for exactly one month. It may be divided into two periods: the first, which lasted five days and was marked by discomfort and fear; the second, which lasted for twenty-four days and may be described as a period of comparative comfort accompanied by acute mental strain.

In Loubianka No. 11, a former insurance company's office, I was kept in a room which was used for the registration and preliminary examination of minor criminals. It had three windows, two of which looked on to an inside courtyard. It was furnished with a table, four wooden chairs, and an old, broken-down sofa, on which, if I was fortunate, I was some-times allowed to sleep. Generally, I slept on the floor. The real hardship, however, was that the room was never empty, never dark. Two sentries were on guard all the time. The work of the minor Commissars, who used the room, never ceased by night or day. Most of these men were Letts or Russian sailors. Some of them were not unfriendly. They regarded me with a kind of detached interest, spoke to me occasionally, and gave me the *Izvestia* to read. Others again were surly and hostile. At night Peters would send for me, and I would have to go through a kind of bantering cross-examination. I cannot say that he treated me unfairly. The want of sleep was a severe strain, and for that reason I found his midnight questions trying. They were mostly urgent appeals to tell him the whole truth in my own interests. He would inform me that my colleagues had confessed (one French agent did write an anti-Ally letter which was published in the Bolshevik Press), and he would urge me to do the same if I wished to avoid being handed over to the Revolutionary tribunal. He was, however, neither brutal nor even impolite. As between prisoner and gaoler, our relations were pleasant. He himself was married to an Englishwoman, whom he had left in England. He seemed interested in my romance with Moura. Occasionally, too, he would come into my room and ask if I were being properly fed. The food—tea, thin soup, and potatoes—was not sustaining, but I made no complaint. On the second day, he brought me two books to read: Wells' "Mr. Britling Sees It Through," and Lenin's "State and Revolution." My one comfort was the official Bolshevik newspapers, which my gaolers took a propagandist joy in supplying to me. Certainly, as far as my own case was concerned, they were far from reassuring. They were still full of the Lockhart Plot. They contained numerous resolutions, passed by workmen's committees, demanding my trial and execution. They gave, too, full prominence to foreign comment on the plot. The German Press, in particular, did itself proud. During the war it had suffered much from similar accusations of undiplomatic conduct, notably, in the von Papen case, and now it made the most of our alleged misdemeanours, which were described as the most scandalous in the history of diplomacy. There were, too, discouraging reports of Bolshevik victories over the Czechs and the Allies, and still more fearsome accounts of the Terror, which was now in full force. It was not these details which relieved my anxiety. From the first day of my captivity I had made up my mind that, if Lenin died, my own life would not be worth a moment's purchase. Only one thing could save me: an overwhelming victory of the Allied armies in France. Knowing the Bolshevik passion for peace at almost any price, I felt that such a victory might moderate the Bolshevik attitude towards us. And the *Izvestia*, to my relief, contained not only bulletins of Lenin's health but also news from the Western Front. Both were comforting. By September 6th Lenin was pronounced to be out of danger. In the West the Allied advance was meeting with real success.

From Peters I learnt that my colleagues had been herded together in the Butirky prison. I alone had been singled out for solitary confinement. It was an additional strain.

Two macabre incidents marked the period of my detention in the "Cheka." On the third day a bandit was brought into my room. He was a tall, powerful fellow not more than twenty-five. I was a silent witness of his cross-examination, which was very different from anything I had experienced at Peters' hands.

At first he laughingly asserted his innocence. No man was a more loyal supporter of the Soviet régime than he. No man had observed the decrees more scrupulously. The accusations of banditry and smuggling, with which he had been confronted, were the acts of counter-revolutionaries, who were seeking to destroy him. He made a brave show, but the Commissar paid no attention. With relentless reiteration he repeated his question: Where were you on the night of August 27th? The bandit blustered, became confused, lied, and, when he saw that the Commissar knew he had lied, began to weep and plead for mercy. The Commissar laughed and scribbled something on a piece of paper. He tossed it to the sentry, while the bandit still grovelled before the table. The sentries tapped him on the shoulder, and in an instant his manner changed. Realising that his doom was sealed, he sprang to his feet, hurled one sentry against the wall, and made a dash for the door. One of the Bolsheviks put his foot out, and the bandit fell sprawling on the floor. He was seized and, still scuffling and shouting curses at his captors, was dragged out of the room.

The second incident, more terrifying in its effect upon my nerves, took place on my last day in Loubianka No. 11. I was reading in the afternoon, when Peters came into the room. I went over with him to the window to talk. When he had a free moment, he liked discussing England, the war, capitalism and revolution. He told me strange tales of his experiences as a revolutionary. He had been in prison in Riga in Tsarist days. He showed me his nails as a proof of the torture which he had undergone. There was nothing in his character to indicate the inhuman monster he is commonly supposed to be. He told me that he suffered physical pain every time he signed a death sentence. I believe it was true. There was a strong streak of sentimentality in his nature, but he was a fanatic as far as the clash between Bolshevism and Capitalism was concerned, and he pursued his Bolshevik aims with a sense of duty which was relentless.

As we were talking, a motor van—a kind of "Black Maria"

—pulled up in the court-yard below, and a squad of men, armed with rifles and bandoliers, got out and took up their places in the yard. Presently, a door opened just below us, and three men with bowed heads walked slowly forward to the van. I recognised them instantly. They were Sheglovitoff, Khvostoff, and Bieletsky, three ex-Ministers of the Tsarist régime, who had been in prison since the revolution. There was a pause, followed by a scream. Then through the door the fat figure of a priest was half-pushed, half-carried, to the "Black Maria." His terror was pitiful. Tears rolled down his face. His knees rocked, and he fell like a great ball of fat on the ground. I felt sick and turned away. "Where are they going?" I asked. "They are going to another world," said Peters drily. "And that man," he said, pointing to the priest, "richly deserves it." It was the notorious Bishop Vostorgoff. The ex-Ministers formed the first batch of the several hundred victims of the Terror who were shot at that time as a reprisal for the attempted assassination of Lenin.

That same night Peters sent for me. "To-morrow," he said, "we are sending you to the Kremlin. You will be alone and you will be more comfortable." In my presence he rang up the Commandant of the Kremlin. "Are Citizen Lockhart's rooms ready?" he asked peremptorily. The answer was obviously in the negative. "Never mind," said Peters, "give him Bieletsky's." Bieletsky was one of the ex-Ministers who had been shot that afternoon. The allusion seemed ominous. The Kremlin was reserved only for the most unfortunate political prisoners. Hitherto, not one had left it alive.

I was taken to the Kremlin on the evening of September 8th. I was placed in an apartment in the Kavalarieski Korpus. My new quarters were clean and comfortable. They consisted of a small hall, a sitting-room, a diminutive bedroom, a bathroom —alas! without a bath—and a tiny kitchen. The rooms in former days had served as a flat for one of the Ladies-in-Waiting. Unfortunately, the windows on both sides opened on to corridors, so that I had no fresh air. Unfortunately, too, I was not alone, as Peters had promised I should be. I had a

companion in misfortune, the Lett, Smidchen, who was the
cause of all our troubles and who was alleged to be my accom-
plice and agent. We spent thirty-six hours together, during
which I was afraid to exchange a word. Then he was taken
away. I never heard what happened to him. To this day I do
not know whether he was shot or whether he was handsomely
rewarded for the part he had played in unmasking the "great
conspiracy" There was one other drawback to my new prison.
On both sides of my quarters I had sentries: one for each
window. They were changed every four hours, and, as each
change had to come into my rooms to certify that I was there,
I was woken up every night at ten, two and six.

My sentries were mainly Letts, but there were also Russians,
Poles and Hungarians. I had also an old man—a former servant
of the Kremlin—who did my rooms. He was as kind as he
dared to be, but our conversation was limited and confined
strictly to requests for the Bolshevik newspapers and for hot
water for my samovar. From the *Izvestia* I learnt that the Allied
Governments had sent a fierce Note to the Bolsheviks, demanding our immediate release and holding them separately and
jointly responsible for our safety. By way of reprisal England
had arrested Litvinoff and thrown him into prison. Chicherin
had replied to this protest with a note which set out our
alleged misdeeds at great length, but which contained an offer
to let us go free in exchange for Litvinoff and other arrested
Russians in France and England. Chicherin's offer was to
some extent reassuring. As, however, other sections of the
official newspaper continued to announce that I was to be
tried for my life, I was still far from certain of my release and
even of my personal safety.

My food in the Kremlin was the same as in Loubianka No. 11
—soup, tea and potatoes. Peters apologised for it, stating that
it was the same as that supplied to himself and his assistants.
From what I had observed during my stay in the Cheka headquarters, his statement was true.

One of my first acts, after my arrival in the Kremlin, was
to write to Peters on behalf of Moura and my staff. Once again

my appeal was to his sense of decency. I told him my staff was in no way responsible for anything I might or might not have done. As far as Moura was concerned, I asked him what satisfaction he could have in making war on women. On the third day he came to see me. He informed me that in all probability I should be handed over to the Revolutionary Tribunal for trial. He had, however, released Moura. What was more, he had given her permission to bring me food, clothes, books and tobacco. Provided it was written in Russian and given to him open, he offered to take a note from me to her. At the same time he gave instructions to the Commandant of the Kremlin that I was to have two hours' exercise daily in the open air. He was in a magnanimous mood. Lenin was now well on the way to recovery. The news from the Bolshevik front was excellent. The Bolsheviks had recaptured Uralsk from the Czechs. Kazan was on the eve of capitulation.

Peters was true to his word. That afternoon I had concrete proof of Moura's release in the form of a basket with clothes, books, tobacco, and such luxuries as coffee and ham. There was, too, a long letter from her. Of course, it contained no news of any sort, but it arrived sealed. It was not to be read by the prying eyes of my guards. Peters himself had stamped it with the official seal of the Cheka with a footnote signed in his own bold handwriting: "Please deliver this letter in sealed form. It has been read by me.—Peters." This strange man, whose interest I had somehow aroused, was determined to show me that a Bolshevik could be as chivalrous in small matters as any bourgeois.

The clothes and the food—but especially the clothes— were a real boon. I had not taken off my suit or washed or shaved for six days. I was not to be relieved of my anxiety for another fortnight. Only the night before, Krylenko, the Public Prosecutor, had spoken at a meeting and, amid loud cheers, had announced that the Allied conspirators were to be tried by him and that the criminal Lockhart would not escape his proper punishment. From now on, however, my prison life was to be tolerably comfortable.

Naturally, time lay heavy on my hands. Gradually, however, I evolved a kind of routine, which made the day pass more rapidly. As soon as I was dressed, I sat down to play a Chinese patience. (With my clothes and books Moura had enclosed a pack of cards.) I played a kind of game with myself. With Celtic superstition I said to myself that, if I did not get it out, the day would end in disaster. It was an unhealthy excitement in which I gambled my life against the cards. Fortunately for my peace of mind, I never failed to get the patience out. Some days, however, it was late in the afternoon before I succeeded.

My card-playing ended, I read. The books I read during my three weeks in the Kremlin included : Thucydides, Renan's "Souvenirs d'Enfance et de Jeunesse," Ranke's "History of the Popes," Schiller's "Wallenstein," Rostand's "L'Aiglon," Archenholtz's "History of the Seven Years' War," Beltzke's "History of the War in Russia in 1812," Sudermann's "Rosen," Macaulay's "Life and Letters," Stevenson's "Travels with a Donkey," Kipling's "Captains Courageous," Wells' "The Island of Doctor Moreau," Holland Rose's "Life of Napoleon," Carlyle's "French Revolution" and Lenin and Zinovieff's "Against the Current." I was a serious young man in those days.

The preparation of my meals was another pastime. After luncheon there was my walk in the Kremlin grounds. My first walk was on September 11th. It was the day on which the Bolsheviks recaptured Kazan, and the Kremlin was a riot of flags and red bunting. In the early days of the Bolshevik régime the Kremlin was a fortress to which visitors were rarely, if ever, admitted. Even at the time of my friendliest relations with the Bolsheviks I had never crossed its threshold. My interviews with Lenin, Trotsky, Chicherin and the other Commissars had always been outside its walls. Now I was able to see the changes which had taken place since the October revolution. The giant monument to Alexander the Second on the parade ground had been dragged down from its huge pedestal. The cross which marked the spot where the Grand Duke Serge had been blown up had been removed.

My sentry on that first day was a Pole. He walked beside me with loaded rifle and was talkative and not unfriendly. He informed me that he had frequently accompanied the Tsarist ex-Ministers on their walks and that few prisoners who entered the Kremlin came out alive. The betting among his comrades was two to one on that I would be shot.

On the whole, my sentries were decent, sensible fellows, who made no attempt to jeer at me. During my whole period of captivity I struck only one really nasty one—a sour-faced curmudgeon, who swore at England, cursed me as an assassin, and refused to allow me even to send a message to the Commandant. He was a Hungarian. The Letts were the best. Most of them were contemptuous of the Russians, whom they regarded as inferiors. One Lett informed me that, if Russia could have put a million non-Russian troops into the trenches, she could not have failed to win the war. Every time the Letts advanced, he said, they were let down by the Russians, who failed invariably to support them. He despised, too, the dirt and laziness of the Russian troops. On the other hand, he had a wholesome respect for the Bolshevik leaders, whom he regarded as super-men.

Not all my sentries were Bolsheviks. They were divided into three classes: first, the ardent Communists, who convinced one by their sincerity and by their devotion to their cause. Of these there were not many. Secondly, the sheep who went with the crowd—Bolshevik to-day, Menshevik to-morrow. And, thirdly—and these were the most numerous—the sceptical, who believed that in Russia anything was possible and everything bad. All, however, were convinced that the revolution had come to stay. Even those Letts, who were anxious to return to Latvia, laughed at the possibility of a successful counter-revolution. To them counter-revolution meant the restoration of the land to the land-owners.

These walks were a welcome relief to the monotony of my existence. They kept me from thinking about myself, and, although at first I could not refrain from indirect questions to my guards regarding my own fate, the answers I received soon discouraged further attempts to satisfy my morbid curiosity. Every day during my walk I paid a visit to a little church built in the wall of the Kremlin. It had a little garden round it and a famous ikon called "Our Lady of Unexpected Joy." Before the war, inspired by the attractiveness of the title, I had written a short story about it, which was published in the *Morning Post*. Now it was to be for three weeks the shrine of my daily prayers.

After my first week in the Kremlin, Karachan came to see me. He was reticent about my own case. He, too, hinted that a public trial was inevitable. He also informed me that René Marchand, a member of the French Mission, had furnished the Bolsheviks with full proofs of an Allied meeting at the American Consulate-General. At this meeting the Allied representatives had discussed such measures as blowing up railway bridges and cutting off Moscow and St. Petersburg from their sources of food supplies. He had given, so Karachan said, a full list of the names of those who were present. I laughed. Most of my conversations with Karachan were conducted in a tone of airy persiflage. "That beats the *Times*," I said. "Believe me or not, as you like, this is another invention of your Cheka."

"It is true," he replied. "We shall publish the letter in a day or two. Fortunately for you," he added with a grin, "you do not seem to have been present."

The story was more or less true. Marchand had thrown in his lot with the Bolsheviks. After the war he returned to France and joined the French Communist Party. He renounced his Communism in 1931.

Karachan also gave me news of the war and of the outside world. The neutral diplomatists had issued a violent protest against the Terror, from which I deduced that they were working to secure our release. The Allied forces were making no progress in Russia. The Bolsheviks had registered further successes against the Czechs and the Russian counter-revolutionary forces. On the other hand, the Allies were driving back the Germans in the West. Austria and Bulgaria were on the verge of collapse. He admitted that the Allies might now win the war.

This was good news indeed. It was further stressed by the

disclosure of the real object of Karachan's visit. He had come to ascertain my views regarding the terms on which England would be prepared to abandon her intervention and to make peace with Russia. The Bolsheviks were prepared to offer an amnesty to all counter-revolutionaries who would accept the régime, and a free exit out of Russia to the Czechs and to the Allies. Obviously, if the Bolsheviks were ready to discuss peace terms with the Allies, they were not going to shoot me. On the other hand, the Allies were not likely to listen to any proposals of this nature. On the whole, my hopes were raised by this visit. Lenin, Karachan informed me, was now able to sit up and to take nourishment.

The week from September 14th to 21st was wet and miserable, and on two days I was unable to have my daily walk. I still received my daily messages and my daily supply of luxuries from Moura. She sent me, too, a fountain-pen and several note-books, and I amused myself by writing bad verse and by keeping a strictly non-committal diary of my prison life. I had, however, no more Bolshevik visitors and no news, and, as I was sleeping badly, I underwent a fresh period of pessimism.

Spiridonova, who was imprisoned in the same corridor as myself, I saw often. We never spoke, although we greeted each other solemnly when we passed on our daily walks. She looked ill and nervous, with great dark lines under her eyes. She was clumsily and very carelessly dressed, but might have been quite pretty when young.

Another prisoner, whom I met occasionally on my walks, was General Brusiloff. He had had an accident to his leg and walked with difficulty with the aid of a stick. My diary states that "he looked ill, haggard, and very old, and that he had a sly, foxy face." Yet another prisoner was Sablin, the former Soviet Commander, who had played a leading part in the Left Social-Revolutionary attempted *coup d'état* in July. Good-looking, with an attractive smile and blue eyes, he looked little more than a boy.

The eminence of their prisoners evidently caused some

amusement to our guards. One day my sentry piloted me to the
shrine where formerly had stood the statue of Alexander II and
with pride pointed out to me a sentence roughly chiselled on
the side of the huge pedestal. The words, carved by one of our
sentries, ran as follows: "Here the Red Army soldiers of the
9th Lettish Rifles had the honour of walking with Brusiloff,
Lockhart, Spiridonova and Sablin." The word "honour" was in
inverted commas. I reflected with grim morbidness that this
was the only statue except a tombstone on which my name was
likely to figure.

On September 21st Karachan came to see me again. He
was in high fettle over the Bolshevik successes on the Volga.
The Red Army had captured Simbirsk and Buinsk and was now
full of confidence. He brought me copies of *The Call*—a
Bolshevik news-sheet, printed in English, which was to be
distributed by airplanes among the English troops on the
Archangel and Murmansk fronts. It contained a lurid account
of the so-called Allied Plot. My name figured largely in it, and
to my other crimes was now added the charge of having concocted a false treaty between Germany and Russia as a means
of inducing the Allied troops to fight against the Bolsheviks.
The account, so the paper said, read "like a tale from the
Arabian Nights." I pointed this passage out to Karachan and
congratulated him on the aptness of the simile. It was a fine
example of imaginative fiction. Karachan, who knew the circumstances of my arrest in every detail, smiled blandly.
"Your Government," he said, "is supporting the war against
the revolution. Every kind of irregularity has been committed
by Allied agents in this country. You have become the symbol
of these irregularities. In a clash between two world forces the
individual has to suffer."

The next day I received a surprise visit from Peters. He
brought Moura with him. It was his birthday (he was thirty-
two), and, as he preferred giving presents to receiving them, he
had brought Moura as his birthday treat. In more senses than
one this was the most thrilling moment of my captivity.
Peters was in a reminiscent mood. He sat down opposite me

Allied invasion of Russia to suppress Workmens Revolution, and re-establish Tsarism.

Sensational plot discovered to overthrow Soviet government.

Allied complicity in counter-revolutionary plot proved

British diplomat in Moscow discovered at conspirative meeting.—Lavishly distributing bribes. Fabricating forged documents.

The following is a summary of a statement issued by the Soviet government, which discloses a widespread plot instigated by the Allied governments to overthrow the Russian revolution.

On August 14 th. at twelve o'clock, at the private room of Mr. Lockhart, the representative of the British government in Russia, an interview took place between him and a commander of one of the Soviet detatchments in Moscow.

At this meeting it was proposed to organise a rebellion against the Soviet government in connection with the British landing on the Mourman. In order to maintain close relation between the British diplomatic agents and this comm ander of the Soviet troops, an English lieutenant, Sydney Reiley was delegated to act under the alllas of «Reis». It was proposed that certain parts of the Moscow garrison should be sent to Vologda to open the road for the English, while the rest of the garrison should arrest the Council of the Peoples Commissioners in Moscow, and establish a military dictatorshrip.

For this purpose on Aug. 14 th. Mr .Lockhart handed 700,000 roubles to his agents. On Aug. 22nd another meeting took place at which 200,000 roubles were assigned for the purpose of arresting Lenin and Trotsky, and members of the Council of Public Economy, seizing banks, posts and telegraphs. On Aug. 28th 300,000 roubles was paid over to this commander of Soviet troops who was to go to Petrograd to establish connection with the English military group working there together with a group of Russian counter-revolutionaries.

At the same time in Moscow, meetings under the auspices of the agents of the Allied Powers were held with the object of intensifying the famine. It was proposed to blow up certain bridges on the railways, and wreck food trains, in order that the population of Moscow and Petrograd should become so maddened by hunger as to rise in revolt against the Soviet government.

Letters have been discovered with Mr. Lockhart's signature on official British government paper, delegating this commander of Soviet troops to act on behalf of the British government.

The plot was discovered by the commander disclosing the whole scheme to the Soviet authorities.

Acting on this information the Soviet authorities on the night of Aug. 31st surprised a conspirative meeting at which Mr. Lockhart was present. Although Lockhart was arrested, some of the conspirators escaped and are now at large. They have carried out a portion of the ir plans. Trainloads of food were blown up by them at Voronezh. Documents were seized at this meeting which shows that the intention of the Allies as soon as they had established their dictatorship in Moscow was to declare war on Germany and force Russia to fight again. In order to find a pretext for this, a fictitious treaty between Russia and Germany was concocted which presented the Soviet government as selling the independance of Russia to Germany. This forged treaty was to have been printed and scattered broadcast.

FELLOW WORKERS!

Here is positive evidence of the real purpose for which you have been brought to Russia.

You are being used as the tools of your capitalists who are working here in close unity with the agents of bloodstained Tzarism, for the overthrow of the first Socialist Republic, and the re-establishment of the former reign of oppression.

YOU ARE NOT FIGHTING FOR LIBERTY. YOU ARE FIGHTING TO CRUSH IT.

FELLOW WORKERS !

Be honourable men. Remain loyal to your class, refuse to be the accomplices of a great crime. Refuse to do the dirty work of your masters.

G. TCHITCHERINE,
Peoples Commissary for Foreign Affaivs.

at the small table near the back wall and began to talk of his
life as a revolutionary. He had become a Socialist at the age of
fifteen. He had suffered exile and persecution. I listened only
fitfully. Moura, who was standing behind Peters and in front
of me, was fiddling with my books, which stood on a small
side table surmounted by a long hanging mirror. She caught my
eyes, held up a note, and slipped it into a book. I was terrified.
A slight turn of his head, and Peters could see everything in
the mirror. I gave the tiniest of nods. Moura, however, seemed
to think that I had not seen and repeated the performance.
My heart stopped beating, and this time I nodded like an
epileptic. Fortunately, Peters noticed nothing or else Moura's
shrift would have been short. Although he gave me no news
about my own fate beyond saying that preparations were being
made for my trial, he treated me in every other respect with
great courtesy, questioned me several times about my treatment by my sentries, and asked me if I were receiving Moura's
letters regularly and if I had any complaints to make. Then,
excusing himself on account of pressure of work for the
shortness of his visit and promising to bring Moura again, he
left me. Moura and I had hardly exchanged a word, but already
I felt a new hope. It was as if I had left the world and come
back to it again. As soon as they had gone, I rushed to the book
—it was Carlyle's "French Revolution"—and took out the
note. It was very short—six words only: "Say nothing—all
will be well." That night I could not sleep.

The next day Peters came again. His second visit explained
his first. This time he was accompanied, not by Moura, but by
Asker, the Swedish Consul-General, a man of great charm and
high ideals, who had laboured night and day to secure our
release. Peters went straight to the point. The neutral diplomatists had expressed concern about my fate. They had been
much perturbed by rumours that I had been shot, that I was
being subjected to Chinese torture. He had, therefore, brought
the Swedish Consul-General in order that he might persuade
himself by the proof of his own eyes (1) that I was alive, and
(2) that I was being well-treated. My conversation with Asker

was restricted. We had to talk in Russian, and his knowledge
of the language was limited. Moreover, he was not allowed to
discuss my case with me. Having satisfied himself that I was
not being starved or tortured, he managed to say that everything
possible was being done on my behalf, and then he left.

On the following morning the Bolshevik Press broadcast a
statement that, while the bourgeois Press throughout the world
was spreading rumours of the terrible tortures to which I was
being subjected, I myself had denied them and had admitted
to the Swedish Consul-General that I was being treated with
every courtesy.

My interview with Asker was not altogether satisfactory.
The fact that he was not allowed to discuss my own case with
me depressed me. If I was no longer afraid for my life, the
probability of a public trial and of a long term of imprisonment impressed itself more strongly than ever on my mind.
My apprehensions were increased by the publication in the
Izvestia the next morning of the disclosures of Marchand, the
French agent. It took the form of an open letter to Poincaré
and denounced in strong terms the counter-revolutionary
activities of the Allied agents in Russia. Although my name
was not mentioned in the letter and although I had never had
any connection with the activities, which had turned Marchand
against his own country, the Bolshevik Press seized on this
opportunity to rake up all the mud they could against me.
Once again I was denounced as the instigator of everything
true or untrue and as the arch-criminal of diplomacy. I suppose
I should have felt flattered. I was by far the youngest of the
Allied representatives. Yet I had been singled out for solitary
confinement in the Kremlin, and my name had figured in every
newspaper as the ringleader of the Allied representatives.
Doubtless, the Bolshevik attitude, so different in public and in
private towards myself, was determined solely by reasons of
policy. I had known them more intimately than any other Allied
representative. I had opposed intervention almost to the end.
It was necessary that they should do their best to discredit in
advance any evidence I might bring against them. The American

officials, who were far more deeply implicated in Marchand's disclosures than I was, escaped not only arrest but all abuse. The Bolsheviks knew that President Wilson, who was a historian and who, therefore, remembered Napoleon, was very lukewarm in his attitude towards the Russian policy of the Allies. They were determined to do nothing to prejudice that attitude.

The weather at this period was very trying. There were days when the sun shone and when the temperature was as high as in July. These were days of hope. There were other days when the wind blew and the rain beat down mercilessly on the Kremlin walls. Winter was already in the air, and the cold and the damp added to my depression. My diary tells me that my nerves, which hitherto had stood the strain of these strenuous months remarkably well, were beginning to suffer.

On September 26th Karachan came to see me again. He was, as always, courteous and affable. We had a further discussion about the Allied situation in Russia and the possibility of opening up negotiations for peace. He informed me that the question of my trial had now been settled. It was not to take place. He assumed that eventually I should be set free.

When he had gone, I sat down and translated into blank verse the Tell soliloquy from Schiller: "Through this deserted valley must he pass."

Two days later Peters came in with Moura. It was six o'clock on a Saturday evening. He was dressed in a leather jacket and khaki trousers. An enormous Mauser pistol was strapped to his side. There was a broad grin on his face. He told me that I was to be set free on Tuesday. He would allow me to go home for two days to pack. I thanked him, and then he looked at me rather sheepishly, put his hand into his pocket, and pulled out a packet. "I have a favour to ask of you," he said. "When you reach London, will you give this letter to my English wife?" At the same time he gave me a signed photograph of himself and showed me some snapshots of his wife. Almost before I could say "of course I will," he drew back. "No," he said, "I shan't trouble you. As soon as you're

out of here you'll blaspheme and curse me as your worst enemy."
He seemed incapable of crediting any bourgeois with feelings of
humanity towards the proletariat.

I told him not to be a fool and to give me the letter. Politics
apart, I bore him no grudge. I would remember his kindness
to Moura all my life. I took the letter. Later, of course, I
delivered it. Then he began to talk, first, about politics and the
plot. He admitted openly in front of Moura that the Americans
were as greatly compromised in this business as anyone else.
(Since my arrest an American agent had been detected with
plans, concealed in a hollow walking-stick, of the disposition
of the Red Army.) He confessed that the evidence he had been
able to collect against me was not very damaging. I was either
a fool or very clever. "I don't understand you," he said. "Why
are you going back to England? You have placed yourself in a
false position. Your career is finished. Your Government will
never forgive you. Why don't you stay here? You can be happy
and make your own life. We can give you work to do.
Capitalism is doomed any way."

I shook my head, and he went away, wondering. He could
not understand how I could leave Moura. He left her alone
with me.

The reaction was wonderful. Although, except during the
first few days before it was clear that Lenin was going to recover, I was not really afraid that I should be shot, the strain
had been severe, and I had never been sure that some little straw
would not change everything against me. We laughed and
cried alternately. Then we settled down to talk. There was so
much to tell—a whole month's gap during which I had heard
nothing of the outside world, of my colleagues, of Moura
herself.

It was an incoherent, disjointed conversation, interrupted
by numerous digressions, but little by little I pieced together
the whole story. Moura had been in the women's prison.
My colleagues and a goodly number of the French had been
incarcerated in the "Butirky." Wardwell, the American, had
been heroic. He had wrung concessions from the Bolsheviks.

Daily he had fed all the Allied prisoners and Moura as well with his own provisions. He had not lessened her alarm by telling her that I was to be shot. For ten days there had been great anxiety about my fate. My solitary confinement had baffled the neutral diplomatists. There had been a terrible scene between the Dutch Minister and Chicherin, during which both men lost their tempers. The Dutch Minister was persuaded that I was going to be shot and had telegraphed his conviction to London. The British Government had replied with a menacing note to the Bolsheviks. The whole situation seemed hopeless until Lenin was able to take a hand in affairs. After he recovered consciousness, his first remark, it was said, was: "Stop the Terror." Gradually the hot-heads on both sides cooled down, and out of chaos a scheme had been evolved whereby we were to be exchanged for Litvinoff and other Bolsheviks in England. There had been a long hitch before an agreement could be reached. The British Government, who had arrested Litvinoff, were not prepared to trust the Bolsheviks. They would not allow Litvinoff to leave English soil until I had crossed the Russian frontier. For days the negotiations were side-tracked in this cul-de-sac. I had foreseen this difficulty when I had first read of the proposal in the *Izvestia*. I knew that the Bolsheviks cared little about Litvinoff, but much about their own prestige. The only way to deal with them successfully in a matter like this was to take them at their word. They would act up to it. Treated like bandits, they would behave as bandits. I realised that the British Government would prefer the bandit treatment. This was precisely what had happened. Fortunately, Rex Leeper, who advised Mr. Balfour during the negotiations, understood Bolshevik psychology. He persuaded Mr. Balfour to agree to let Litvinoff leave London at the same time as I left Moscow, and Mr. Balfour, in face of the opposition of the majority of the Cabinet, took his advice. The Swedes and Norwegians had now taken charge of the negotiations. We were to be allowed to cross the Russian frontier as soon as Litvinoff and his party reached Bergen.

During this exciting month there had been one episode in

connection with our imprisonment which had made all Russia laugh. When the mass arrest of the Allied representatives began, half a dozen officials, including Hicks and Grenard, the French Consul-General, had taken refuge in the American Consulate-General, which since the rupture of relations had been taken over by the Norwegian Minister. Officially it was now the Norwegian Legation.

The Bolsheviks soon tracked down the missing Allied officials. They wanted to arrest them. At the same time, disturbed by the consequences of their raid on the British Embassy in St. Petersburg, they had no wish to create another breach of the law of nations. They would be correct. They would not infringe diplomatic extra-territoriality. But they would force the refugees to surrender by starving them out.

The Norwegian Legation was a large house with a small dower house, where the besieged Allies slept, and a large garden. It occupied the whole space between two side streets and both sides were entirely exposed to the public view. The Bolsheviks surrounded the whole place with troops, allowed no one to enter the gates, and shut off the water supply and the electric light. Every day half Moscow assembled in the streets to see the fun. But the Allies never surrendered. They took their exercise daily in the garden. Whenever it rained they rushed out with bath tubs to collect the drops. So far from looking starved, they seemed to have grown fatter. They held out to the end.

The bath tubs were, in fact, make-believe. The dower house cellars contained the stores of the American Red Cross: bully beef, milk, biscuits, butter, candles, tobacco. In cutting off the water supply the Cheka had forgotten one tap, which was apparently connected with another main. Ample supplies of food, clean and well-furnished quarters, and poker, played by night behind heavily draped windows so as not to destroy the Bolshevik delusion, made the lot of the besieged more comfortable than that of their other colleagues in misfortune.

That night, when Moura left me, I sat up late, smoking and reviewing the situation. After the first joy of relief had evaporated, my feelings changed to a deep depression. My whole future seemed without hope. My nerve had gone. Now that I was to be set free, or rather to be sent out of Russia, I did not want to go. I found myself coming back again and again to Peters' proposal that I should remain in Russia with Moura. I gave it more consideration than the English reader may imagine. It was not so madly impossible as it seemed. Sadoul and Pascal, a young French officer of almost saint-like character, had accepted a similar proposal. There was Marchand. These men were not wilful traitors. Like most of us, they had been influenced by a cataclysm which they realised would shake the world to its foundations. There were moments when I asked myself what I should do if I had to choose between the civilisation of Wall Street and the barbarism of Moscow. Now, however, I was not a free agent. I had become the centre of a miniature world storm—a something over whose body two world systems had been wrangling. I could never be a Bolshevik. At this stage, when the telegraph wires of half Europe had been working to secure my release, I could not forego my official obligations.

The decision left me helpless and indifferent. Some time before, an American newspaper, in criticising American diplomacy in Russia, had compared the American Ambassador unfavourably with the "cold, experienced Lockhart with his calculated and relentless pursuit of British interests." What a satire it now seemed on my conduct. How futile were the personal wishes of the individual in this maelstrom of international conflict.

Moura herself was wonderful. She was ill. She had a temperature of over 100, but she made no complaint. She accepted the parting with Russian fatalism. She knew that there was no other way.

For two more days I was kept in the Kremlin. Moura was with me from morning till sundown. Together we packed my belongings: my books, the pack of patience cards, the notes and letters—some of them written on Cheka notepaper—which she had sent me. We talked mainly of the past, avoiding as far as possible all discussion of the future.

On Tuesday, October 1st, Karachan came to see me and to say good-bye. He told me that we were to leave the next day. At three that afternoon I was released and taken back under escort to my flat. A sentry was posted at the door, and I was informed that I was under "house arrest."

The flat was in a sad state. Since my second arrest it had been occupied by a Cheka guard. I discovered that my pearl-studs, my links, my new waterproof and a considerable sum of money had disappeared. The soldiers, too, had drunk all our wine and appropriated our supplies of provisions. In their search for compromising documents they had taken out the linings of my chairs and sofa. They had even probed the wall-papers. Yet in the closed typewriter in my study I found a piece of paper, which had escaped their attention and mine. It bore the words: "I hereby certify that the firm of . . . . is good for the sum of . . . ." Fortunately, the secretary, who had been typing, had gone no farther.

Although I was not allowed to go out, there was no ban on visitors. That evening Asker came to see me. He had been the most efficient and level-headed of all the neutral representatives. He told me that at one moment I had been in serious danger of being shot. I thanked him as best I could. He was a splendid type of Swede, and to him more than to anyone we owed our release. Wardwell, too, was another whose efforts on our behalf left us with a debt we could never repay. Later, when we returned to England, the British Government conferred the Knighthood of the Order of St. Michael and St. George on the neutral Ministers who had conducted the negotiations for our release. I was able to secure for Wardwell, who as an American could not accept an Order, a piece of silver-plate with an inscription conveying the gratitude of the British Government for his services on our behalf.

Yet another visitor was Liuba Malinina, the niece of Chelno-koff. She informed me that she had become engaged to "Hickie," who was still beleaguered in the Norwegian Lega-tion. Could I secure his freedom for an hour the next day in order that she might marry him?

I promised to do what I could, and later in the evening, when Peters came in to say good-bye, I put the question to him in the half-joking, half-sentimental way which I knew would appeal to him. He was amused. "No one but a mad Englishman," he said, "would make a request of this nature at a time like this. Nothing is impossible to such a race. I'll have to see what I can do." He did, and "Hickie" and Liuba were duly married the next day.

The Wednesday of our departure was a busy day. There was a letter from Peters apologising for the theft of my belongings and enclosing compensation, which I returned with a polite note of thanks. There were long conversations with Asker about the control of British interests and about the protection of British subjects in Moscow. At six o'clock in the evening the sentry was taken away from my front-hall, and at nine-thirty Asker came with his motor car to take me to the station. There I found my French and English colleagues, most of whom had been taken straight from prison to the train. The train itself was drawn up at a siding outside the station. As I walked down the line, I wondered vaguely whether my colleagues would blame me for all they had endured. Everyone was strangely silent and subdued. The train was in charge of a platoon of Lettish soldiers, who were to conduct us to the frontier. Their presence created an atmosphere of restraint. I think we all felt that until we were out of Russia we could not breathe freely. There were a few friends to see us off: Moura, Wardwell, and some Russian relations of the newly-married Mrs. Hicks. There was nothing tense or dramatic about our farewell. There was the usual Russian hitch about the time of our departure, and we were kept waiting for several hours. In the cool, starlit night Moura and I discussed trivialities. We talked of everything except ourselves. And then I made her go home with Wardwell. I watched her go until she had disappeared into the night. Then I turned into my dimly-lit carriage to wait and to be alone with my thoughts. It was nearly two in the morning before our train, with many snorts and several false starts, steamed slowly out of the station.

The end, however, was not yet. After skirting St. Petersburg —the *Izvestia* declared that our train had been diverted lest the infuriated populace should tear us limb from limb—we reached Bieloostroff, the Russo-Finnish frontier station, on the Thursday evening. Our rejoicings were premature. There was no Finnish train to meet us. The commander of our Lettish escort had received the strictest orders not to allow us to proceed until he had received definite confirmation of Litvinoff's arrival at Bergen. There was no news of Litvinoff. There was nothing to do but wait.

These three days at Bieloostroff seemed more trying than my imprisonment. Now that everything was over, I had given a free rein to my depression. We were cooped up in a dingy, unheated train. We had provisions for several days but not for longer. Although I had no real fears that the Bolsheviks would change their mind and take us back to Moscow, the possibility of a hitch could not be excluded. As the delay dragged itself out, nerves became strained and tempers frayed. There were even hot-heads who counselled making a dash by night across the narrow strip of no-man's land.

For me personally the nights were the worst ordeal. Now I could hardly sleep at all. I talked with Lavergne and Hicks. Rather feebly we tried to justify ourselves, repeating all the old arguments and consoling ourselves with the reflection that, if the Allies had only taken our advice, they would not have landed themselves in such a mess. I think we all realised that in any circumstances intervention would have been a mistake. We foresaw clearly that we should be blamed and that both the generals and the politicians would shelter themselves behind the excuse that they had been badly informed.

Mostly, however, I walked the platform by myself. I wanted to be alone. I dreaded the home-coming and the questions I should have to face. Fortunately, the weather was fine, and under the starlit Northern sky I must have walked for miles. Hope was dead in my heart. I had no illusions about my reception at home. For a few days I should figure in the front page of the news. There would be newspaper men and photographers. I should be received by the Crown Princess of Sweden, by The King, by Mr. Balfour. There would be relief at my escape. Had anything happened to me, there would have been unpleasant complications and perhaps some twinges of consciences in Whitehall. Then I should be laid on the shelf. My knowledge, at that time unique, of a complicated situation would be allowed to go to rust. There is no one more quickly neglected than the man on the spot whose policy becomes discredited. And my policy was already discredited in the eyes of both the pro-Bolsheviks and of the interventionists. My future was not pleasant to contemplate, and I subjected my conscience to a severe cross-examination. Months before, when we had had a slight altercation about a question of principle, Moura had described me as "a little clever, but not clever enough; a little strong, but not strong enough; a little weak, but not weak enough." Peters himself had described me as the man of the "zolotaia seredina"—the man of the golden mean—and had despised me. It seemed then, it seems to-day, a fair definition of my character. And now I had left her. My cup of unhappiness was full.

If these were my inmost thoughts, I had to keep a brave face in public. The piece had to be played through to the end. There were some forty or fifty French and English on the train. We had to keep on good terms with the Lettish commander and endeavour to induce him to expedite our departure. To keep our spirits up, I organised a great series of test matches between the French and ourselves at pitch and toss. We played the series out with the platform for our pitch and with the Lettish soldiers and the Russian station officials as our crowd. They became almost as excited as we did. And, doubtless, to them the sight of a silver-haired French general bending down on his knee on the platform and measuring the distance between the various rouble pieces with a pocket-handkerchief was thrilling. If they thought us mad, they became quite human, and it would have required little persuasion to induce the Lettish commander to take a hand in the game himself. He refused, but there was obvious reluctance in his refusal.

Perhaps he was afraid that Moscow might consider his participation unproletarian. England, or rather Scotland, won the
series. In my Presbyterian youth I had played the game
diligently on the Scottish Sabbath, and, like the curate in the
music-hall song, who "won three out of four 'cause he'd
played it before," we were the more experienced players.

The end of the test matches saw the end of our troubles.
As we were picking up our coins, the commander came up with
a telegram in his hand. Everything was in order. The Finnish
train was ready, and we were to leave immediately. He also
brought us the Russian newspapers from St. Petersburg. They
were full of great news. Bulgaria had collapsed and had signed
an armistice. Austria was a suppliant for peace. The Hinden-
burg line in the West had been broken. On my companions
the news acted like a tonic. Most of them regarded their departure as a happy release, as a nightmare that had been swallowed
up in a glorious morning. They could look forward to the
future with a new hope. In my heart there was no elation. My
physical body was going forward, but my thoughts were back
in Moscow and in the country which I was leaving—probably
for ever.

FINIS

INDEX